MACRO PROCESSORS

MACRO PROCESSORS
and Techniques for Portable Software

P. J. Brown

Reader in Computer Science,
University of Kent at Canterbury

A Wiley–Interscience Publication

JOHN WILEY & SONS

London · New York · Sydney · Toronto

Library of Congress Cataloging in Publication Data

Brown, Peter J
    Macro processors and techniques for portable software.

    (Wiley series in computing)
    A Wiley–Interscience publication.
    1. Macro processors.   2. Software compatibility.
I. Title.
QA76.6.B77   001.6'425   73–17597
ISBN 0 471 11005 1

Set on Monophoto Filmsetter and
printed by J. W. Arrowsmith Ltd., Bristol, England

To

Heather of the West

Preface

This book covers two subjects: macro processors and software portability. Each of these subjects has the great merit that the current state of knowledge is of manageable proportions, and it has been possible to make a comprehensive study of both of them within one book. Both studies start from scratch, not assuming any more knowledge on the part of the reader than a familiarity with the nature of high-level languages and assembly languages. The reader may be a student, a research worker or someone professionally engaged in the production of software.

It is a notorious weakness of authors and research workers that they think their own subject, be it cheese-making in Western Tibet in the early sixth century or the production of hydrogen bombs, is of universal importance and interest. But let me state my case. Macro processors are a powerful software tool, which has so far been under-exploited. A study of them can be both intellectually stimulating and practically rewarding. Software portability, or the moving of software from one machine to another, is obviously of supreme practical importance, since huge sums of money are currently spent in reprogramming for new environments. Many ingenious ways of attacking this problem have been developed, and they are well worth examining. The two subjects of this book therefore merit the attention of every computer scientist.

The book is split up into three Parts.

Part 1 covers macro processors. The aim is not to survey every macro processor in existence, but to present a reasoned exposition of the subject, extracting the most interesting and useful concepts and developing these to the full.

Part 2 covers software portability. The relationship of this to Part 1 is that one of the most important uses of macro processors is to aid software portability, and, conversely, a good proportion of portability techniques centre on the use of macro processors. It would certainly be short-sighted, however, to think that all techniques for software portability should use a macro processor, and Part 2 covers several techniques that do not. The primary aim of Part 2 is to bring all the techniques together and to evaluate their relative merits. I hope that, as a result, a reader who himself has some software to make portable can select which method or combination of methods suits him best.

Practical experience is one of the best ways of learning, and the purpose of Part 3 is to give the reader a chance to do something for himself. It describes, in full detail, how a specific piece of portable software can be implemented on virtually any computer. This project can be undertaken by the reader, or a group of readers. It involves using a macro processor to map a given software description to the order code of a computer. Both the computer and the macro processor can be selected by the reader.

Relationship between the Parts

Few people ever read a technical book from beginning to end. Certainly, some readers of this book will be more interested in macros than portability, and some will have the opposite preference. Some may be keen to undertake the project in Part 3 without wading through a lot of chit-chat first.

I have therefore tried to allow as much flexibility as possible in the order in which the three Parts are read. In particular, anyone who already knows what a macro processor is can read Parts 2 and 3 without reading Part 1. Moreover those who are temperamentally doers rather than thinkers can attack Part 3 before Part 2.

The best way to understand the relationship between the Parts is to note that they are set at decreasing levels of generality. To start at the bottom, Part 3 is concerned with one piece of software and one portability method. At a higher level, Part 2 describes portable software in general terms. At the top, Part 1 discusses a general-purpose tool, the macro processor, one of the uses of which is to make software portable. Each Part should therefore help to illuminate the other two; the particular illustrating the general, and the general giving a deeper understanding of the particular.

Acknowledgements

I would like to thank Tony Burbridge and Martin Healey of IBM Hursley, who provided useful comments about my descriptions of IBM software. (I would not claim that they necessarily agree with everything I have said.) Calvin Mooers was helpful in answering my queries about references to trademarked software. I had many useful discussions with John Lowe of the University of Kent about the design of the ALGEBRA program. I am also very grateful to Mrs Ruby Herting, who undertook most of the typing.

Above all, I am indebted to Mrs Heather Brown who spent many hours checking the material and arguing with me over the best methods of presentation.

P. J. BROWN
Canterbury, April 1973

Contents

Preface

Part 1. MACRO PROCESSORS

Part 1

MACRO PROCESSORS

Chapter 1.1

Basic Concepts

A study of macro processors is rewarding at two levels. Firstly, from a purely utilitarian viewpoint, macros are a valuable and powerful tool which every serious computer user should know how to exploit. Secondly, from an intellectual viewpoint, macros form a relatively small and self-contained subject of study that produces many challenging and stimulating problems. Now that the information explosion has become a major problem for the computer scientist, it is good to be able to isolate a subject where only three or four significant new papers are published each year and where anyone can master the whole subject.

The purpose of this Part of the book is to introduce the reader to the most important features found in macro processors and to describe some particular macro processors that are either typical of their class or outstanding in themselves. In this introductory chapter, we identify, mainly by means of examples, the main facilities that a macro processor should possess. The second chapter continues this groundwork. There follows a sequence of chapters describing various individual macro processors, evaluating what is new or good about them and explaining how they realize some of the facilities described in this first chapter. After this we return to general topics and summarize the uses of macro processors and some implementation problems associated with them. Two specialist chapters deal with inter-macro communication and macros that are integrated into compilers.

A reader who already knows what a macro is will be bored to tears by the introductory material in this chapter. Having read the next three sections, which define terminology and present sample macros, he would do well to skip as far as the section on nesting, pausing only to skim through the section on base languages. Even more knowledgeable readers may wish to skip to the 'Summary of requirements' section near the end of this chapter.

Terminology

Unfortunately the use of terminology for describing macros is very varied. Even the term 'macro processor' is not standard; alternative terms that can be found in the literature include 'macro generator', 'macro expander' and 'macro compiler'. The problem of varying terminology is not, however, as bad as it may seem, because the number of different terms is relatively small. The terminology that is adopted throughout this book is defined in the next section. This terminology is used even when talking about macro processors which, when described in the literature, have had their own, different, terminology.

Definitions

A *macro* is a facility for replacing one sequence of symbols by another. A piece of computer software for supporting macro activity is called a *macro processor*. The logical action of a macro processor is illustrated in Figure 1.1A.

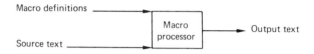

Fig. 1.1A. The basic action of a macro processor

There are two inputs to the macro processor, the *macro definitions* and the *source text*. Each macro definition defines a pattern of symbols that is to be replaced and what it is to be replaced by. The latter is called the *replacement text* of the macro. The source text is the sequence of characters in which the replacements are to be made. The action of the macro processor is to scan the source text for occurrences of the macros that have been defined.

Each such occurrence is a *macro call*. On finding a macro call, the macro processor identifies the replacement text of the macro and replaces the call accordingly. The text that replaces a macro call is said to be *generated* by the call. The *output text* is derived from the source text by replacing all the macro calls that occur in it.

The above definitions make no assumptions about the nature of the source text. It might, for example, be a computer program in any programming language, a book or a sequence of replies to a questionnaire. There exist many different macro processors. Some of them are tied to individual programming languages and will only process source text in that language, whereas others are more general.

An example of a macro

Many people who have only a superficial understanding of macros imagine that macros can only operate on computer programs. In order to discourage this limited view from the start, our first examples of macros will be ones that can be applied to source text in the English language.

For better or for worse, there is not much variety in the letters one writes. For business letters in particular, one has a set of a few dozen standard paragraphs and to compose a letter one strings together a selection of these, filling in a few of the words that are variable. (The same possibly applies to one's personal letters as well.) We will consider how this process might be automated using a macro processor. A macro would be defined for each of the standard paragraphs, and given a suitable name, preferably mnemonic. Thus SEEYOU might be a macro with the replacement text 'I will look forward to meeting you, and hearing about your proposals'. Most paragraphs will require certain arguments to be inserted in the fixed text, for example 'I suggest you catch the train which leaves Victoria at ... and reaches Canterbury at .... I will arrange to meet you at the station.' Each call of this macro, which will be named TRAIN, will require two arguments to be supplied, namely the departure and arrival times of the train.

The simplest way of writing a macro call is to write the name of the macro first and to follow this with the arguments (if any), separated by commas. We will assume this convention is adopted here and a typical call of the TRAIN macro would then be

$$TRAIN \quad 9.40, 11.03$$

Argument one is the text '9.40' and argument two the text '11.03'.

The replacement text for the TRAIN macro would be expressed in the following way.

> Output 'I suggest you catch the train which
>   leaves Victoria at'
> Output the first argument
> Output 'and reaches Canterbury at'
> Output the second argument
> Output '. I will arrange to meet you at the station.'

(The exact notation used in practice to specify replacement text would, of course, be rather more concise than this. Questions of notation are discussed in more detail in subsequent chapters.)

A complete example of source and output text

For the benefit of those readers who are completely unfamiliar with macro processors, this section shows a complete example of how the SEEYOU and TRAIN macros could be used.

The example is this. The definitions of the SEEYOU and TRAIN macros have been fed to a macro processor. The following source text is then supplied:

> 'Dear Mr Jones,
>   Thank you for your letter of January 16th.
> I will be happy to see you on January 30th.
>   TRAIN   10.40, 12.03
>   SEEYOU
>   Yours sincerely
>   ...'

The resultant output text would then take the form:

> 'Dear Mr Jones,
>   Thank you for your letter of January 16th.
> I will be happy to see you on January 30th.
>   I suggest you catch the train which leaves
> Victoria at 10.40 and reaches Canterbury at 12.03.
> I will arrange to meet you at the station.
>   I will look forward to meeting you and
> hearing about your proposals.
>   Yours sincerely
>   ...'

Within the source text, pieces of text to be copied literally can be intermixed with macro calls in any way the user chooses. Each of the macro calls in the above example generates a complete paragraph, but it would be possible to design other macros which generated sentences, clauses, or indeed any sequence of characters. The same macro can be called any number of times from within the source text, though in our example it is unlikely that one would want to repeat anything in this way.

Macro-time facilities

We will now elaborate this example in order to introduce a further important property of macro processors. Assume that there were some visitors who did not merit meeting at the station. For them the second sentence generated by the TRAIN macro would read 'You can then catch a 32 bus.' There are various ways of adapting the macro to deal with this. Perhaps the simplest is to add a third argument, which would read either MEET or BUS, depending on which of the sentences was to be generated.

This places an added requirement on the macro processor. In previous examples the form of the replacement text was fixed except for the insertion of the arguments, but in this case the arguments determine the very form of the replacement text. The replacement text would be specified in the following form.

> Output 'I suggest you catch the train which
>   leaves Victoria at'
> Output the first argument
> Output 'and reaches Canterbury at'
> Output the second argument
> Output a full stop
> If the third argument is MEET go to label L1
> If the third argument is BUS go to label L2
> Print the error message 'Illegal third argument to TRAIN macro'
> Finish
>
> L1:   Output 'I will arrange to meet you at the station.'
>   Finish
> L2:   Output 'You can then catch a 32 bus.'

In this example, therefore, the replacement text is not simply a series of output statements but consists of a small program which generates the appropriate output. The macro processor needs to provide a programming language in which such programs can be written. The facilities available in this language that are not output statements are called *macro-time* facilities, since they are executed at the time the macro processor is in operation and are totally local to it. In this example the two labels L1 and L2 and the two conditional statements to go to these labels are macro-time facilities.

Optional arguments

Before leaving the TRAIN macro, it is worth mentioning one more useful facility. Assume that 95% of visitors were met at the station, and therefore the third argument of TRAIN was almost always MEET. It would be much more convenient if MEET were then the default option. This could be done by saying the third argument could be omitted if the MEET option was to be assumed. Most macro processors cater for such optional arguments. In such cases there needs to be a macro-time facility of the form

> If argument n exists then go to ...

Note that there is a difference between an argument that is present and is null and one that is omitted. Thus in the macro call

> TRAIN   10.15, 10.30

the third argument is omitted whereas in

> TRAIN   10.15, 10.30,

the third argument exists but is null. An argument is absent only if the character(s) delimiting it are absent. In practical terms if a macro processor allowed arguments to be null but not to be omitted, the TRAIN macro would need to be called in the second of the above forms, which would not be a natural one to write and would doubtless lead to errors.

Concepts of emptiness, nullness, etc. are, in fact, a ripe field for erudite papers. Mooers (1968) gives a detailed discussion of this question with regard to one macro processor.

If the same symbol is used as a separator between each pair of successive arguments (as in our examples, where the comma is used) it is necessary to have fixed rules to resolve ambiguities about which argument is omitted. Thus if a macro usually has three arguments but is called with two, is it the first, second or third argument that is omitted? The normal rule is only to allow arguments to be omitted from the end of the argument list.

Base languages

Now that the basic concepts of macros, their arguments and their replacement texts have been explained, it is possible to examine other fields of application of macros.

By far the most popular application of macros is in conjunction with programming languages. This happens as follows. A programmer is using some programming language and finds that, when he is writing a certain program, he is continually repeating similar sequences of instructions. He therefore defines, for each such instruction sequence, a macro that generates the instructions for him. For example, assume his program is an assembly-language program that deals with linked lists, and every time he wishes to advance a pointer *PTR* to point at the next item on a list he needs to write

```
LDINX   PTR
LDMOD   1
STORE   PTR
```

(We are not concerned here with the exact meaning of these instructions, or with the nature of the machine on which the program is to run.) It would be much better to use a macro for this. It might be written

ADVANCE   *PTR*

where *PTR* is the argument. This has many advantages. In particular it is more concise, easier to remember, less error-prone and more comprehensible.

A macro processor can be used in conjunction with any programming language. If L is a programming language then, when using a macro processor with L, it is possible to mix, within the same program, macro calls and ordinary statements in L. The program is first passed through the macro processor, which replaces all the macro calls and produces as output text a program in the language L. This program is then fed in the normal way to the compiler for L. In such a situation the macro processor is a *pre-processor* to the compiler for L. This is illustrated in Figure 1.1B.

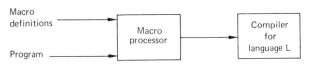

Fig. 1.1B. A macro processor acting as a pre-processor to the compiler for a language L

The language L is called the *base language*, since it is the base on which the macros are built. The action of the macro processor is to extend the base language by introducing new facilities, in our example the ADVANCE macro.

Shared and local definitions

It is very likely that if the ADVANCE macro were used in a program it would be used many times. The effort of defining the macro might still be worthwhile even if the ADVANCE macro was only used in one program, and it is indeed very common for macros to be defined that are local to a single program. In such cases the macro definitions are often prefixed to the start of the program, and the two are regarded as a single entity. The form of the input to the macro processor might be

> Definition of ADVANCE macro
> Definitions of other macros
> Start of program in L
> .
> .
> .
> ADVANCE X
> .
> .
> ADVANCE Y
> .
> .
> .
> End of program in L

(Many macro processors even allow definitions to be interspersed with the rest of the source text, and perhaps allow them to be switched on and off. One might then have macros that are local to a certain section of the source text.)

The letter-writing macros, on the other hand, are only useful if they are shared between many different letters. A macro local to a particular letter would rarely be worth the effort of defining it, as single letters virtually never contain repetitions of similar phrases or paragraphs.

There are thus two different levels of using macros

(a) Locally to one piece of text.

(b) Shared between several pieces of text.

The two levels are not mutually exclusive; both may be used in processing a single piece of text. Our example of the programming language macro was presented as a local one. However it is quite common to use shared macros in programming languages. Macros analogous to the letter-writing ones could be used to generate data structures or routines common to several programs. Indeed the ADVANCE macro itself might be elevated to become a shared macro if it turned out that several programs needed it, just as an actor may rise from amateur theatricals in his home village to international film fame.

Libraries of macros

Macros that are useful to a number of different people are often made available in public *libraries* of macros which are maintained on backing store. At a more specialized level, some macros may only be used by one person, but might be used by him in several different contexts (e.g. different programs or different letters). These might be stored in the user's own library.

It is much easier to use macros than to define them. The letter-writing macros, for example, could be used by anybody but it would require someone with programming experience to define them. For macros associated with programming languages the spectrum is shifted. The users of the macros would, of course, be programmers but these people still might not have the experience and knowledge to define macros for themselves, particularly in some of the more complex situations we shall be examining later. It is one of the uses of libraries that a skilled systems programmer can prepare a suite of macros and then these can be used by people with less specialized knowledge.

The use of macro libraries, in fact, mirrors almost exactly the use of subroutine libraries for programming languages. There are the same levels of specialization, from publicly shared subroutines to special subroutines within a single program, and there is the same need for a programmer with particular skills to define the subroutines, for example those using special numerical methods.

Points of confusion

We will now mention two matters that often cause confusion to users of macros. In each case there are two concepts that are superficially similar but really quite distinct. Some people, especially beginners, mix them up. There is a danger, however, in bringing this to the attention of the reader. If the reader is exceptionally perceptive and clear-thinking he will not confuse the concepts. Therefore to present him with some material about why the concepts should be confused may introduce confusion when there was none before. It may be like having a philosopher explain to you what is 'truth'; you understood it before he explained it but not after.

Some readers may therefore choose to skip the next three sections.

Confusion between macro-time and run-time

The first point of confusion is concerned with macro-time facilities and is best introduced by an example.

Assume that the base language is some high-level programming language and that there exists a macro DEMOTE, which has two arguments. The first is the name of a variable and the second is one of the words OFFICER, NCO or ALL. The action of the macro is to generate a statement to decrease the value of the first argument by one. However, if the second argument is OFFICER demotion should take place only if the value of the variable is greater than five and, if it is NCO, only if this value is less than or equal to five. ALL means demote unconditionally. (Thus the macro demotes a soldier one rank if he belongs to the class indicated by the second argument.) The three calls

1.   DEMOTE X, OFFICER

2.   DEMOTE Y, NCO

3.   DEMOTE Z, ALL

might generate

1.   IF $X > 5$ THEN $X = X - 1$;

2.   IF $Y < = 5$ THEN $Y = Y - 1$;

3. $Z = Z - 1$;

The replacement text of this macro would include macro-time statements of the form:

If argument two is OFFICER then output 'IF argument one > 5 THEN'

If argument two is NCO then output 'IF argument one $< = 5$ THEN'

The point about this is that there is an IF statement in the replacement text of DEMOTE which generates an IF statement in the base language.

It is easy to confuse the two. The distinction is that the two statements are executed at different times, one at macro-time and the other at run-time for the base language. Similarly it is possible, if one does not think carefully, to confuse other macro-time facilities, for example labels, with their run-time equivalents.

Confusion between macros and subroutines

The second possible point of confusion is between macros and subroutines, and can arise when a macro processor is being used as a preprocessor to any programming language. The difference between the two is often said to be that a macro generates in-line code whereas a subroutine is a call of some code that is remote from the point of invocation. This explanation may be good for the beginner, but becomes shaky when one comes to more advanced situations, for example where a macro generates a subroutine call.

It is better to compare macros and subroutines at the 'what they are' level rather than the 'how they work' level. This yields a clear distinction: a macro is a replacement facility that is applied before a program is compiled (or assembled) whereas a subroutine is a replacement facility that is applied when a program is run. A major use of macros is to provide a shorthand notation in which programs can be expressed, whereas a major use of subroutines is to make the size of a program smaller at run-time, i.e. to provide a shorthand run-time form. Other attributes of macros, such as the improved comprehensibility and flexibility that they provide, are also mirrored in subroutines. Some of the restrictions are also similar, for example the restriction present in some macro processors that a macro call must be a statement in the base language. One dissimilarity is that macros can be applied to data as well as programs. (Actually, since data structures may mirror program structures it might be possible to generalize the subroutine concept and apply it to data.)

It is interesting to note that the distinction between macros and subroutines is simply a special case of the distinction between macro-time facilities and run-time facilities described in the previous section.

Although the difference between macros and subroutines may be clear cut, it can be difficult in some situations to choose which tool to use, i.e. whether to effect a replacement at macro-time or at run-time. Consider, for example, the ADVANCE macro. It would have been possible to encode this as a subroutine call so that to 'advance' a pointer PTR the following two instructions were used

LOAD   *address of PTR*

CALL   ADVSUB

where the subroutine ADVSUB consisted of three instructions similar to those that were specified earlier as the replacement text of the ADVANCE macro. This subroutine would, in addition, require a 'RETURN' instruction. Hence on a typical computer the ADVSUB subroutine would require two instructions for each call plus four for the subroutine itself. The ADVANCE macro required three in-line instructions. (Macros are often called 'in-line subroutines', a description which fits this situation well but which is nevertheless a confusing one when examining more general situations.) In this case, therefore, the subroutine form makes the overall program length shorter if there are more than four calls of it. However the program would run more slowly, and so it may be difficult to decide whether to use a macro or a subroutine.

The advantages of subroutines are clearly overwhelming for routines that are rather longer than ADVANCE. Similarly, for routines that are highly parameterized, macros can have overwhelming advantages. Consider a macro of form

ADD   A,B,C

which sets A as the sum of B and C. This takes three instructions on a typical one-address computer whereas the calling sequence of a subroutine to achieve the same effect would take at least four.

A macro to generate a subroutine call

It should be emphasized that it is only a subset—and a small subset at that—of the applications of macros that can be compared with subroutines. The uses of macros to improve the notation of programs or to 'create' programs by means of macro-time statements are in no way comparable to uses of subroutines. A good way of illustrating this is to show an example of macros and subroutines in tandem.

Assume that it is decided to use the ADVSUB subroutine to 'advance' pointers. It would still be useful to have an ADVANCE macro. The user would still write

ADVANCE   PTR

but the ADVANCE macro, instead of generating in-line instructions, would generate a call of ADVSUB. (The first call of ADVANCE would need to generate the ADVSUB subroutine itself, so that the other calls could use this.) This is an instance of macros and subroutines working happily together, the former providing notational advantages (one statement instead of two) and the latter providing run-time advantages. The macro also gives the advantage of flexibility. If it were decided at a later date that it was, after all, a bad idea to have an ADVSUB subroutine since the extra speed of in-line code was required, then the definition of the ADVANCE macro could simply be changed accordingly. It would *not* be necessary to search the program for all occurrences of the ADVANCE macro and change each of these.

More specialized features

We have now covered the basic mechanisms needed by macro processors, and have hopefully cleared up some points of confusion commonly associated with them. We will now move on to more specialized facilities, the kind of facilities one can do without in simple applications but which are needed when the going gets tough.

Lists of arguments

It is often useful to have macros that allow an arbitrarily long list of arguments, all to be processed in a similar way.

To illustrate this we will choose an example where a macro processor is being used as a pre-processor to an assembly language in order to generate data declarations.

Assume that one is writing a program that manipulates linked lists of numbers. Each list element consists of a number followed by a pointer to the next element of the list. The last element on the list has the value zero in its pointer field. In order to declare fixed lists it would be useful to have a macro called LIST, say, that generated a list consisting of the numbers supplied as arguments. Since each list would tend to contain a different number of elements it would be necessary for the LIST macro to have a variable number of arguments. Thus it should be possible to write

LIST   3,9

to declare a list consisting of the two numbers three and nine, and

LIST   1,5,26,7,3,126,109

to declare the given list of seven numbers.

Consider how the replacement text for LIST might be written. We will assume that the assembly language is such that the number 23 is declared

NUM   23

and an address field pointing at the label P is declared

PTR   P

In this case

LIST   3,9

would be replaced by

```
NUM    3
PTR    * + 1
NUM    9
PTR    0
```

where '*' means the address of the current location.

The replacement text of LIST would take the following form.

```
        Set N as 1
L2:     Output 'NUM' and some spaces
        Output the Nth argument
        Output a newline (i.e. an end of line marker)
        Output 'PTR' and some spaces
        If N is equal to the number of arguments then go to L1
        Output '* + 1' and a newline
        Set N as N + 1
        Go to L2
L1:     Output '0' and a newline
```

This illustrates some further macro-time facilities. The variable N is a macro-time integer variable, and serves as a loop counter. Most macro processors provide macro-time variables and facilities for manipulating them. These should include an assignment statement, arithmetic operators, and comparisons of their values in IF statements. It is useful, though not imperative, to have a macro-time looping statement of a similar nature to the DO (or FOR) statements found in high-level programming languages. Many macro processors have a variant of the DO statement that will repeatedly evaluate a piece of replacement text for each of a sequence of arguments, and this would make the above example much more concise to express.

Note that the example requires that it be possible to refer to the Nth argument, where N is a variable, and also that macro-time statements can find out how many arguments there are.

Communication between macros

It is sometimes necessary to relay information from one call of a macro to another.

We will illustrate this with a further example using assembly language. Assume that macros are used to introduce a simple looping statement into an assembly language. (Note that we are *not* postulating a macro-time looping statement, as described in the previous section, but macros which generate assembly language instructions that cause a program to execute a run-time loop.) Assume that a loop is introduced by a macro named DO, which has three arguments as follows:

(a) the controlled variable,
(b) its starting value,
(c) its final value.

The step size is always one. (If we were ambitious we could have allowed for an optional fourth argument to specify the step size if it was not one.) The end of the loop is indicated by a macro ENDO, which has no arguments. A loop might therefore be written

```
DO   K,1,10
assembly language statements
ENDO
```

We will assume that the DO and ENDO macros are such that this will generate the assembly language text

	Label	Instruction	Operand	(Comment)
		LOADL	1	(Load Literal value 1)
	DOLB1:	STORE	K	
Replacement		LOAD	K	
for		COMPL	10	(Compare with literal
DO				value 10)
		GOGR	DOLB2	(If K > 10 go to
				DOLB2)

		assembly language statements		
Replacement		LOAD	K	
for		ADDL	1	(Add Literal value 1)
ENDO		GO	DOLB1	
	DOLB2:			

The first point about this example is that the assembly language output contains two labels, DOLB1 and DOLB2. If there is a second call of the DO and ENDO macros, these macros cannot reuse the same label names or the assembler will object. They have to use two new names, say DOLB3 and DOLB4. Similarly the third call should use DOLB5 and DOLB6 and so on. This can be implemented using a macro-time integer variable that is initialized to the value one and incremented each time a label is generated. The value of this variable is concatenated with the string 'DOLB' to form a unique label name. The variable needs to be *global*, which means that it can be referred to within the replacement text of any macro and its value is maintained throughout macro processing (as distinct from a local variable whose value may be destroyed between one macro call and the next). In this example the value of the variable is needed by both the DO and the ENDO macros.

The second point about the example is that the controlled variable, in this case K, is used in the ENDO macro but supplied as an argument to the DO macro. Hence there needs to be a global character variable to relay this information from the DO macro to the ENDO macro.

The third point concerns nesting. Consider the following calls of the macros

```
        DO   K,1,10
        DO   J,2,5
         .
         .
         .
        ENDO
        ENDO
```

In this case it is not possible to use single global variables to relay information from DO to ENDO because the inner call of DO will clobber the information to be relayed between the outer DO and ENDO. Instead an array or stack is needed. (Some macro processors might be clever enough to regard DO and ENDO as one single macro, in which case the problem could be solved using local variables.)

Communication between macros is actually a subject that merits considerable study. This study will, however, be delayed until Chapter 1.7 and we will content ourselves for the moment with having simply identified some of the tools that are needed.

Created symbols

The labels DOLB1, DOLB2, etc., in the previous example illustrated a general point about macro processors. It is common for macros to need to create a series of unique symbols. In the DO macro there was a risk that the programmer might inadvertently use, say, DOLB4 as one of his own label names, unaware that a macro might generate the same label. One way of lessening the risk would have been to choose 'unusual' names such as XQZY1, XQZY2 for the labels generated by macros, but this is neither pleasing nor wholly satisfactory. There is, however, no completely general solution to the problem, and macro users will often have to put up with rules such as 'do not use any names starting with XQZ as the macros may use these'.

The nearest thing to a solution to this problem arises with macro processors that are specially interfaced with particular assemblers. In this case the assembler may reserve some special internal symbols that can be used for macro generated names but not for names supplied by the original user.

Some macro processors even have a special automatic facility for so-called *created symbols* to make it specially easy to do this.

Nesting

It is often useful to call one macro from within the replacement text of another. For example, if we wished to design some macros for sophisticated list processing operations, it would be convenient to express these in terms of the ADVANCE macro mentioned earlier, which finds the next element of a list. Defining one macro in terms of another has advantages in conciseness and flexibility, though it complicates the job of the macro processor and slows it down.

A second, rather different, example of nested macro calls could arise with the letter-writing macros. Assume that one letter is a joint letter, and each occurrence of 'I' is to be replaced by 'We'. This could be done simply by defining 'I' as a macro with 'We' as its replacement text. (If we were aiming to be very clever we might replace 'I' by 'we' rather than 'We' if it did not occur at the start of a sentence, but in this example we are not aiming to be clever.) Since 'I' occurs in the replacement text of other macros, some nested calls would arise. For example a call of the TRAIN macro results in the scanning of the text:

I will arrange to meet you at the station.

This contains a call of the I macro, and thus the final output text is:

We will arrange to meet you at the station.

As well as illustrating nesting this example also shows a new type of usage for macros, namely the making of a systematic change throughout a document.

Recursion

A special case of nesting is *recursion*, which means calling a macro from within its own replacement text. A simple example of a recursive macro definition is as follows. The macro is called CURSE and uses a macro-time variable called COUNT.

If COUNT = 0 then Output '0' and exit
Output '('
Output value of COUNT
Output '+'
Decrease COUNT by one
Call CURSE
Output ')'

If this were then called by the sequence

Set COUNT = 6

Call CURSE

then the resultant output text would be

$$(6+(5+(4+(3+(2+(1+0))))))$$

(If the macro processor allowed arguments to be manipulated as numbers rather than as strings of characters, then the above call could have been written CURSE 6 and the replacement text could have been written without the need for the variable COUNT.)

This specification of the CURSE macro in terms of itself is a simple and natural one. It would, of course, be possible to specify it without the use of recursion but this would require two macro-time loops.

Recursion is often felt to be an academic plaything, and not a suitable tool for good red-blooded users with real problems to solve. Within certain scientific and business fields there is some truth in this. Recursion really comes into its own, however, when the data to be analysed or synthesized contains some structuring. In such cases the best way of defining the structuring is often in terms of itself. Thus for example an arithmetic expression may itself contain other arithmetic expressions, and a recursive definition and recursive methods of evaluation are natural ones. Similarly in a tree structure each branch is itself a tree structure, so recursive methods are again the most natural ones. Thus, unless a macro processor is only used in a restricted field of application, it should contain recursive capabilities.

The position could be summarized thus. If recursion were added to COBOL it would be little used as most programmers would find they could get by without it. If recursion were added to a general-purpose macro processor, users would soon find it was just what they needed for certain of their problems.

A use of recursive macros

An instructing and amusing description of a use of recursive macro calls is provided in a paper by Fletcher (1965). The problem he considers is that of fitting a set of pieces of different shape into a rectangular space. In his example the pieces are 'pentominos', i.e. shapes made up of five touching squares, and the size of the rectangular space in terms of these squares is six squares wide and ten squares long. There are, in fact, twelve different pentominos. These therefore total sixty squares, the same area as the rectangular space. Figure 1.1C shows the shapes of some of the pentominos.

The details of the problem are not relevant here, but, in essence, Fletcher solves it by a trial and error method. The heart of the program that does,

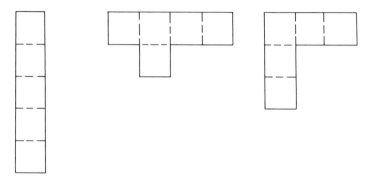

Fig. 1.1C. Three of the twelve possible shapes made up of five squares

this is the routine that takes a given square of the rectangle and finds which shapes can be fitted to cover it. This obviously depends on which of the adjacent squares are free. The easiest way of specifying the relationship between which squares are free and which shapes can be fitted is by means of a tree structure. Fletcher has designed a macro which converts this tree structure into a set of assembly language instructions, thus creating the routine to test which shapes can be fitted. The specification of the tree structure is supplied in the form of an argument to the macro, and is represented using nested parentheses in the same way as would be done in a list processing language such as LISP. The macro calls itself recursively to deal with each level of nesting. All this is done using the standard macro-assembler supplied by IBM for their 7090 computers.

As well as illustrating the use of recursion, Fletcher's work provides an example of the use of macros to convert a language suited to a particular problem into a standard programming language. The specification for his problem (i.e. the criteria for fitting each of the twelve pentominos) is best expressed as a tree structure and the macros convert this into an assembly language program consisting of a very large number of branch and test instructions. In fact a single macro call, with a tree structure as its argument, generates seven hundred assembly language instructions. It would be highly tedious to write these directly and almost impossible to get them right. Even in a high-level language, with nested IF statements, the task would be formidable.

Calls within arguments

A special case of recursion is where one macro can be called within an argument to another. This may arise in macro processors where macros are not written one to a line, but within some fixed delimiters that act as brackets. For example a macro to add A to B might be written

ADD(A,B)

(This is, of course, a similar notation to that used for subroutine calls in programming languages.) It is useful to allow an argument to be a macro call and even to be a call of the same macro to which it is an argument, for example

ADD(ADD(B,C),A)

In this case the macro processor, while evaluating the first argument of the outer call of the ADD macro, executes the inner call.

Local variables

An implication of nesting and recursion is that a macro processor needs to provide for macro-time variables and labels that are local to a given call, in the same way as many high-level languages support variables that are local to a subroutine call. These local macro-time variables should remain unchanged whatever nested calls occur within the call to which they belong, even when a macro calls itself recursively. Since the treatment of local macro-time variables exactly mirrors the treatment of local variables in high-level languages, we shall not go into any more details here.

String manipulation

Up to now arguments to macros have been regarded as indivisible sequences of characters that can be inserted into the replacement text, compared with other sequences of characters, and perhaps assigned as values to macro-time character variables. It is often desirable to regard an argument as a string of individual characters or perhaps as the concatenation of two substrings. This occurs particularly when a macro processor is acting as a pre-processor to a programming language and a macro argument is a character constant rather than a variable or an expression. For example, a macro named PERSON might map

	PERSON	A. J. SMITH	
into	CHAR	A	(Initials of the person)
	CHAR	J	
	NUM	0	(Special marker to indicate end of initials)
	CHAR	S	(Surname of the person)
	CHAR	M	
	CHAR	I	
	CHAR	T	
	CHAR	H	

where CHAR and NUM are statements for generating single characters and numbers, respectively. This macro would need to examine its argument character by character, finding the dots that separate the initials, and splitting up the surname.

To take an example from a different field, an argument might be a score at some game, being two numbers separated by a dash, e.g. 36–0. It might be convenient to regard this as two separate substrings, namely the two scores.

The facilities required by a macro processor to make it capable of manipulating strings are very simple. Three basic operations are needed, as follows.

(a) An operator that gives the length of an argument, i.e. the number of characters it contains.
(b) An operator that selects the substring given by the Mth to Nth characters within a string, where M and N are integer values.
(c) A concatenate operator to build up strings from a number of substrings.

These facilities, or their equivalent, are exceptionally well worth having in a macro processor as they add a new dimension to the kinds of argument that can be processed and therefore to the potential application areas. Indeed some macro processors have been utilized almost exclusively as string manipulation systems.

It is actually possible to process string arguments even if a macro processor has no string processing facilities, provided the user of the macro does all the work. Thus in the PERSON macro the argument could be split into separate characters by the writer of the macro call, e.g.

PERSON   A,.,J,.,S,M,I,T,H,.

This is, however, roughly equivalent to asking your dinner guests to grind their own coffee with a nutcracker because you do not possess a coffee grinder.

Created definitions

The last facility we shall consider is that of dynamically created macro definitions. This happens when a macro call creates a new macro definition, perhaps using the arguments of the call in building up the definition.

The need for dynamically created definitions is not immediately obvious and is best introduced by reference to fundamentals. A macro processor is a tool for extending a language by adding new facilities that can be expressed in terms of the existing ones. It should be able to extend itself. In particular the means for writing macro definitions should be extensible. It should therefore be possible to write a macro which creates a macro definition.

(It should similarly be possible to create macros that define new macro-time statements.)

A macro call that creates a new macro which in turn causes further replacements in subsequent text has the nature of a declarative statement. For example, assume there exists a very crude language where variables need to be given names that consist of the letter V followed by a unique number. Given a facility for dynamically created definitions, it would be possible to use a macro processor to introduce identifiers as variable names. Each such identifier would be declared using a macro such as

ALLOCATE X

This would have the action

Define X as VN

Increase N by 1

where N was a macro-time integer variable with a suitable initial value. Thus if N had the initial value 1 then the statements

```
ALLOCATE X
ALLOCATE PI
ALLOCATE VALUE
LET PI = 3·1416
INPUT X
LET VALUE = X*X + PI/(2 − X)
```

would generate macro definitions to replace X by V1, PI by V2 and VALUE by V3 and would therefore produce the final output

```
LET V2 = 3·1416
INPUT V1
LET V3 = V1*V1 + V2/(2 − V1)
```

(We are assuming here that the macro processor is one that allows macro calls to occur anywhere. Some macro processors are more restrictive and would be unsuitable for the above task.)

This example is rather over-simplified, but should give the reader an impression of how dynamically created macro definitions might be used to introduce declarative macros into programming languages. Realistic examples might not be declarations of simple variables but might involve subsets of arrays or subfields of words.

The scope rules that apply to dynamically created definitions are unusual, at least to those familiar with block structure in high-level languages. In our example a call of the ALLOCATE macro creates a definition of a macro but, contrary to the practice of high-level languages, this is *not* local to the replacement text of the ALLOCATE macro but is a global definition that applies to all subsequent macro processing. Some macro processors also support dynamically created definitions with local scope but these have somewhat esoteric uses. They are certainly no use for implementing statements of a declarative nature since the scope of a declaration is never local to the declare statement itself.

Summary of requirements

To summarize this chapter, the following is a list of the main features that it is desirable for a macro processor to possess.

(a) Insertion of arguments, including the treatment of optional arguments and arbitrarily long lists of arguments.
(b) Libraries of macros.
(c) Macro-time variables, both local and global and both integer and character. Arrays or stacks of these are useful.
(d) Macro-time statements for assignment, and conditional testing of macro-time variables and arguments. Arithmetic facilities for integer variables.
(e) Macro-time GOTO statements and labels, with perhaps a special looping facility.
(f) Nesting and recursion.
(g) String manipulation.
(h) Dynamically created macro definitions.

A word about (e). There has been a continuing argument about whether GOTO statements are desirable in programming languages. It is certainly true that the use of a good program structuring is much preferable to a large number of GOTO statements. Some claim fiercely that GOTO statements should be completely eliminated, whereas others hold that they still have some uses. The argument is reminiscent of the wars in *Gulliver's Travels* between those who opened eggs at one end and those who opened them at the other. However to prevent this book being destroyed by the nogotoists, we had better say that (e) can be replaced by any equivalent facilities.

Uses

The basic use of any macro processor is to extend languages or bend them towards particular classes of users. In addition, some macro processors have successfully opened up further important applications and we will introduce these when talking about the macro processors concerned.

The ADVANCE macro provided an example, albeit rather trivial, of extending a language. It often happens that users, once they have accustomed themselves to the idea of macros, use them increasingly in their programs.

This may be taken to the extent that a program is made up exclusively of macro calls with no direct use at all of the base language. In this case the set of macros might be considered as representing a programming language in its own right. Indeed, many programming languages have been constructed in this way, though such languages must, of course, be designed to have the syntax that the macro processor supports. For example it might be that each statement had to consist of a unique name followed by an argument list separated by commas.

As we have seen, it is possible for a set of macros to be designed with one particular application in mind, for example list processing, or even one problem, say the simulation of a hospital. This is what is meant by *bending* a base language towards a particular class of users. In a sense the letter-writing macros bent the English language towards a specific problem by introducing new constructions such as TRAIN and SEEYOU.

For really powerful high-level languages the need for extension may not be very great and the role of macros for such a purpose would therefore be small. However the bending of languages towards particular users is an application of macros that can be applied to all languages.

When we have said more about individual macro processors we shall return to the subject of the uses of macros, and will, in addition, look at some of the limitations as well.

Chapter 1.2

Special-purpose and General-purpose

We have seen that macro processors can be used with any base language. Historically macro processors started life tied to particular assembly languages, each assembly language having its own macro processor. The macro processor and assembler were, and still are, often regarded as a single unit, called a *macro-assembler*. More recently macro processors such as GPM (Strachey, 1965) have been designed to work on any strings of characters and are therefore suitable for any base language. These macro processors are called *general-purpose*, to distinguish them from *special-purpose* ones tied to individual base languages. The development of general-purpose macro processors has continued over recent years, and they are now widely available. Nevertheless the general-purpose macro processors have not rendered the special-purpose ones obsolete. Far from it. Macro-assemblers continue to be designed, and, more recently, special-purpose macro processors tied to high-level languages have appeared. These will be examined in more detail in later chapters.

It is worth looking more closely at the relative usefulness of special-purpose and general-purpose macro processors as they illustrate a more general principle of software design.

Some thoughts on software design

Many software designers—the author included—have been trained as mathematicians, and may well have had more experience of writing mathematical proofs than of writing programs for the products they have designed. A mathematician is trained to generalize. If he can combine two concepts into one he is greatly pleased. He is also trained to minimize the number of primitive operations or axioms in his system. His ideal is hence to build a massive structure on a few foundations.

When these ideas are applied to software for practical use they are not always successful. Programming languages that are mathematically beautiful and programming languages that lend themselves to mathematical study are not generally the ones that have been popular with people with real problems to solve and real money to spend.

The desire to generalize has been applied to compilers, and attempts have been made to produce compilers that compile all languages for all machines. Again, these do not tend to be the compilers that people actually use.

The underlying reason why generality and minimization of primitives are sometimes inappropriate ideals in software is probably because software always involves a host of trivial practical details, often concerned with the apparently irrational characteristics of physical devices or the habits of programmers. These details, by the force of their numbers and their refusal to fall into any kind of pattern, make up the bulk of the work in software writing, and any attempt to sweep them under the carpet will end in disaster.

It would be wrong, however, to outlaw the mathematician's ideals completely. They are certainly good ones to be applied in moderation. The danger comes when other considerations are not properly balanced against them.

Application to macro processors

Having generalized about the dangers of generality, we will see how this applies to macro processors.

Macro processors are just within the limits to which generality is practical. General-purpose macro processors have been used with success for almost all base languages, but if extensive macro work is to be done with a given base language then this can be done more easily using a macro processor specially designed for that language.

The advantages of a general-purpose macro processor are obvious. It is cheaper for the software writer. Moreover, the user, once he has mastered how to use the macro processor, can apply it to all existing programming languages and to any new languages that come along later. Thus the general-purpose macro processor starts the contest with a healthy lead over its special-purpose rivals.

As foreshadowed in the previous section, the disadvantages are concerned with details. We will illustrate the problem by examining one such detail.

The problem of fields

Many programming languages, particularly the older ones, tend to require information to be in fixed fields, often corresponding to columns of a punched card. If, as a result of macro processing, the size of one field is changed, then all subsequent fields will be out of alignment, with disastrous results.

When such problems arise, special-purpose macro processors, which are designed to process information in the exact format required by the programming language concerned, have obvious advantages. General-purpose macro processors are not, however, a complete write-off in these applications. Most problems can be solved by writing special input and output modules. The input module replaces sequences of blanks that are used to separate fields by 'tab' characters, and the output module converts these back into blanks again. If a field size has changed, the number of blanks generated on output will differ from the number on input. These special-purpose input/output modules do, of course, represent an erosion of the concepts of generality. General-purpose macro processors are therefore beginning to lose their healthy lead over their rivals.

Syntax

A second disadvantage of general-purpose macro processors is concerned with the syntax of the macro facilities. An advantage of special-purpose macro processors is that the notation in which macro calls and their replacement text are written can be made to look like a natural extension of the base language. This applies in particular to macro-assemblers. The syntax of a macro call can be made to look exactly like an ordinary assembly language instruction, so that a user can invoke a library of macros and use these macros as if they are ordinary instructions. Indeed there might be no need to know which instructions are macros and which are not.

The same advantage applies to the treatment of symbols. A special-purpose macro processor for Algol 60 would treat symbols such as ':=' and '**begin**' as single entities since these are basic symbols in Algol 60 whereas a general-purpose macro processor would not. Treating ':=' as two separate symbols might well lead to problems, particularly if a colon was taken as the terminator of a label.

Finally there are usually contexts in which macro processing should be inhibited. When the base language is a programming language, comments and character string constants are best ignored by macro processors. This is more easily done with a special-purpose macro processor.

With all these upsets, general-purpose macro processors are no longer way ahead. They may even be behind—it depends on the nature of the course.

Interface with base language

When the base language is a programming language, the macro processor needs to interact with the compiler for the base language. This interaction can take place at various degrees of intimacy.

The most common situation is that the macro processor does all its work, producing the complete output text, and then hands this over to the compiler for the base language. In this case we will say the macro processor is a *complete pre-processor*. The interaction between a complete pre-processor and a compiler is absolutely minimal.

Partial pre-processors

Interaction can be made closer if the macro processor hands text over to the base language compiler as it generates it. In this case we will say that the macro processor is a *partial pre-processor*. Partial pre-processing may be realized by organizing the macro processor and the compiler as co-routines. Alternatively the macro processor might be regarded as the input subroutine for the compiler. The unit of communication would depend on circumstances. A reasonable choice would often be for the macro processor to supply the text to the compiler one line at a time. This has the advantage that if the compiler detects an error in a line, the error message will be given against the source line that caused it. In the case of a complete pre-processor, on the other hand, all the compiler error messages are given against the intermediate output text. Ideally the user should not have to know about this intermediate output text. The advantages of partial pre-processing are even more manifest in a conversational environment, where it is highly desirable for a user to be informed of any errors he has made as he types his program in.

If a special interface is designed, a partial pre-processor can be made to interact very closely with the compiler that follows it. There is really no limit to the information that can be passed between one and the other, particularly in the case of a special-purpose macro processor. One possibility is for the macro processor to doctor any messages the compiler produces, and perhaps to convert them into a form that is more comprehensible to the user. The macro processor can then act as a flexible front-end to the compiler. Mandil (1972) provides examples of this application.

Compiler-integrated macros

The closest interaction of all occurs when the macro processor is made an integral part of a compiler or assembler. We will call such macro processors *compiler-integrated*. Compiler-integrated macro processors have two main advantages. Firstly, it may be possible to specify replacement text at a lower level than the source language. Thus macros for a high-level language might be expressed in assembly code or the like and macros for an assembly language in loader code. This can surmount a fundamental limitation of macro pre-processors, namely, that they can only extend the base language *in terms of itself.* Thus if a high-level language contains absolutely no primitive operations for, say, graphics, then it would be impossible to use a macro pre-processor to introduce graphics into that language. (Many high-level languages permit the use of assembly language subroutines, and this offers a possible escape from this restriction. However, the interface is not always sufficiently flexible to be exploited by macros; sometimes it is only possible to call assembly language subroutines *between* the execution of high-level language statements, not *within* the statements.)

The second advantage, which only applies to relatively high-level languages, is that compiler-integrated macros can potentially use any information the compiler has extracted from the source text. For example a compiler might convert its source text into a tree structure, extracting all declarations and building these into a dictionary. This should make the source text much easier to manipulate. It is a disadvantage of macro pre-processors (both complete and partial) that the source text is simply a sequence of symbols with no natural structure. Many desirable extensions or replacements that macros should be able to perform depend on context. For example one might wish to achieve the following tasks by macros.

(a) Replace 25 by N wherever it occurs as the limit on a FOR statement.
(b) Print the value of variable X immediately after any assignment statement with X on the left-hand side.

To accomplish such context-dependent replacements the macro processor has to examine the structure of the source text. Some macro pre-processors are capable of doing this, at least to a limited extent, but the user needs to do all the work of writing macros to find the structuring. With compiler-integrated macros, on the other hand, the macros might be able to work on the source text when it was in a form from which information was much easier to extract. The difference is that the compiler might automatically do what, to the user of a macro pre-processor, would be a laborious task. In later chapters we will encounter some tasks which, while not impossible to perform using a macro pre-processor, are difficult or even impractical. Many of these could be performed much more easily by suitable compiler-integrated macros.

At this point we might be expected to say that macro pre-processors, given their limitations, are of no further interest and the rest of the discussion is to be concentrated on compiler-integrated macros. In fact we are going to say almost the reverse. This is why.

Compiler-integrated macro processors are highly specialized, being not only dependent on one single language but also on one single compiler for that language. In spite of the fact that the basic ideas have been around since the mid-sixties, there are very few compiler-integrated macro processors that are in regular production use, though many have been, and are continuing to be, the subject of research projects (often under the heading of 'extensible languages'). It is an area where research is still to the fore, and ideas have not yet converged.

We have therefore concentrated this discussion on macro pre-processors, where the state of the art is better advanced and less volatile. However in the last chapter of this Part we will return to compiler-integrated macro processors and examine them in more detail.

Until this last chapter, the term 'macro processor' should be taken to mean 'macro pre-processor'. (We count most macro-assemblers as pre-processors, even though the macro processor might be fairly closely integrated with the assembler, since the macro facilities can usually be regarded logically as coming before assembly. The exceptions are the so-called meta-assemblers.)

In summary, compiler-integrated macros are powerful tools, but expensive to implement, rare and underdeveloped. Macro pre-processors are less aristocratic—they are common and cheap—and have been developed to a stage where a study of them is rewarding. They have plenty of power, which has been exploited in diverse areas, but have limitations in two areas: context-dependent replacement and the introduction of new facilities for which no primitives exist.

Individual macro processors

Our general discussion is postponed at this point and we will consider some individual macro processors. Our treatment is selective. We describe one representative macro-assembler rather than every one, one macro processor for a high-level language and four general-purpose macro processors. For a more comprehensive treatment the reader is referred to a separate survey (Brown, P., 1971b).

Chapter 1.3

The IBM OS Macro-assembler

IBM System /360 and System /370 are very widely used computers and, as a consequence of this, the macro processors that IBM provides for them are probably the most widely used of their type. We will examine two of these, each of which contains interesting and important features. The two are the macro-assembler than runs under the OS operating system and the macro processor for the high-level language PL/I. The latter will be considered in the next chapter. It will not be assumed that the reader has any detailed knowledge of IBM computers or of PL/I. A reader who is familiar with any assembly language and any high-level language should be able to understand the material.

Data types

We will start by examining a facility of the OS macro-assembler which, though not the most important to a user, is the one most worthy of study. This is the facility for examining *attributes* of arguments.

One characteristic of the IBM System /360/370 architecture is that it supports a large proliferation of data types. An integer can, for example, be stored in a binary representation as a full word or as a half word or in a decimal representation as an arbitrarily long series of digits.

In a high-level language, operators tend to be *polymorphic*, which means applicable to all appropriate data types. Thus one can write 'A + B' irrespective of whether A and B are fixed or floating, binary or decimal, single length or double length or even a mixture of these. In an assembly language, operators are not polymorphic; on System /360/370 there is one set of instructions for binary full-word data, another for binary half-word data, and so on. If the wrong type of instruction is used, horrible errors in the running of the program may result. (This problem applies to almost all kinds of computer, since they mostly support more than one way of representing data, but is worse than usual on System /360/370 because of the relatively large number of data types.)

The OS macro-assembler sets out to alleviate this problem. It performs a pre-pass through the entire text looking for assembly language statements that declare variables and constants and builds a dictionary which contains the name and data type attributes of each of them. It then performs the replacement of macro calls on a second pass through the source text. Within the replacement text of a call it is possible to look up a symbol in the dictionary and find out what type of data it represents. This is done in the context of a more general facility for examining the 'attributes' of arguments to macros. Many other macro-assemblers also have this facility, but it is often confined to manifest attributes, like the number of characters in an argument string.

As an example of the use of data type attributes, consider a simple macro of form

ADD   A,B

which adds two variables together. There are two ways of writing this. One way is to design it to work only with one data type, say binary integers that occupy a full word. Even in this situation, data type attributes are useful since a macro can examine its arguments to make sure they are of the correct type and give a warning message if they are not.

A more ambitious way of writing the ADD macro would be to make it cater for all types of data by examining the attributes of the arguments and generating code appropriately, thus giving the macro-assembler a dash of the power of a high-level language. In general terms the ADD macro would take the following form. (We do not show it in exact terms as we are not assuming the reader knows System /360/370 assembly language or the precise syntax of macro-time statements. Readers interested in details should look at the examples given in a paper by Kent (1969).)

> If first argument is of type 'full word binary'
> and second argument is of type 'full word binary'
> then generate 'Load first argument
>   Add second argument'
> If the first argument is of type 'single length floating'
> and second argument is of type 'single length floating'
> then generate 'Floating-load first argument'
>   Floating-add second argument'
> etc.

From the discussion so far, it might appear that the facility to examine data attributes is a highly effective one, but there is unfortunately a limitation to its use. In practice, arguments to macros will not necessarily be variable names or literal constants. They may, for example, be indirectly addressed data, and the type of such data is not decidable in an assembly language program. Hence if the ADD macro were made to cater for all data types there would be serious limitations on its use.

The change-of-meaning problem

There is also a more fundamental problem. The pre-pass can only process data declarations that are in proper assembly language form at the time the pre-pass is made. It may be that some of the declarations are generated by macros—for example the LIST macro used as an example in Chapter 1.1 generated a set of declarations—and therefore would not be there on the pre-pass. This is a general and very important problem. If macro activity is a multi-pass process any information extracted on the first pass might be invalidated by subsequent macro activity. In some macro processors the problem can be even nastier than in OS macro-assembler. Assume, for example, that, in some programming language, an integer variable I is declared thus

INTEGER   I

and a real variable X thus

REAL   X

It might be possible for macros to replace 'REAL' by 'INTEGER' and/or vice-versa, thus making the data type entirely different from that apparent on a pre-pass. Thus a dictionary built on a pre-pass would be worse than incomplete: it would be downright wrong.

This general problem will be referred to later. It is called the *change-of-meaning problem*.

Further facilities

Although the pre-pass facility is perhaps the most interesting feature of the OS macro-assembler, it is only a comparatively small part of the whole. We will now describe some of these other features.

Taken as a whole the OS macro-assembler is utilitarian rather than conceptually beautiful; not the girl you would dream about, but the sort you might marry. Macro calls are written in the commonly used notation of specifying an identifier as the macro name and following it with a list of arguments separated by commas. This is the same as the format of assembly language instructions. A label may precede the macro call and this can be referred to in its replacement text.

To cater for macros that require a variable number of arguments, any argument can be made to represent a list of subarguments. In this case the list is enclosed in parentheses. For example it would be possible to specify a macro of form

MAX (A,B,C, . . .), RES

which would generate code to find the maximum value of the variables listed as subarguments of the first argument and put the result in RES, the second argument. There are facilities within replacement text to set up loops to proceed one by one through a list of subarguments. Specifically each argument is referred to by a name and if this name is subscripted then the argument is treated as a list of subarguments, and the subscript acts as an index for the list.

Lists of arguments can be nested (at least in some of the implementations of OS macro-assembler). For example a macro call might be written

INVITE   (JOAN,(JOHN,MARY),PETER,(AL,JIM,DON))

In such cases the corresponding replacement text must contain macro-time statements to unravel the structuring and generate the appropriate code. Macro-time statements are available for testing whether an argument is a list and, if so, how many elements it contains.

In Fletcher's (1965) use of recursive macros to solve the pentomino problem, which was described in Chapter 1.1, his tree structure was represented by nested lists of subarguments using exactly the same notation as the OS macro-assembler (though Fletcher was, in fact, using an earlier IBM macro-assembler).

Keyword arguments

There is a good facility for dealing with optional arguments, and this surmounts the ambiguity problem, mentioned in Chapter 1.1, that if one argument is missing from a list of arguments it is not apparent which one it is. Instead of being identified by its position in an argument list, an argument may be identified by a *keyword* that is written in front of each occurrence. An equals sign is written between the keyword and the argument itself. We will call such arguments *keyword arguments* (and the corresponding parameters will be called *keyword parameters*). As an example of keyword arguments, assume it is desired, for debugging purposes, to have a macro called PRINTV which generates instructions to print a vector V containing 100 values. To prevent output getting too voluminous it might be useful to limit the printing where appropriate to a part of V. To achieve this the macro could be given two optional arguments denoted by the keywords FROM and TO. The following would then be sample calls of the PRINTV macro

```
PRINTV
PRINTV  TO = 10
PRINTV  FROM = 90
PRINTV  FROM = 6,TO = 16
PRINTV  TO = 16,FROM = 6
```

Within the replacement text, a keyword parameter can be declared as having a default value. In this case the FROM parameter might default to 1 and the TO parameter to 100.

Keyword arguments have other advantages in addition to facilitating optional arguments. In particular they have the following properties.

(a) They can be written in any order.
(b) They may make a program easier to read. The meaning of the PRINTV example above would be obvious to the most casual reader.
(c) They can be combined with ordinary positional arguments.
(d) If a user is content with the default value corresponding to a keyword argument, he can forget about the existence of that argument.

One very heavy use of macros on System /360/370 is for communicating with the operating system. Complicated I/O instructions can be generated by a simple macro call. A characteristic of I/O is the very large number of optional features that may apply. With keyword arguments a user may specify just those options that he wants. He does not even need to know about the special options that he does not require. Macros for communicating with the operating system are available in a standard library which is normally incorporated into any macro-assembly. This library can be changed or replaced, thus allowing the method of communication with the operating system to be altered without affecting the source program.

Replacement text

Facilities for writing replacement text are comprehensive and straight-forward. There are simple macro-time statements and both local and global macro-time variables. Macro-time variables may be of three types, integer, Boolean and character, and it is possible to declare single-dimensional arrays of any of these.

A few global macro-time variables are used for the macro processor to provide information that may be of use in replacement text. For example, System /360/370 programs are divided into units called 'control sections' and it may be necessary for a macro to know the name of the current control section. This is maintained by the macro processor in a system variable called SYSECT.

Base language dependence

The OS macro-assembler is not greatly dependent on its base language. In other words it would not need to be changed much to make it a general-purpose macro processor. Dependence on the base language is confined to the following features.

(a) The pre-pass and the attribute facility.
(b) The format of the macro call. In particular the label, which precedes the macro call, is taken as part of the call and can be referenced in the replacement text.
(c) The use of system variables such as SYSECT.
(d) Certain choices of character representations.

It is actually implemented as a complete pre-processor to the assembler itself. The dictionary created by the macro processor is not used by the assembler because of the possibility, mentioned earlier, that it might be incomplete.

Further reading

Kent (1969) has written a very good tutorial paper on the OS macro-assembler, and it is well worth reading this before attacking the IBM manual. The IBM manual is not badly written, but it may be difficult for a reader to extract the wheat from the chaff on a first reading. Freeman (1966) describes the System /360 macro facilities from a system designer's viewpoint.

Compiling of macro-time statements

A feature of the implementation that has caused some discussion is the fact that macro-time statements are not precompiled. Similar considerations apply to most other macro processors so we will discuss the problem in general terms first.

Consider a macro-time assignment statement of form

$$\text{SET} \quad \text{VAR} = 0$$

which means that the macro-time variable VAR should be given the value 0. When a statement such as this occurs within a macro definition the macro processor can treat it in two alternative ways. One way is to leave the statement in a form close to or identical with the original source form, and to interpret this every time the macro is called. The other way is to pre-compile it into machine instructions and execute these when the macro is called. Our example of setting the variable VAR to zero might compile into a single machine instruction.

The reader is probably already familiar with the pros and cons of compiling versus interpreting in the context of high-level programming languages. In short, interpreting is easier, more flexible and gives better error messages but compiling gives much faster run times. In the context of macro-time statements, which can be regarded as a programming language for generating the replacement text of macros, similar considerations apply. The relative balance of the factors may, however, be different, and, in particular, the flexibility offered by interpretation may have added importance. If, when a macro definition is encountered, all the macro-time statements within it are to be compiled then the components of those statements must be fixed in advance and must remain unchanged. For example, if macro-time variables need to be declared, they would have to be declared either before or within any macro definitions that used them, and could not subsequently be redeclared. (By carrying out the compilation process in two passes it is possible to remove this problem.)

The limitations imposed by compilation become more serious when one considers macro-time statements that are created and changed by other macros. For example, assume that there exists a macro called MTDO which acts as a macro-time DO statement. A sample call might be

$$\text{MTDO I, VAR} + 1, \text{ N, } statement$$

which means that the *statement* should be executed successively with I starting with the value of VAR + 1 and going in steps of one until it reached the value of N. The definition of the replacement text of MTDO might contain a statement of form

$$\text{SET   PAR1 = PAR2}$$

where PAR1 and PAR2 are the first and second parameters of MTDO, respectively. When arguments were substituted for parameters in the above call of MTDO this would expand into

$$\text{SET I = VAR} + 1$$

The point of this somewhat laborious example is this. Any attempt to precompile the statement

$$\text{SET   PAR1 = PAR2}$$

as it appears in the definition of MTDO would end in disaster as what appears at this stage to be a simple assignment, involves, after substitution of arguments, some arithmetic calculations, namely the addition of one to the value of VAR.

It is easy to think up more abstruse ways of negating the efforts of a compiler. It is possible, for example, in many macro processors to re-define the meanings of macro-time statements. Moreover it may be possible to create them dynamically by concatenating two pieces of text, for example appending 'T I = 0' to 'SE'.

These examples are illustrations of a fundamental point. Macro processors are concerned with making replacements in text and therefore potentially changing its meaning. Any attempt to extract information from text before it has been subjected to macro activity is dangerous. We have already encountered this problem, the so-called change-of-meaning problem, in the context of the building of a dictionary by the OS macro-assembler. The dangers of pre-compiling macro definitions is another instance of the same problem.

Having spent so long in the case against compilation, it is fair to put some arguments in favour. These can be explained much more simply. When attempts are made to exploit the full power of a macro processor, this usually means creating macros that contain a good deal of macro-time conditional statements and loops. If these are interpreted the macro processor becomes very slow indeed—most users of macro processors have had practical experience of this fact—and as a result the use of the macro processor might become impractical. The majority of macro-time statements do not involve parameters and their meanings are virtually never changed in practical use. Anyone who creates a macro-time statement by appending 'T I = 0' to 'SE' is asking for trouble. Indeed in some macro processors it is forbidden to do such things. Thus it should be possible to compile at least 80% of macro-time statements and this would speed up a macro processor considerably, thus extending its practical uses. Compiling may therefore be thought of as taking a short cut along a fast road that has some dangerous pot-holes in it, and some driving restrictions as well, but most drivers get through unscathed.

To return to the OS macro-assembler, this was implemented with a very low degree of pre-compilation, much less than in some previous IBM macro-assemblers. This prompted Maurer (1969) to implement a version that attempted a large amount of pre-compiling. He then tried to compare relative speeds, and found that compilation might give an improvement of an order of magnitude.

Chapter 1.4

The PL/I Macro Processor

The macro processor for PL/I was not the first macro processor to be attached to a specific high-level language, but previous efforts were almost all undertaken as research projects, and the PL/I macro processor therefore had a pioneering aspect in that it was issued as a piece of production software by IBM. Moreover, not only was its very existence something of a breakthrough, but its central design concept is an exciting one. The basic idea is that the syntax and semantics of the macro-time statements should be exactly the same as the corresponding PL/I statements. The two are distinguished from one another by prefixing the macro-time statements by a special marker, the percent sign, within any context where there might be ambiguity between the two. Thus for example

%DECLARE A FIXED;
%LABEL: A = 1;

are two macro-time statements that declare a macro-time variable A and set it to one. The latter statement has a label which could be the subject of a %GOTO statement. Macro-time statements can be mixed in an arbitrary way with ordinary PL/I text. All this PL/I text is copied over to the output, in the same way as most macro processors work.

The attractions of this idea are obvious. It is a great saving if the user of a macro processor can employ a language he already understands. The idea is actually an old one, as it originated in a classic paper by McIlroy (1960). (For this and for other reasons, McIlroy's paper still remains the most important one yet published on the subject of macro processors.) There had, however, been no extensive effort to exploit the idea before the PL/I macro processor came along.

Facilities available

As the reader probably knows, PL/I is a large and comprehensive language that includes most of the facilities of COBOL and ALGOL 60, plus a lot more. Only a subset of its facilities is carried over into its macro processor, but, although this subset is small relative to the whole of PL/I, it is still extensive by most standards. Actually it is not quite a proper subset as changes have been introduced into a few of the macro-time facilities. Character variables, for example, are declared differently. Moreover there are some extra macro-time statements that have no counterpart in PL/I.

There are two distinct types of macro. One type is treated as a macro-time procedure (subroutine) and is declared and called like a PL/I procedure. The other type, which is useful for macros that have no arguments and involve no macro-time activity other than replacement, is treated simply as a macro-time variable. When a macro-time variable is declared, all subsequent occurrences of it in the source text are replaced by the current value of the variable. (Note that the percent sign is only used to prefix macro-time statements, not macro calls.) Thus the source text

```
A = 6;
%DECLARE A FIXED;
%A = 7;
TAG = A;
%A = 9;
IF A = B THEN GO TO START;
```

would generate the output text

```
A = 6;
TAG = 7;
IF 9 = B THEN GO TO START;
```

Note that the creation and re-definition of macros occurs dynamically as the source text is scanned. Changing the value of a macro-time variable acts as a re-definition of the macro.

There are facilities for both integer and character macro-time variables, and the two work in a very similar manner.

It is worth examining how macro calls are recognized, since this is so different from the normal macro-assembler where the macro name can occur in one fixed field and the arguments in subsequent fields. In the PL/I macro processor, replacement occurs everywhere except within comments and string constants. However, going back to the example above, it can be seen that the A in TAG was *not* replaced; TAG did not become T7G. This is because the source text is not treated on a character-by-character basis. Instead a sequence of letters and/or digits is treated as a single indivisible atom.

If it is required to inhibit replacement of certain macros in parts of the source text, this can be done by some special statements called ACTIVATE and DEACTIVATE. If, for example, the macro-time variable A had the initial value 9, then the source text

    P = A;
    %DEACTIVATE A;
    Q = A;
    %ACTIVATE A;
    R = A;

would generate the output text

    P = 9;
    Q = A;
    R = 9;

ACTIVATE and DEACTIVATE are, incidentally, two of the statements that are unique to the macro-time part of PL/I.

Since macro calls with arguments are treated like PL/I procedure calls, arguments are separated by commas and the entire argument list is enclosed in parentheses. A sample call is therefore

NAME(ARG1,ARG2,ARG3)

Within the replacement text of the macro, all the power of the macro-time statements can be used to examine the arguments and generate the appropriate output text.

Uses

There is a facility in PL/I for switching the input stream so that pieces of a PL/I program can be included from a library. This has been made part of the macro processor rather than PL/I itself. Ironically, it is for this facility rather than for any true macro processing capability that the PL/I macro processor has been mainly used.

When the true macro processing facilities have been used, the main applications seem to have been:

(a) Taking an existing PL/I program and replacing every occurrence of one identifier by another. For example BINARY could be replaced by DECIMAL. This is a simple example of *systematic editing*, which is discussed further in Chapter 1.6.

(b) *Delayed binding.* It may be that a programmer wishes to specify a constant in his program, but wishes to be able to change the value of the constant if he needs to. One way of doing this, of course, is to use an ordinary PL/I variable in place of the constant but there may be objections to this either for reasons of efficiency or because the syntax of the language requires a constant in a certain position (e.g. the size of a data item). A better solution is to use a macro-time variable to stand for the constant and to replace it by the appropriate value during macro processing. The PL/I compiler would then see it as an ordinary constant. The purpose of the macro processor is to delay the binding of a value to the constant until the last possible moment.

Systematic editing and delayed binding are popular uses of macro processors in all contexts and are in no way particular to PL/I. Indeed, apart from some minor formatting conventions, the PL/I macro processor could be used just as well to pre-process programs in any language. The PL/I macro processor is implemented as a complete pre-processor and can therefore be regarded as logically separate from the PL/I compiler.

Further reading

There are two IBM manuals that contain descriptions of the PL/I macro processor. One chapter of the PL/I manual is devoted to the macro processor. This is a comprehensive description, but one gets that impression that the writer was really stuck for some examples of uses that the thing could be put to. The introductory student text (IBM, 1968) is better, and contains some good examples. Nicholls (1969) has written a short overall summary of PL/I as an extensible language.

Evaluation

The macro-time facilities are not a true subset of the full language, so some of the advantages of using a common language are lost. Indeed it could be argued that if two facilities are almost the same but not quite, it is better to use two totally different languages to avoid confusions. (The whole subject of designing languages to minimize programming errors is a neglected one and is well worthy of further research.)

In many ways the power of the macro processor is much degraded by the attempts to tailor it to the full PL/I facilities. PL/I may possess a good range of clothes for ordinary climates, but when it ventures into the arctic wastes of macro processing wearing only a selection of its regular clothes, albeit with a little extra padding here and there, it gets frostbite.

The syntax of macro calls is a good instance of this. Since names in PL/I must be identifiers, macro names also have to be identifiers, and as a result the power of the macro processor in the field of systematic editing is severely limited. (It is only possible to replace identifiers, nothing else.) The parallelism between macro calls and PL/I procedures also has unfortunate repercussions. The facilities for defining procedures in PL/I are geared to allowing great generality; little of this is needed for macros, but the cumbersome syntax remains. Worse still, PL/I procedures must have a fixed number of arguments. This restriction may be satisfactory for PL/I but it is not for a macro processor. Indeed several of the examples in the PL/I macro processor manuals are devoted to showing ways to overcome this restriction. The tactics are to write a macro-time program to look at an argument and split it up into its constituent parts.

The whole process is taken to the ultimate in farce by the following example from the IBM student text. They wish to define a macro of form

$$ADD \; X \; TO \; A,B,C, \ldots$$

which will generate

$$A = A + X; \; B = B + X; \; C = C + X, \ldots$$

It takes 45 lines plus comments to define this macro. The notation required for a macro call is

$$ADD \; ((X \; TO \; A,B,C, \ldots))$$

the double parentheses being needed to prevent the commas being taken as argument separators (since the macro would then have a variable number of arguments).

The PL/I macro facility is heralded as providing a shorthand notation, in other words a means of avoiding laborious writing. Actually, in the examples of the ADD macro quoted in the student text, it turns out to be a 'longhand notation' as the output is shorter than the source, thus contributing a negative amount towards paying off the investment in 45 lines of macro definition. The only possible advantage of the ADD macro is that it might be easier to write or to understand than its replacement, but even this is doubtful.

It would be wrong to end on a note of ridicule. (I should declare an interest at this point. I played a part, though a minor one, in the development of the PL/I macro processor.) The macro processor has seen some good use in the field, and maybe has pioneered the way for better things. The basic idea of drawing a parallel between macro-time and base language statements may still turn out to be a good one in spite of what I have argued to be its comparative failure with PL/I. This will be discussed further in Chapter 1.8.

Chapter 1.5

GPM and the TRAC Language

In the year 1965 the first two general-purpose macro processors were described in the literature. They were called GPM (Strachey, 1965) and the TRAC* language (Mooers and Deutsch, 1965, Mooers, 1966, 1968). The two were developed independently but are remarkably similar in nature. Each has a fine economy of concept, and a study of both of them is a prerequisite for a sound understanding of macro processing principles.

GPM

GPM stands for *General-Purpose Macrogenerator*. Strachey's description of it is well worth reading. It contains a definition of GPM itself with examples, some intellectually amusing and some practical, together with a full description of how GPM can be implemented. As a result of this, GPM has been implemented many times, but most of these implementations have been done purely as an exercise in implementing software, and GPM is widely known but not extensively used.

There are just three basic constructions in GPM: these correspond to calling a macro, inserting an argument and designating a string as literal. A macro call is written

$$\S\text{name, arg1, arg2}, \ldots, \text{arg}N ;$$

Within replacement text the insertion of an argument is represented by the character $\sim$ followed by a digit denoting the argument number. (The macro name counts as argument zero.) The enclosing of a string in the *literal brackets* $\langle \ \rangle$ causes the string to be copied literally and not evaluated. Thus $\langle \S \sim 1 ; \rangle$ stands for the string $\S \sim 1 ;$. The literal brackets prevent the character $\S$ being taken as the start of a macro call or the character $\sim$ as meaning the insertion of an argument.

---

* TRAC is the service mark and trademark of Rockford Research, Inc., Cambridge, Mass.

Macro-time statements in GPM are represented and processed in the same way as macro calls. In particular, a macro is defined by calling a built-in macro called DEF. For example

§DEF,SIZE,6;

would define SIZE as 6. The following are some examples of calls of the SIZE macro

(1) §SIZE; would be replaced by 6.
(2) X(§SIZE;,§SIZE;) would be replaced by X(6, 6).
(3) SIZE§SIZE;SIZE would be replaced by SIZE6SIZE.

As an example of a macro with arguments, the definition

§DEF,SQMATRIX,⟨REAL ARRAY (1 : ~1,1 : ~1)⟩;

would cause §SQMATRIX,13; to be replaced by REAL ARRAY (1 : 13,1 : 13). (We will explain the literal brackets surrounding the replacement text of SQMATRIX in a minute.) The § character is reserved as a unique marker to introduce macro calls and to separate them from other text. In fact the § character together with the semicolon that occurs at the end of a macro call may be regarded as a pair of brackets that is used to enclose all macro calls.

Calls may be nested within arguments to other calls and thus, continuing the above example, §SQMATRIX,§SIZE;; would generate REAL ARRAY (1 : 6,1 : 6).

Before being processed, arguments themselves are evaluated. Thus

§DEF,P,PI;
§DEF,COW,A§P;B§P;C;

would define COW as APIBPIC, the nested calls of P being replaced by PI. Moreover if a definition were written

§DEF,OPP,UN~1;

the use of the character ~ would cause an attempt to be made to insert argument one at the time the call of DEF was being scanned. Since arguments only exist within the replacement text of a macro call, this would be an error if it occurred in the source text. If, on the other hand, the macro were defined

§DEF,OPP,⟨UN~1⟩;

then the replacement text of OPP would be defined as the string UN~1 and argument one would be inserted when the macro was called. For example

§OPP,READY;

would generate UNREADY. The purpose of the literal brackets is therefore to delay evaluation to a later stage. Literal brackets may be nested. Thus

$$\S DEF,DUB,\langle\langle \sim 1\rangle\rangle;$$

would define DUB as $\langle \sim 1\rangle$. When DUB was called, this string would be evaluated and yield the result ~ 1. Hence this is a way of placing the symbol $\sim$ in the output. Each evaluation of a string strips off one level of literal brackets.

A good rule for writing macro definitions is to always enclose the second argument of DEF in literal brackets unless something clever is being attempted.

One of the discoveries that comes out of Strachey's paper is the power and generality of the simple replacement facility that macros provide. In particular, replacement can be used to perform arithmetic and conditional generation.

Strachey's examples of this are initially hard to understand, but it is worth persevering. The following example illustrates the arithmetic capability. The macro definition

$$\S DEF,SUC,\langle\S 1,2,3,4,5,6,7,8,9,10,\S DEF,1,\langle \sim \rangle \sim 1;;\rangle;$$

is such that if it is called with a single digit as argument then the result will be that digit increased by 1. Thus, for example, §SUC,5; is 6. We will consider how this call would be processed. The replacement text of SUC simply consists of a call of a macro which has the name 1. The way GPM works is that when it finds a macro call it goes through all the arguments of the call evaluating any macro calls nested within them. (This method of scanning is what a later chapter terms 'call by value'.) Hence, when the 1 macro is called, its arguments are scanned in this way. The last argument is §DEF,1,$\langle \sim \rangle \sim 1$;. This has the effect of defining 1, the macro that is just about to be called, as ~ 5. (Note how this ~ 5 is built up. When $\langle \sim \rangle \sim 1$ is evaluated, the first $\sim$, being in literal brackets, is copied over as part of the value whereas the ~ 1, which is not in literal brackets, is evaluated and causes the first argument of SUC, in this case 5, to be inserted.) When the macro 1 is called, its replacement text, which has just been defined as ~ 5, causes the fifth argument to the call of SUC to be inserted. This is 6. Clever stuff.

Note how 1 is a temporary local macro that is re-defined every time SUC is called. The name of the temporary macro is an added subtlety. If it had been called, say, NEXT instead of 1, the SUC macro would have worked except when its argument was the digit zero. §SUC,0; would have as its value argument 0 of the NEXT macro. Argument 0 is the macro name so the value would be NEXT. Hence the choice of 1 as the name.

Conditional evaluation can also be achieved using local macro definitions. The effect of

$$if \ A = B \ then \ C \ else \ D$$

where A, B, C and D are strings possibly containing macro calls, can be achieved by the definition

$$§A,§DEF,A,\langle D \rangle;§DEF,B,\langle C \rangle;;$$

This generates a call of A and creates two local definitions, one of A and then one of B. If B is the same as A these two definitions define the same macro, and since the second overrides the first, the string C is taken. If B is not the same as A the first definition holds.

Strachey's paper goes on to combine these facilities to create a macro to add one to a two-digit number, the algorithm being that the second digit is incremented unless it is nine, in which case the first digit is incremented and the second digit set to zero. One can then proceed to a more general arithmetic capability.

It is truly amazing that so much can be done with so little, but there is, unfortunately, a negative side. Macro definitions become more and more complicated and harder and harder to understand. When there exist macros to create macros to create macros it becomes a mind-bending task to decide which parts to enclose in one pair of literal brackets, which in two, and so on. Moreover the amount of machine-time used to process macro calls becomes exorbitant. To quote Strachey about GPM: 'It contains in itself all the undesirable features of every possible machine code—in the sense of inviting endless tricks and time-wasting through fascinating exercises in ingenuity—without any of the *ad hoc* features of real machines'.

The TRAC language

Although the TRAC (*T*ext *R*eckoning *A*nd *C*ompiling) language is logically similar to GPM, it does not use the same notation nor are its primitive operations identical. The TRAC language is more widely used than GPM, perhaps because it has been more heavily promoted. It has been presented as a tool for on-line use and this has doubtless helped its popularity.

It contains a set of built-in functions, which are called in the following way

$$\#(\textit{function name},string1,string2,\ldots,stringN)$$

One of the functions is called *ds* (*d*efine *s*tring) and this defines a macro. A macro call is written

$$\#(cl,\text{macro name},arg1,arg2,\ldots,argN)$$

cl is a built-in function that calls a macro. In the TRAC language, therefore, calling a macro is a particular example of a built-in function whereas in GPM the built-in functions (the DEF macro, etc.) are particular examples of macro calls. The TRAC language view of the world is more logically consistent, since there is an inherent difference between a macro, which performs string substitution, and a built-in function (or macro-time statement), which performs a pre-defined action. The TRAC language notation is more verbose, however. In complicated cases huge nests of macros build up, and programmers tend to spend time working out whether it needs twenty-one closing parentheses or twenty-two to terminate one of the constructions they have built up.

The TRAC language method for specifying where arguments are to be inserted into replacement text is interesting. Consider the definition

$$\#(ds, \text{SENT, THE ANIMAL SAT ON THE MAT})$$

This defines a macro called SENT with replacement text THE ANIMAL SAT ON THE MAT. This macro can be parameterized by the operation

$$\#(ss, \text{SENT, ANIMAL, THE})$$

This segment string operation has the effect, when SENT is called, of causing the first argument of the call to be substituted for each occurrence of ANIMAL and the second argument for each occurrence of THE. Thus the call

$$\#(cl, \text{SENT, CAT, A})$$

would generate

A CAT SAT ON A MAT

Although this mechanism for parameter definition might appear cumbersome in simple cases, it has advantages in flexibility and generality.

The following is a slightly more complex example of a TRAC language macro and gives more of an impression of the appearance of the language. It is the most popular example in computing: the recursive definition of the factorial function. The following, which is reprinted from Mooers (1966) by permission of Rockford Research, Inc., shows how this would be done in the TRAC language.

$$\#(ds, \text{Factorial},(\ \#(eq,1,X,(1),$$
$$(\ \#(ml,X,\#(cl, \text{Factorial}, \#(ad,X,-1))))$$
$$)))\ \#(ss,\text{Factorial},X)'$$

The parentheses that are not part of function calls act like literal brackets in GPM. The function *eq* is such that $\#(eq,X,Y,(S1),(S2))$ means *if* $X = Y$ *then* S1 *else* S2, and *ml* and *ad* are the multiply and add functions, respectively.

Given this definition of factorial, the call

$$\#(cl, \text{Factorial}, 2)$$

would cause the replacement text of Factorial to be evaluated with X replaced by 2. This would lead to a call of *eq* of form

$$\#(eq, 1,2,(1),(\,\#(ml,\text{X},\#(cl,\text{Factorial},\#(ad,\text{X},-1))))))$$

Since the first two arguments of *eq* are unequal, the string given by the value of the last argument would be evaluated. This would call *ml* to multiply 2 by the result of $\#(cl,\text{Factorial},1)$. The recursive call of Factorial would give the result of one, thus yielding two as the final answer.

There is an important distinction in the TRAC language between *active functions* (which we have assumed up to now) and *neutral functions*. Neutral functions are called with two sharp signs instead of one at the start, for example

$$\#\,\#(cl,\text{SENT},\text{CAT},\text{A})$$

The essential difference between the two is the treatment of the value of the function. If the function is active the value is re-scanned to see if it contains macro calls; if it is neutral it is not re-scanned. This is rather different from GPM; in particular, activeness or neutrality is a property of a macro call, not of a definition. Moreover in GPM argument insertion proceeds as replacement text is evaluated and literal brackets inhibit both argument insertion and macro calls, whereas in the TRAC language arguments are inserted into the replacement text as the first action of a macro call and then a decision is made as to how the resultant text is to be treated.

The TRAC language is one that has attracted a distinguished band of fervent disciples. (APL is another language with this property.) You either like it or hate it. Devotees would point to the underlying simplicity and versatility of the language; cynics think people use it just to impress the neighbours.

In addition to the papers previously cited, further information about the TRAC language is given in papers by McKinnon Wood (1968) and Williams (1968).

Comparison of usage

GPM was developed explicitly as a macro processor. In its normal use, GPM macro calls are embedded in a program expressed in some programming language. GPM replaces these macro calls and the program is then compiled normally. Although Strachey noted some of the other applications of GPM, such as the macros to perform arithmetic, conventional macro processing remained its main use. Probably the most extensive use of GPM has been to create a set of macros, based on assembly language, that aid the encoding of systems programs.

The TRAC language, on the other hand, is presented as a general-purpose text processing language, and has been used for such jobs as parsing of natural language. Macros are regarded as string variables, and, indeed, the word 'macro' rarely occurs in descriptions of the TRAC language since the word 'string' is preferred.

Why, if GPM and the TRAC language are so similar, do their uses appear to be so different? The first point to be made is that macro processing is a specialized field of text manipulation, and so the two application areas are not as different as may appear. Many of the primitives of the TRAC language, in particular the segment string function mentioned earlier, have been specially designed to cater for text processing in general rather than macro processing in particular.

The second point concerns a feature of the TRAC language that we have not mentioned yet. This is the read string function, which reads the next string from the input stream. (An input string, which is normally typed by a user at a conversational console, is an arbitrarily long set of characters terminated by a quote sign.) Thus the reading of input text is entirely under the control of the macro writer. In GPM, on the other hand (and in most other macro processors too) input flows by in an inexorable stream and is all treated in a uniform manner, i.e. it is scanned for macro calls and those that are found are replaced. We will call these two manners of working *controlled input* and *uncontrolled input*, respectively. Uncontrolled input is fine for conventional macro processing, since the input text is usually best analysed in a uniform manner and it is a bore to have to specify explicit input statements. However, when one moves into general text manipulation the flexibility of controlled input is needed.

With uncontrolled input the only way an item of data can be passed to a specific macro is for a call of the macro to be written with the item of data as an argument. This may be highly inconvenient in general text processing. It is like working with a numerical language which required that, every time a number was supplied as input to a program, the label within the program of the corresponding INPUT statement had to be specified. Perhaps the following example will clarify this point further.

Assume that a program in the TRAC language is to analyse data which consists of a series of records each of which consists of up to four items as follows:

(1) YES or NO. This is the answer to a question about whether a given person has a son.
(2) A number. This is the age of the eldest son, and is only supplied if the answer to (1) is YES.
(3) and (4) Similar items for a daughter.

The program might take the following form

(a) The SON macro is called and inputs a data item. It checks that the answer is YES or NO. If YES it calls the AGE macro to input and process the next item. In a conversational environment these macros might issue prompts (e.g. SON?) and might ask for corrections if any data item is wrong (e.g. PLEASE ANSWER YES OR NO). The SON macro processes the answers and exits.

(b) The DAUGHTER macro is called and performs a parallel action to the SON macro. When it has finished, a check is made to see if there is any more data. If so, the SON macro is called again and the process is repeated.

In GPM, on the other hand, the macro names would have to be built into the data. The data might look like this:

§SON,YES;§SONAGE,16;§DAUGHTER,NO;
§SON,NO;§DAUGHTER,YES;§DAUGHTERAGE,17;

. . .

Alternatively each record could be made into a single macro, e.g.

§RECORD,YES,16,NO;
§RECORD,NO,YES,17;

This latter form, however, would be less convenient in a conversational environment as it would not be possible to prompt each item in turn, nor to correct items individually as they were typed in.

Moreover, things might well get out of hand with GPM if a macro name was wrongly specified (e.g. §SIN,YES;) or if macros were called in the wrong order. In the TRAC language the appropriate macro is already in control when the input is requested, and an appropriate structure is forced on the data. All in all, GPM is simply the wrong tool for the job, as indeed any macro processor with uncontrolled input would be.

Chapter 1.6

ML/I and STAGE2

We will now examine two general-purpose macro processors, ML/I and STAGE2, which might be called 'second generation'. They may lack some of the elegance of the first-generation models but they cater for wider usage.

ML/I

It is hard for me to review ML/I in a dispassionate way since I developed it myself (Brown, P., 1967). The reader is therefore advised to view what follows as they would a mother's description of her only child.

ML/I is a general-purpose macro processor, and is closer to GPM than to the TRAC language. It has been implemented on a number of machines, though, as in the case of GPM, some of the implementations were performed by software jackdaws who like to collect implementations of all the software they can lay their hands on.

The aim of ML/I is to allow a much freer notation for macro calls, and to let the notation have some meaning. There are two reasons for this. Firstly, if a macro processor is used to extend a programming language, it is best if the new statements look like the old. If the programming language has all the grace of Georgian architecture it is a sin to build a concrete and glass extension. It is easy for a special-purpose macro processor—especially a macro-assembler—to achieve this, but a general-purpose macro processor needs to be flexible to achieve the same aim.

Secondly, notational freedom adds a new dimension to the uses of a macro processor. In the traditional way of working, a set of macros is written and then people write programs that use them. ML/I allows this order of events to be inverted. Macros can be used to make changes in programs that have already been written. This use of macros to replace one pattern of symbols by another throughout a program is called *systematic editing*. It should not be confused with the kind of editing where a set of isolated changes is being made to a program. This latter kind of editing is not a job for a macro processor.

Uses of systematic editing arise in many ways. Perhaps the most common is for modifying a program obtained from elsewhere; even if this is written in a so-called standard language it always seems to be necessary to make some systematic changes to the program before it can be run. For example, the rules for FORMAT statements in some FORTRANs allow the character string XYZ to be written 'XYZ' whereas others require the form 3HXYZ. Input/output statements are also often subject to local variations. Uses of systematic editing also arise in personally developed programs; as specific examples, it may be required to replace the number 20 by 30 wherever it occurs as an array bound or a limit on a loop or it may be required to add an extra argument to all calls of a certain subroutine.

ML/I does not, therefore, have a fixed notation for writing macro calls, but allows each macro to have its own *delimiter structure*. The delimiter structure defines the macro name, which comes at the start of the call, the delimiters that are to follow each argument, and the closing delimiter that is to end the macro call. If it is desired, for example, to write a macro to replace all strings of the form '...' then the macro name would be a quote sign and the closing delimiter would also be a quote sign. If it is required to create a macro of form

$$\text{SET} \ldots = \ldots + \ldots$$

then the macro name would be SET, the first delimiter an equals sign, the second delimiter a plus sign and the third delimiter the newline character at the end of the line.

It is possible to specify alternatives for the same delimiter. We could, for example, allow either a plus sign or a minus sign as the second delimiter of the SET macro. Within the replacement text of a macro it is possible for a macro-time statement to examine which delimiter occurred in the call and generate code accordingly. The notation therefore has meaning. This is an important point; it would be worse than useless to allow either a plus sign or a minus sign in the call of SET if they both generated the same text.

Lastly it is possible for a delimiter structure to loop back on itself. (A delimiter structure is, in fact, a directed graph.) This is done by placing a *node* at a certain point in the structure; this node can then be defined as the successor of any delimiter. In other words it can be specified that, after a given delimiter is found, the state of scan should be taken as that specified by the node. Since a delimiter structure can contain any number of nodes, this allows any combination of optional or repeated arguments. Assume, for example, that we wished to extend the SET macro to allow any number of arguments, separated by plus or minus signs, to appear to the right of the equals sign. This can be represented pictorially thus

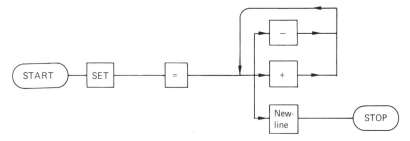

This in turn could be encoded as an ML/I delimiter structure. We will not describe details here except to say that, like any one-dimensional representation of a two-dimensional structure, the appearance of a delimiter structure is not immediately appealing. Full details can be found in the *ML/I User's Manual* (Brown, P., 1970).

Given this delimiter structure, the following would be sample calls

SET ... = ...
SET ... = ... + ... − ... + ...
SET ... = ... − ... − ... − ...

Within the replacement text of SET there would be a macro-time loop which went through each argument in turn, examining the delimiter that preceded it and generating appropriate code.

Warning-mode

We have seen from the previous discussion that some macro processors require a certain unique character to precede a macro call. Thus in GPM all macro calls start with the § character. We will call characters such as the § in GPM *warning markers* and we will use the term *warning-mode* to describe the scanning mechanism of macro processors that require warning markers.

Those macro-assemblers that require the macro name to appear in the operation field can be regarded as working in a variation of warning-mode. The fields of an input line can be regarded as being separated by a set of invisible 'field marker' characters—cf. the 'newline' character at the end of a line—a different field marker being used to herald each field. With this assumption the operation field marker acts as a warning marker. This is, however, slightly different from the use of § in GPM. The § character is a *compulsory* warning marker in that it *must* be followed by a macro call; the field marker is an *optional* warning marker in that it *may* be followed by a macro call. The use of optional warning markers to restrict the context of macro calls has advantages in faster implementation and in avoiding ambiguities (a variable which is referenced only in operand fields can have the same name as a macro). The disadvantage is precisely that the context is restricted. If traditional macro-assemblers are examined in their role as extenders of assembly language they have a serious limitation: they can only add new facilities of one type, namely new statements; they cannot introduce new ways of writing such elements as constants, variables or addresses since macro names cannot occur in the operand field.

It is worth mentioning the third type of warning marker that is logically possible. This is the type that must be followed by a macro call, but without the requirement that each macro call must be preceded by a warning marker. If * were a warning marker with this property then each occurrence of * would herald a macro call but there might be macro calls not preceded by a *. It may seem pointless to describe a facility of so little obvious use, but it is a well-known phenomenon among language designers that apparently useless facilities that have been included only for logical completeness in a language always turn out to be just what is needed for some particular application.

Free-mode

ML/I and the PL/I macro processor do not require warning markers and these are said to run in *free-mode*. If SET has been defined as a macro name the normal action of ML/I is to take any subsequent occurrence of SET, whether in the source text or in replacement text, as the start of a call of the SET macro. Experience has shown that macro processors that run in free-mode usually do best to analyse text in units larger than single characters. ML/I works in units of *atoms*, where any sequence of letters and/or digits counts as an atom. The use of atoms prevents macros being called in an unintended way. Thus the SET macro would be called only if it occurred as an atom, and so names such as ASSET and SETH would not cause the SET macro to be called. A parallel may be taken with the analysis of natural language: one does not take 'damage' as referring to the age of a female horse.

The concept of atoms does not solve all the problems with free-mode macro processors. If the user of the SET macro writes a comment in his program of the form

/* INITIAL LOOP TO SET UP TABLE */

he would be upset if the macro processor took this occurrence of SET as part of a macro call, and tried to replace it and the text that followed. The same would apply to a statement of form

PRINT "ANSWERS USING FIRST DATA SET"

To combat these problems, ML/I contains a construction called a *skip*, which is a generalization of the literal brackets found in GPM. Skips inhibit macro activity in a given context. They have the same delimiter structure facilities as macros have. Thus in the above example /* would be defined as a skip name with */ as its closing delimiter, and this would have the effect of keeping comments out of the clutches of macro replacement. A similar skip could cover literal character strings. Thus the use of skips can curb the enthusiasm of a free-mode macro processor to replace everything that comes in its sights.

ML/I macro names can be any sequence of atoms, and this leads to potential ambiguities. If, for example, both GO and GO TO are the names of macros (or skips), then is the text

GO TO Y

treated as a call as GO, GO TO, or both? The ML/I rule is that the longest possible name is matched, so the above call would be taken as a call of GO TO. This rule works well in practice, and can be useful in limiting the context of replacement. For example if one wanted a macro to replace each occurrence of GO that was not followed by TO, then GO could be defined as a macro and GO TO as a skip.

However, even with all these mechanisms to hand, free-mode macro processors still have their dangers. If a free-mode macro processor is being used to extend a programming language, then it is often necessary to place restrictions on the choice of names in the extended language (e.g. do not use SET as the name of a variable unless you really have to, and, if you do, enclose it in literal brackets).

To summarize, therefore, if we consider the application of a macro processor to extend a base language, a warning-mode macro processor requires the user to insert an extra symbol everywhere he wishes a macro to be called, whereas a free-mode macro processor may necessitate the insertion of extra symbols (literal brackets) when it is desired to inhibit a macro from being called.

ML/I actually allows the user to choose whether to run in free-mode or warning-mode, though the warning-mode facility is not greatly emphasized in the documentation. In practical usage, free-mode has been chosen almost invariably. It is felt that this is less likely to lead to errors. Warning-mode users are more likely to suffer from omissions or mistypings of warning markers than free-mode users are likely to suffer from unintended macro calls.

In the field of systematic editing warning-mode is useless, so the free-mode macro processors have the field to themselves.

Pattern matching and prefix notation

A limitation of the ML/I notation for macro calls is that each macro call must start with a pre-defined symbol, the macro name. In other words, macro calls are written in *prefix* notation. Programming languages often use *infix* notation, which, in the case of a binary operator, means the operator is written between its operands. For example, addition is written in the form $x + y$ rather than in some prefix notation such as $+ xy$ or $+ (x,y)$. ML/I is not good at dealing with infix syntax. It is sometimes possible to save the day by processing the infix notation in a wider context (e.g. the infix plus and minus operators within the SET macro), but this is not always so. Often the ML/I user has to resort to such devices as defining the newline symbol as a macro with the next newline as its closing delimiter. This provides the wider context mentioned above, but is a clumsy device.

Macro processors that recognize macro calls by a pattern-matching method help solve these problems. The best known of these is STAGE2 (Waite, 1970b), which is a development (and to some extent a subset) of an earlier macro processor called LIMP (Waite, 1967). STAGE2 is mainly designed as an aid to portable software, and this aspect will be discussed in detail later, but is interesting as a macro processor in its own right.

STAGE2

STAGE2 analyses the source text line by line. With each macro is associated a template, which consists of some fixed strings (delimiters) with gaps between them for the arguments. Every source line is compared with the template associated with each macro. It may be that several templates fit the same source line; in this case a notion of the closest fit resolves ambiguities, in a similar way to the rule in ML/I described earlier. To quote an example from Waite's paper, the source line

$$\text{ALPHA} = (\text{BETA} + \text{GAMMA}) * \text{DELTA}$$

would match the templates

$$\text{ALPHA} = (') * \text{DELTA}$$
$$\text{ALPHA} = {}^{\text{'}*\text{'}}$$
$$\text{ALPHA} = {}'$$
$$' = '$$
$$' = (') * '$$

where the quote sign stands for an argument. The first template gives the closest fit and so it would be the macro associated with this that was called.

A similar, slightly extended method for matching macro calls is used in MP/I (Macleod, 1971).

STAGE2 also provides interesting facilities for use in replacement text. Each time a macro call is processed, a set of nine local character variables is created. These are given initial values corresponding to the argument strings—if there are less than nine arguments then the remaining character variables are initialized as null. (It is not permissible to have more than nine arguments.) Two separate facilities, the passing of arguments and the use of local character variables, are thus combined into one.

Global character variables are provided in STAGE2 by an associative memory. This can be used, for example, as a dictionary. This concept of associative memory is not, in fact, dissimilar to the use of global macros to pass information between macros. (The latter works as follows. One macro creates a global macro which has, as its replacement text, some text to be looked at by a second macro. This second macro may then call the global macro and perhaps examine its value to extract certain information from it.)

A further good point about STAGE2 is that it makes provision for the use of temporary files during macro processing. They are useful for storing comparatively large blocks of information that are generated by a macro for insertion into the output at a later stage.

Comparison

Macro processors that operate on a line-by-line pattern-matching basis have the obvious limitation that a macro call must correspond exactly to a line, and it is not possible to have one macro call nested within another. It may be possible to program round these difficulties, just as it may be possible to program round ML/I's limitations on infix notation, but the results are not pleasing.

Macro processors of the ML/I type and those of the STAGE2 type complement each other's limitations. Some installations maintain implementations of both ML/I and STAGE2 and pick the better tool for each individual macro processing job.

Grant (1971) has proposed a completely different way of matching macro calls. A macro is recognized by its name and has two arguments: the entire source text occurring before the call and the entire source text coming after. These are named L and R, respectively. Macro-time statements can scan L and R for given symbols. For example, R could be searched for the next comma and the text up to this point could be taken as the true argument of the macro. Macro-time statements can change L and R—for example new declarative statements could be added at the start of L—and can specify where scanning is to re-start after a macro call has been processed. There are, of course, considerable practical problems in implementing Grant's proposal efficiently since L and R might be very long strings.

I have used a text processing language called SCAN (Brown, P., 1972a) to act as a macro processor in the way Grant describes, albeit with a limitation on the size of L and R. My experience was that it was very good at certain relatively simple jobs (some of which ML/I found difficult), but problems arose with nested calls.

Chapter 1.7

Communication Between Macros

Having described a representative sample of individual macro processors, we will now continue the general discussion. In this chapter we will examine some of the problems that arise when macros need to communicate with one another, and will show how the use of global variables and other tools helps to solve these problems.

Problems of communication arise in most types of macro activity, but it is convenient to illustrate them with respect to a specific application area. The application area we will use for most of the problems is the use of macros to extend an assembly language. We will assume that the assembly language is for a simple computer called BASECOMP. BASECOMP has one accumulator and its instruction repertoire consists of a set of single-address instructions, two of which are

> LOAD   *V*   Load accumulator with value of *V*.
> STORE   *V*   Store accumulator in *V*.

End-to-end communication

One of the simplest, but nevertheless most important, uses of inter-macro communication arises when two macros are called in immediate succession and it is desired to relay some information from one call to the next. A particular case of this that has aroused much attention is the problem of eliminating redundant instructions at the boundary between macros that generate machine instructions. This is a good problem to look at since even a fairly superficial examination shows up most of the difficulties that arise when a macro tries to communicate with a succeeding one. The problem can be illustrated thus. Assume that a macro

> SET   *argument1* = *argument2*

maps into the instructions

> LOAD   *argument1*
> STORE   *argument2*

Then the successive calls

$$\text{SET}\quad P = Q$$
$$\text{SET}\quad R = P$$

generate

$$\text{LOAD}\quad Q$$
$$\text{STORE}\quad P$$
$$\text{LOAD}\quad P$$
$$\text{STORE}\quad R$$

The second LOAD instruction is redundant. This redundancy can be eliminated by using a global macro-time character variable to indicate the current contents of the accumulator. If this variable has the name CACC then SET might be written

> If CACC ≠ *argument2* then generate "LOAD *argument2*"
> Generate "STORE *argument1*"
> Set CACC = *argument1*

CACC would need to be initialized to some suitable value, for example a null value, to show that the accumulator contained no fixed value at the start of the program.

The problem is not, of course, likely to be confined to one macro. If a call of SET is followed by any macro call that starts by generating a LOAD instruction or if it is preceded by any macro call that ends by generating a STORE instruction, then the same problem occurs. Thus all such macros should use CACC in the same way as SET. For example if there existed a macro of form

SWOP   argument1, argument2

which interchanged the values of its arguments, then this would use CACC to ensure that if SET followed SWOP or SWOP followed SET then any possible optimization would be done.

This is all very simple. Unfortunately it is too simple—it ignores a number of potential pitfalls. Firstly if the second of the two successive macro calls is the object of a GOTO instruction then it cannot be assumed that the accumulator contains what the previous macro put in it, and so optimization must be suppressed. (Macro processors simply do not have the facilities to look at the dynamic behaviour of a program and optimize on the basis of this.) If we assume that it is only possible to GOTO an instruction that is labelled, then the existence of a label can be made to cause CACC to be set to null. The exact mechanics of doing this depend on the macro processor concerned. Surprisingly, a general-purpose free-mode macro processor might do better than a macro-assembler. In the former case it might be possible to define a macro which matched the label field. This macro would test if its argument was not null, i.e. if a label was present, and set CACC to null if this was so. The typical macro-assembler would not have this facility; instead the label name, if any, would be passed as an argument to each macro. Hence each macro would need to contain a test of whether the label was null. This is an example, therefore, of the defects of the inflexible format found in macro-assemblers.

The second pitfall is illustrated by the following example

```
SET     P = Q
LOAD    S
STORE   T
SET     R = P
```

Here the two calls of SET do not occur in succession, and the user has inserted extra machine instructions between them which change the accumulator.

There are two ways of dealing with this, both of which make demands on the macro processor.

The first way is to associate with CACC a second global variable called CLINE which gives the line number (or instruction number or location counter value) where CACC was last set. As mentioned earlier, many macro processors provide system variables that supply information about the current context of a macro call and one such variable might usefully correspond to the line count. Given this, a macro would only suppress a LOAD instruction if CACC corresponded to the variable to be loaded and CLINE was one less than the current line number. This solution is still not perfect as intervening comments or blank lines would needlessly cause optimization to be suppressed.

The second way is to define LOAD and STORE as macros such that a call of either generates an identical copy of itself but, as a side effect, maintains the value of CACC. This way is better than the first as it allows elimination of the redundant LOAD instruction generated by the SET macro in a context such as

```
STORE P
SET X = P
```

Unfortunately this technique is impossible in those macro-assemblers in which the names of machine instructions are sacred and cannot be overridden by macros. This is a serious deficiency.

Even now we are some way from perfect optimization. After the macro call

```
SET   P = Q
```

the accumulator contains the values of both P and Q and an instruction to load either should be suppressed if it follows. Hence CACC should be a list of names rather than a single one.

One might begin to question whether the effort is worthwhile. As hardware becomes cheaper and people more expensive, the efforts to save a few instructions in a program become less and less economic unless the program is to be used very widely. However people are slow to change, and react adversely when they see blatant inefficiencies in macro-generated code, so optimization may be justified on psychological grounds. Compilers do not tend to reveal the generated object progam to the user and hence can get away with murder.

The overall lessons to be learned from this example are

(a) Optimization of macro-generated code is difficult.
(b) It is often necessary to find out about the context of a macro call. System variables may be useful here, but a flexible macro processor that can perform its own examination of context (e.g. by looking at label fields) is the only really satisfactory answer.

Communication between nested calls

It is a common practice for the replacement text of one macro to contain calls of other macros. There should be few problems of communication in this situation as the entire situation is under the close control of the macro writer.

A more interesting situation arises when one macro call occurs within an argument of the call of another macro. If the user is allowed to nest calls in this way the replacement text of the relevant macros has to be written to cater for all the combinations that can occur. Many macro processors, in particular those (like most current macro-assemblers) where a macro call occupies exactly a line, do not allow calls to be nested in this way. We must therefore assume in this section that we are dealing with one of the somewhat restricted class of macro processors which does allow such nesting. Examples are GPM and ML/I.

To illustrate the situation, we will assume there exists a macro of form IND(X), which means the indirect address pointed at by X. This macro can be called within an argument to the SET macro. A sample might be

$$\text{SET} \quad \text{IND(X)} = Q$$

(or whatever equivalent notation the macro processor uses, e.g. §SET, §IND, X ;, Q ; in the case of GPM).

We will first assume that BASECOMP supports indirect addressing and that this is achieved by writing :I after the instruction name. The above call would then map into

<pre>
LOAD   Q
STORE:I   X
</pre>

The replacement text of the IND macro could then be defined simply to be :I followed by the argument. It could be called from within either argument of the SET macro or of any other macro of a similar nature without changing these macros in any way. (We assume the BASECOMP assembler is flexible enough to cater for any variations in spacing between the fields of the generated instructions.) The power of the SET macro and similar macros has therefore been greatly increased by defining this trivial new macro.

An Elysian picture is emerging. It would seem that by adding more and more simple macros one could build up a flexible language as powerful as, say, Algol. For example one could supplement IND by macros for referencing arrays or for extracting subfields from words. With some macro processors one could extend the SET macro to allow any number of arguments separated by arithmetic operators, and one could add macros corresponding to high-level language IF statements, DO statements, etc. This has indeed been successfully done, but the technique has its limitations and there are often serious problems involving the interrelation between macros. To illustrate these we will consider how the IND macro would be dealt with if BASECOMP had no indirection facility, but required instead the use of an index register. (Even if IND did not need an index register, some of the other macros we have postulated, such as those for referencing arrays, would. Hence the problems we are about to highlight are bound to come up at some stage.) We will assume, therefore, that to load the contents of the word pointed at by P it is necessary to execute the two instructions

<pre>
LINDEX   P   Load value of P into index register.
LOAD:X   0   Load accumulator with word at offset zero from
               where the index register points.
</pre>

Similarly for the STORE instruction and other BASECOMP instructions. The interrelation of the SET and IND macros now becomes rather complicated. Consider the generation of the LOAD instruction within the SET macro. It is not possible to say

<pre>
Generate   "LOAD   argument2"
</pre>

as it was before, because if the first argument happens to involve indirection it is necessary to add an instruction before the LOAD and then add the text :X 0 after the LOAD. In other words the text generated by the SET macro and the IND macro are not neatly nested but are interspersed.

One potential solution to this problem is not to make IND a macro at all but to make the SET macro examine whether each of its arguments is a call of IND and act accordingly. This is not satisfactory as it means that every macro that can have IND nested within it must do the same thing. Moreover there may be other macros of a similar nature to IND that would require the same treatment.

In fact there seems to be no generally good solution to this problem at all. It is true, however, that if one considers any single macro processor one could probably find a solution that worked for that macro processor, but the solution would be one of those that appeared to be held together precariously with lots of bits of string and sticky tape.

It may be that this particular problem is not a serious one. For example if the assembler was one of those rare ones that allowed the operand field to appear before the operation field then the problem would vanish. (This is a typical experience with the use of macros. Some marginal facility in the base language often turns out to be of crucial importance.) Nevertheless it is unlikely that there would be no problems at all with nesting of independent macros.

The overall point of this example may be illustrated by an analogy from the building trade. Bricks are a good building medium for structures up to a certain height, but they did not use bricks to build the Eiffel Tower. Similarly, macros are good for building programming languages up to a certain complexity, and a facility for nested macro calls helps a good deal, but it would be foolish to expect the relatively simple replacement facilities that macros offer and the relatively superficial analysis of syntax and structuring that macro pre-processors perform to be adequate for building an elaborate compiler.

Call by name and call by value

We will continue our examination of communication problems that arise when macros are called from within arguments of other macros by introducing a further complication, which frequently arises in practice.

Assume that a macro called LASTBIT is used to reference the last bit of a word, and that LASTBIT, like IND, can be nested within the SET macro. A sample call, which involves two nested calls of LASTBIT, is

$$\text{SET} \quad \text{LASTBIT(X)} = \text{LASTBIT(Y)}$$

If BASECOMP is a conventional computer the set of instructions to extract the last bit of a word will be different from the set of instructions to store into the last bit of a word. Hence LASTBIT will have to generate different code depending on whether it occurs as the first or second argument to the SET macro, or, more generally, whether or not it is to be used as an operand to a STORE instruction.

The ease with which this problem can be tackled depends on how the macro processor orders its operations and, in particular, at what stage it evaluates macro calls that occur within the arguments of other macros. One possible approach is *call by value*, where arguments are fully evaluated before the macro that contains them is entered. This would make the encoding of the LASTBIT macro difficult, since it would be impossible for it to foretell whether it was ultimately to be used as the operand of a STORE instruction or not—it could even be inserted twice into the replacement text, once as the operand of a STORE instruction and once not.

The other possible approach is *call by name*, where arguments are passed exactly in the form they are written, and are evaluated only when they are inserted. With this approach the problems of communicating with the LASTBIT macro could be solved using a global variable. If this global variable were called STORING and took the value TRUE or FALSE depending on whether a STORE instruction was being generated, then the replacement text of SET might be written in the form

> Set STORING = FALSE
> Generate instruction to LOAD *argument2*
> Set STORING = TRUE
> Generate instruction to STORE into *argument1*

and LASTBIT could then examine STORING and generate code accordingly.

This example therefore shows that call by name can be an invaluable feature. If arguments are called by name, call by value can be partly simulated by evaluating all the arguments and assigning their values to temporary variables immediately a macro is entered. Hence it could be argued that all macro processors should support call by name. However call by value tends to be faster in execution than call by name, particularly if an argument is referenced more than once in a piece of replacement text, and it is presumably for this reason that many macro processors call all arguments by value. (Of course, if nested macro calls are not allowed, there is no difference between the two approaches.)

It should be pointed out that call by name cannot totally simulate call by value, since call by value may have effects before the macro call is entered. GPM uses call by value, and this is specially exploited by the SUC macro quoted in Chapter 1.5. In the SUC macro a nested macro call is used to define the macro in which it is embedded. The nested macro therefore *must* be evaluated before the outer one is entered. A more commonplace example is as follows. Assume BOYS is a macro with replacement text

JOHN, JAMES, COLIN

and ROOMS is a macro that takes a variable number of arguments and works in such a way that the call

$$\text{ROOMS \quad JIM, BERT, \ldots, ALF}$$

generates

$$\text{JIM WILL HAVE ROOM 1}$$
$$\text{BERT WILL HAVE ROOM 2}$$
$$\vdots$$
$$\text{ALF WILL HAVE ROOM } n$$

Now consider the call

$$\text{ROOMS \quad ALAN, BOYS, DEREK}$$

If arguments are called by value, BOYS will be called while the call of ROOMS is being scanned. The call of BOYS has two commas in its replacement text and these will be taken as delimiters of the ROOMS macro. The effect will then be exactly as if the call had been

$$\text{ROOMS \quad ALAN, JOHN, JAMES, COLIN, DEREK}$$

The result will be that 5 rooms will be allocated.

If arguments are called by name then ROOMS will have three arguments and BOYS will only be called when the second argument is inserted. The call will generate

$$\text{ALAN WILL HAVE ROOM 1}$$
$$\text{JOHN, JAMES, COLIN WILL HAVE ROOM 2}$$
$$\text{DEREK WILL HAVE ROOM 3}$$

with the result that three poor boys will have been lumped together in the same room.

It is interesting to note that this ambiguity is not one that has been conjured up by artificial languages. It also occurs in natural language. If one said to the hotel receptionist that one wanted rooms for 'Alan, the boys and Derek', the receptionist would do well to ask whether arguments were called by value.

There is a parallel between 'call by name' and 'call by value' in macro processors and 'top-down' and 'bottom-up' methods used by syntax-directed compilers. Syntax-directed compilers, however, make a more complete analysis of the structure of the source text and problems of intercommunication are lessened. If the source text is converted into a tree representation, for example, it is easier to analyse how one syntactic form relates to another.

Overlapping calls

We will conclude our discussion of inter-macro communication by examining the case where one macro call may overlap another. To illustrate this it is convenient to change the application area from generating BASECOMP programs to simplifying algebraic expressions.

When computers are used to perform algebraic manipulations one of the problems is to eliminate redundant terms. If the computer tried to differentiate $(2*x)+1$ it might end up with

$$(0*x)+(2*1)+0$$

If we consider how a free-mode macro processor might be used to simplify such expressions, some interesting points arise.

Assume that some macros are written to recognize and eliminate redundant symbols and that in particular three of the macros are $0+$, $+0$ and $1*$, each of which has a null replacement text, and a fourth is (0) which generates 0. Hence $(1*x)+0$ would be mapped into (x) since both $1*$ and $+0$ would be replaced by null strings. How would the text $(0)+x$ be processed? The (0) macro would be mapped first and would generate 0. The vital question is where scanning re-starts after this macro has been called. If it re-starts at the plus sign that follows the call of (0) then the end result will be that $0+x$ is generated. Hence the macro $0+$ has been missed since it did not occur in the original source form. If, on the other hand, scanning restarts by re-scanning the 0 that has just replaced the (0), then $0+$ would be recognized and the final result would be x.

The situation can be more complicated than this. Consider the text $x+(0)$. Here again (0) is the first macro call to be found and is replaced by 0. Even if scanning re-starts with this 0, the result will be $x+0$ and the $+0$ macro will thus be missed. If this occurrence of $+0$ is to be caught, the rule must be that the text generated by a macro call is re-scanned in the context in which the original call was encountered.

If this latter scanning rule is adopted, the logical foundations really begin to rock if macros can re-define other macros. One cannot re-start a scan in a previous context if this context has changed in the meantime. If we reconsider the $x+(0)$ example the reader might care to ponder what should happen if the (0) macro, as a side effect,

(a) defined $+$ as $-$, or
(b) deleted the definition of $+0$, or
(c) defined a macro $x+0$.

The problem is that if definitions are changed or created, this should apply only to the text that follows. If, however, on the re-scan of the output from a macro, account is taken of what preceded the call, logical problems arise. This is another occurrence of the change-of-meaning problem.

The problems of missed macro calls illustrated by these examples have an alternative solution. This is to perform the simplification in several passes. The entire output from one pass through the macro processor is fed back in again and the process is repeated until there are no macro calls on a pass, which means that all simplifications have been performed. This solution has the merit of simplicity but the disadvantage of slowness. Large sections of source text containing no macro calls might be re-scanned many times in order to eliminate a few isolated macro calls from other parts of the source text.

In conclusion, it can be said that a macro processor should allow, perhaps as an option, the output from a macro call to be re-scanned, but there are logical problems if account is taken of the context before the call as well as that after it. One macro language that has explicit mechanisms for controlling re-scanning is the TRAC language, but, since it works in warning-mode rather than free-mode, it cannot be used to perform algebraic simplification in the way described above.

Chapter 1.8

Implementation

When attending computer conferences and the like I have listened to (and probably delivered) my full share of boring lectures, but there is one class of bore who easily outshines all the others: this is the man who talks in full detail about the way his system has been implemented. Typically one is presented with huge diagrams of meaninglessly labelled boxes joined together with a maze of lines, and with a mass of tables showing such things as what bit 17 of word 3 contains.

Nevertheless there are always some features of implementation techniques that are relevant and important. The way a macro processor is implemented may have a vital bearing on the facilities the macro processor offers. When discussing these considerations we will try to keep to the general principles and to avoid the details. We will pay particular attention to the effects that the method of implementation has on the design of the macro processor itself.

If the reader is interested in getting down to the guts of a macro processor, several descriptions exist in the literature or can be obtained by writing to the appropriate author. Perhaps the best place to start would be to look at the full description of the implementation of GPM that appears in Strachey's (1965) paper.

Types of usage

The user of almost any macro processor will think the macro processor to be slow. This is not, I think, due to some universal design defect, but rather a manifestation of the fact that computers are not as good at manipulating characters as they are at manipulating numbers. Even on a computer that possesses instructions that can process several characters at a time, it is usually necessary to perform a good proportion of operations on a character-by-character basis. Taking a parallel with numerical operations, it would be a poor computer indeed if, to add two numbers together, you had to write a program to proceed through each number digit by digit, yet with character manipulation this is accepted.

Some macro processors are, however, faster than others and it is worth examining some properties that affect speed.

It is convenient to divide the usage of macro processors into two types. The first is the *low-activity usage* of which an extreme example would be a thousand source lines per macro call, and the second is *high-activity usage* of which an extreme example would be that each source line requires the execution of a thousand macro-time operations (macro calls and macro-time statements).

Low-activity usage

We will first consider low-activity usage. Here, the only criterion affecting speed is the algorithm used to recognize macro calls. The quicker the algorithm can reject a symbol or a line as not being a macro call, the better. Obviously, macro processors that require each macro call to begin with a fixed symbol (e.g. GPM) should be very quick, and the typical macro-assembler, which requires macro names to occur in a fixed field, should also be reasonably good. There are potential troubles, however, with free-mode macro processors which need to try to match each line or even each symbol with all possible macros. Nevertheless this process need not be as slow as it sounds. There are two possible optimization techniques, one for macros that are recognized by the occurrence of their names anywhere in the source text, and the other for macros that are recognized by a pattern match.

Hashing

For macro processors that work on a name recognition basis, hashing techniques can be used. A mapping function is applied to each symbol in the source text to yield an integer, usually in the range $[0, 2^n - 1]$ for some n, and the symbol is compared only with macro names which map to the same integer.

ML/I uses this technique, and some figures are quoted for its scanning speed in a paper that evaluates ML/I (Brown, P., 1971a). The figures given below are based on those given in this paper. On the implementation concerned, n had the value 5, thus giving 32 positions in the hash table. The tests were performed on a file containing about 2000 lines, with an average line length of 30 characters. The machine used was an ICL 4130, which has a store access time of two microseconds. A typical instruction takes 4·5 microseconds, and characters are stored one to a word. The timing figures quoted for the tests are measures of CPU time, and do not include time spent processing interrupts or waiting for input/output devices.

Two tests runs of ML/I were performed. In each case a set of macros was supplied and, in order that the timings measured the speed of scanning rather than of macro replacement, the names were chosen so that none of them was ever found in the source file. However, each symbol needed to be compared with the names. For the first test there were nineteen names (in fact the nineteen built-in macros to ML/I), and the run took 35·5 seconds. For the second test the number of names was doubled to 38, and the run took 38·0 seconds, an increase of under 8%.

The same source file was then fed to an editor, with a null set of edits. This took 18·5 seconds. The source file was also processed by a copying program, which took 14·0 seconds to make a copy. Hence both the editor and copying program were roughly twice as fast as ML/I in copying text. This gives a measure of the overheads in ML/I in breaking each line up into atoms and applying the hashing algorithm to each.

It would be wrong to take the results of these somewhat superficial tests too seriously, particularly as hashing is a subject that merits study in considerable depth. One can, however, draw the general conclusion that dividing text into its constituent symbols and hashing each one is reasonably costly, but, once this has been done, the overheads in searching for extra macro names are not high. If some applications require a huge number of macros, with the result that these overheads do get large, this can be remedied (at the expense of a higher storage requirement) by increasing the size of the hash table.

Hashing techniques are commonly used in compilers and assemblers for table look-up. Macro-assemblers may use hashing techniques to see if a given field contains a macro name in the same way that ML/I tests whether each atom is a macro name.

Tree search

With macro processors that work on a pattern matching basis, the overheads are potentially greater, since matching a pattern will take longer than matching a single name. However since the pattern-matching process is normally only applied to each line, rather than to each atom, the overall overheads are of the same order of magnitude in the two cases.

The pattern matching process can be speeded up by the use of tree structures, and these are described in Waite's (1967) paper on LIMP. Similar techniques are used in Waite's more recent macro processor, STAGE2. The advantage of tree structures is that when two patterns have a common content, as is frequently the case in practice, the analysis of the common part is not repeated for each pattern match. Before explaining the tree structures, we will say a little about how pattern matching works in LIMP.

As examples we will take the four following patterns, or, as Waite calls them, templates

(1) ' = '
(2) ACC = '
(3) ' = PC
(4) ACC = PC

In LIMP patterns, a quote stands for an arbitrary string corresponding to an argument of the macro with which the pattern is associated. Thus pattern (1) above will match any line that contains an equals sign. If the line happens to be

LAPWING = PEEWIT

then LAPWING will be the first argument and PEEWIT the second.

All four patterns would match the line

ACC = PC

and there is therefore a potential ambiguity as to which should be chosen. To resolve this, LIMP has the rule, a natural one, that the pattern that minimizes the number and size of the arbitrary strings is the one that is taken to match. Clearly the purpose of patterns such as (2), (3) and (4) would be to select special cases of pattern (1).

In most practical uses of macro processors that use pattern matching, each input line will be matched by several patterns. There is often a 'catch all' pattern consisting of a single arbitrary string, that will match all lines that nothing else matches. For example the patterns might correspond to statement formats in a simple programming language and in this case the 'catch all' pattern will match error lines that fail to match all the other patterns.

We can now return to the subject of the tree structures. It would clearly be inefficient to try to match patterns (1) to (4) in an independent manner. It would be much better to order the patterns in the tree structure shown in Figure 1.8A.

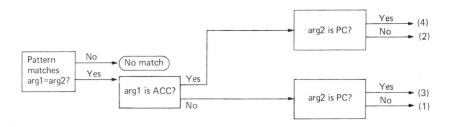

Fig. 1.8A. A tree structure for matching LIMP patterns

Using this, a line is first compared with pattern (1). If there is no match then patterns (2), (3) and (4) can also be rejected, thus saving a good deal of scanning time. If there is a match, then the first argument can be compared with ACC. If this also matches, then the second argument can be compared with PC to see whether pattern (2) or (4) applies. If the first argument is not ACC, then the second argument should be compared with PC to see if pattern (3) applies; if not, then pattern (1) applies.

High-activity usage

In high-activity usage the most important factors in determining the overall speed of a macro processor are its speed of execution of macro calls, once matched, and of recognizing and executing macro-time statements.

There is one supreme consideration here. This is whether replacement text of macros is compiled at the time a macro definition is created or left in its original source form. We have already examined this question in Chapter 1.3, when considering the OS macro-assembler and the relative performance of the 'compiled' implementation. The paper that evaluates ML/I (Brown, P., 1971a), from which the timing figures quoted earlier in this chapter were extracted, also considers the question of compilation. ML/I is purely interpretive, and it is remarked that the statement

$$\text{MCSET} \quad P1 = P1 + 1$$

which is a macro-time statement to increase the integer variable P1 by one, could be compiled into a single machine instruction on most computers, and would then run about one thousand times faster. The only 'loss' would be that the user could not later define P1 as a macro with replacement text P2, thus effectively turning the statement into

$$\text{MCSET} \quad P2 = P2 + 1$$

Not all statements would give such a dramatic improvement, however. The statement

$$\text{MCSET} \quad P1 = argument1$$

could, at best, only be partially compiled since *argument1* would not be known until the macro was called.

This further bears out the conclusions reached in Chapter 1.3, and the position can be summarized thus:

(a) Compilation of macro-time statements may improve speed by an order of magnitude in some cases of high-activity usage.

(b) Not all macro-time statements can be compiled.

(c) Compilation gives a small loss of flexibility, since the binding of a fixed meaning to statements will be performed at an earlier stage, but this is rarely serious in practice.

(d) As a consequence of (b) and (c), if some statements are compiled (thus fixing their meaning) whereas others are not (thus allowing their meaning to be altered) then the precise behaviour of the macro processor will be hard to specify. Its User Manual will therefore be very fat or full of cowardly statements such as 'the effect of . . . is undefined'.

Primitives

We have already said that a macro processor should be able to extend its own macro-time statements. When this facility is available, if the user wants to define a new macro-time statement he may simply create it in the form of a macro which generates an equivalent combination of existing statements. For example if there existed a macro-time IF statement which tested if a single condition held, then the user might create a statement of form

$$\text{IFALL} \quad condition1, condition2, \ldots, conditionN$$

which tested to see whether all of a set of conditions held. This macro would generate a series of ordinary macro-time IF statements.

Given this facility, one can argue that there need only be a few primitive built-in macro-time statements plus a library of macros to extend them. One can then minimize one's primitives, which has the double advantage of appealing to the mathematician's idea of beauty and being easy to implement on a computer. The catch is, of course, that if the execution of ordinary looking macro-time statements actually involves twenty or so macro calls because it is expressed in terms of Turing machine level primitives, then execution is going to be very slow. This was exemplified earlier by Strachey's clever GPM macros for the addition of integers.

Languages that are their own macro language

We will conclude by discussing an implementation technique that has a huge influence on macro processor design, indeed it fixes the design almost totally.

'Something for nothing' offers have great appeal to everyone, though most of us, perhaps as a result of bitter experience, tend to approach such offers with extreme caution. We will now explore an idea whereby one gets a powerful macro processor for nothing, or (and the facade is already beginning to slip a little) almost nothing.

The idea is that if a high-level language offers some reasonable character manipulation features, one can, by adding some trivial extra features to the language, use its compiler as a macro processor. The idea is based on McIlroy's (1960) proposal that was exploited in the PL/I macro processor. In PL/I, the macro-time facilities mirror the facilities in the PL/I language itself. The macro processor for PL/I therefore includes a compiler for a subset of PL/I. (It so happens that it is an interpreter more than a compiler in existing implementations, but it need not have been so. The main point is that it is a processor capable of executing a subset of PL/I. Whether this is done by compiling or by interpreting is irrelevant.) Why implement a subset of PL/I separately within the macro processor? Why not use the PL/I compiler itself as the macro processor, since this provides the whole of PL/I rather than a subset, and requires no extra implementation effort?

The idea—which could of course be applied to any language that contained character manipulation facilities, not just to PL/I—might work like this. If a PL/I program involves macro activity, two passes are made through the compiler. The first pass performs macro activity and the second pass compiles the program generated by the first pass. Clearly there must be some means of identifying which PL/I statements are to be executed on the first pass. There are two ways of doing this, either to mark the statements that *are* to be executed on the first pass or to mark the material that is *not* to be executed on the first pass. The choice is arbitrary, but the second approach has slight advantages so we will select that. We will enclose within square brackets all material that is not to be subjected to macro activity. The following would then be a program

```
FILLTYPE: PROCEDURE OPTIONS(MAIN);
DECLARE TYPE CHARACTER(20) VARYING;
TYPE = 'FIXED BINARY(15)';
[EXAMPLE: PROCEDURE OPTIONS(MAIN);
DECLARE VAR1 ]PUT LIST(TYPE);[...
...DECLARE VAR2 ]PUT LIST(TYPE);[...
   ...
END;]
END;
```

For those not familiar with PL/I this requires some explanation. The line

name: PROCEDURE OPTIONS (MAIN);

may be regarded as a header that must occur at the start of every PL/I program. The *name*, as far as we are concerned, is an arbitrary identifier. Since our macro facilities for PL/I are identical to full PL/I, two header lines are needed. One is for the macro pass and has been given the name FILLTYPE, and the other is for the final PL/I program and has been given the name EXAMPLE. The statement

PUT LIST(TYPE);

means output the value of the variable TYPE. Since, in our example, TYPE is a character string variable—it has been declared as CHARACTER(20) VARYING which means a string of up to 20 characters—the above PUT statement would print a character string. (There are certain details of format, output file attributes, etc., that should be cleared up if the example was to be perfect, but we have suppressed such details for the sake of clarity.)

When the program is run, the material in square brackets is copied over to the output as it is passed over and the remaining statements are executed normally. The final output would be

EXAMPLE: PROCEDURE OPTIONS(MAIN);
DECLARE VAR1 FIXED BINARY(15)...
... DECLARE VAR2 FIXED BINARY(15)...
    ...
END;

Our only extension to PL/I has been the square brackets and even these are not strictly necessary. Their effect is merely to cause the string they enclose to be output. This can be achieved in ordinary PL/I by the statement

PUT LIST('string');

(assuming for the sake of simplicity that *string* itself contains no quote signs). Hence our opening square bracket is equivalent to

PUT LIST('

and the closing bracket to

');

Obviously, however, life would become incredibly tedious for the user if he had to write these out in full each time. In fact, it is already bad enough having to write

PUT LIST(TYPE);

to insert the value of the macro variable TYPE and if the proposal was to be a practical one there would have to be a shorthand form of this.

Our proposal is actually more general than we have so far shown it to be. Firstly, we have presented it as a two-pass process. However, any number of passes could be performed, using nested square brackets to indicate the level at which each set of material was to be performed. One could then have a macro language to extend the macro language to extend the ... to extend the macro language for PL/I, though it is not obvious how such generality could usefully be exploited. Secondly, although our proposal requires the first pass to go through the PL/I compiler, there is no reason why the material in the square brackets should be a PL/I program at all or that the second pass should be through the PL/I compiler rather than, say, the COBOL compiler. The macro facility is therefore a general-purpose one.

It is true to say that we have got something for almost nothing since the only changes we have proposed for PL/I are really trivial notational ones like the square brackets. One might question, however, if the something is worth much. Our proposed facility is weaker than the real PL/I macro processor, which was described in Chapter 1.4, because it rules out one of the major uses of the latter, namely systematic editing, and its notation is clumsier. Our proposal has the merit of making all the facilities of PL/I available during macro processing, but few of these would be needed in practice. In Chapter 1.4 we came out as unenthusiastic about the PL/I macro processor, so we can hardly rave about something worse, however cheap it may be to implement. What we can say is this. It would be highly interesting and perhaps very fruitful to build a high-level language which was designed from the very start to be a good macro language for itself. The language would need to contain string manipulation facilities, so the technique would not be suitable for purely numerical languages, but there is no reason why the language should be exclusively devoted to string processing.

Chapter 1.9

Uses and Limitations

In this chapter some of the uses and limitations of macro processors will be described. Since the use of a macro processor cannot be considered a separate issue from the design of the macro processor itself, many of the applications of macro processors have already been introduced in previous chapters. Hence this chapter acts somewhat as a summary of past material.

The range of possible uses of macro processors that run in free-mode is a superset of the uses of those that run in warning-mode. (This is not to say, of course, that free-mode is 'better'. We have already made the point that a general facility is not always superior to a more specialized one.)

This chapter will begin by examining the uses that can be exploited using either mode of macro processor, and will then examine the extra uses that free-mode brings.

The accepted way of describing anything diverse is to divide it up into classes, and, although there may be a degree of arbitrariness about the divisions, a better alternative is hard to find. In this chapter the uses of macro processors are divided into neat little boxes. However, it should be recognized that many applications, instead of falling cleanly into one of the boxes, will straddle several of them.

Uses of all macro processors

By far the most important use of macro processors is for adding flexibility to a base language. This takes the form of allowing something that is fixed in the base language to be altered, to be dynamically varied or to be extended. The terms *language bending*, *delayed binding* and *language extension* are used, respectively, to describe these situations.

Language bending

A general-purpose programming language cannot suit all users. Hence a macro processor has a role to play in bending a language towards a particular user's view of the world. Such bending need not add any new facility to the language. In fact the opposite is sometimes the case, in that the macros provide a more restricted, more specialized, version of existing facilities.

Assume that a highly financed research group wishes to investigate algorithms for playing the game of noughts and crosses (also called tick-tack-toe). If these people were not familiar with programming, it would be much easier for them to write their algorithms in terms of some natural model of the noughts and crosses game, rather than in some fixed high-level programming language. For example, the statement

PLACE CROSS IN MIDDLE

would be much more comprehensible to them than the equivalent high-level language statement, which might be

$$BOARD(2,2) = 1 :$$

similarly

IF TOP-RIGHT IS FREE THEN . . .

and

IF BOTTOM-MIDDLE IS CROSS THEN . . .

would be better than

$$IF \ BOARD(1,3) = 0 \ THEN . . .$$

and

$$IF \ BOARD(3,2) = 1 \ THEN . . .$$

The research group might therefore decide to employ a programmer to write some macros to bend a high-level language towards their needs. In a day or two, this programmer should be able to create a complete language for noughts and crosses programs, including I/O, declarations (perhaps the users would not specify any declarations as the macros would supply them automatically) and looping statements.

This whole example is, of course, a gross oversimplification. In practice the application area will not be a trivial game, but will be some complicated physical situation. The same principles hold, however. What the macros do is to adapt a programming language towards a group of users, which goes against the usual trend of expecting users to adapt themselves towards a particular programming language.

All this sounds very good. One has a picture of the computer becoming easily accessible to almost any group of lay users. Perhaps grandma can use the computer to solve her knitting problems and grandpa for specifying crop-rotation programs for his vegetable patch. There is no need to write program packages for each type of computer usage. Instead a few simple macros can bend a programming language towards the user, and this can cover an application area in a much more general way than a specialized package.

There is, however, a catch to this Elysian picture. The catch is that there is more to communicating with the computer than simply specifying a program. Firstly it is necessary to specify some control commands for running a program, and these may be fairly complicated, particularly when a macro processing step precedes compilation. Secondly, it is necessary to understand the error messages the computer gives and to correct the program accordingly.

The first problem is the less serious. Many job control languages contain a macro facility—these are discussed at the end of the next chapter—and thus it may be possible to bend a job control language towards the user in the same way as a programming language.

The second problem is the really intractable one. If grandma gets the error message

FLOATING OVERFLOW

she may take it to mean the milk has boiled over, and, worse still, many compilers produce messages like

ERR   116   AB67   294

which will totally baffle her. Hence the macros should be designed to pre-empt the system by detecting errors before they reach the system and giving an error message in the user's terms.

In looking at whether this can be done, it is best to distinguish four different types of error. Firstly there are syntactic errors in a macro call. Errors such as illegal macro names will be detected by the macro processor and will give rise to messages such as

...   IS AN INCORRECT MACRO NAME IN LINE ...

This may not be quite comprehensible to grandma, but at least some lay users should be able to understand it. Unfortunately there may be some errors in macro calls that the macro processor will not be able to pick up. For example, if the macro processor works in warning-mode and the warning marker is omitted, then the call will not be recognized and the macro processor will pass the text on to the next stage of compilation. The result will be an error message from the compiler for the base language. Hence this is one case where macros cannot pre-empt the system message. There are more to come.

The second type of error is a syntactic error in the argument to a macro. Most macro processors treat arguments as arbitrary strings, but allow the arguments to be analysed within the replacement text of a macro call. However, the facilities for syntactic analysis are usually rudimentary. It should be possible to check that an argument is, say, NORTH, SOUTH, EAST or WEST but it is usually impossible to check that an argument is a syntactically correct arithmetic expression. For the errors that are caught, the situation is good. Most macro processors have a means for the macro writer to send error messages to the user, and these can be in the user's terminology. Errors that are not caught will be passed through to the compiler for the base language.

The third type of error arises when the user intermixes base language statements with macro calls. Any syntactic errors in the former will obviously have to be caught by the compiler for the base language.

The last type of error is a run-time error. In all but the very simplest languages there will be some errors that cannot be detected until the program is run. It may be that the macro processor can generate code to check for these errors and catch them before the system does. Hence if grandpa has 12 plots in his vegetable patch and can refer to an individual plot by saying

PLOT X

where X is a variable, then the macro might map this into a sequence of statements that checks whether X is between 1 and 12 and, if not, prints a friendly message like

YOUR PLOTS ARE NUMBERED 1 TO 12, GRANDPA, BUT
IN LINE... YOU REFER TO PLOT 13

If the base language contains special routines that are called when an error is detected (such as some of the ON conditions in PL/I) then it may be possible to do a reasonable job in explaining errors to the user, even though they may initially be detected by the system. However, there will always be some errors (e.g. time expired) which cannot be intercepted and these will give rise to system error messages.

Thus in all but the simplest cases there will be some messages that will be fixed 'system' messages (i.e. generated by a compiler or its run-time system or by the operating system) which will not be expressed in the user's terms. Worse still, if these messages include line numbers or statement numbers that identify where the error occurred, then these numbers will refer to the program generated by the macros, not to the source text as the user supplied it. Grandma and grandpa should not need to know about this intermediate program any more than the user of a compiler needs to know about the intermediate forms into which his program is translated.

Since the system messages cannot be pre-empted by the macros, the next best thing is for the macros to post-process the system messages to convert them to the user's terms. This possible use of macros to process *output* from the computer rather than input to it is itself a radical departure from normal practice. It requires a free-mode macro processor together with an operating system that allows the macro processor to slip in and tamper with its output. Even given all this it might be hard for the macros, given a system error message, to deduce what the user's original error was.

The conclusion must therefore be that this problem cannot be satisfactorily solved, and macros cannot be used by completely lay people. This limits the use of macros not only in the field of language bending, but in many other applications as well. The only possible solution is a closer integration of the macro processor with the compiler for the base language, as discussed in the next chapter.

Delayed binding

Experience has shown that, during the lifetime of a program, almost every aspect of it is liable to change. Thus when one originally writes a program one wants to fix as few details as possible. Unfortunately every programming language requires details to be fixed, sometimes out of logical necessity and sometimes because of limitations in the language. A macro processor can be used to reconcile these clashing requirements by forming an intermediate stage. The programmer defines macros corresponding to all the details he thinks might change at a later stage. The following are some examples.

(a) The base language requires array sizes to be fixed. A macro is therefore used to insert array sizes. (A specific example of this was given in Chapter 1.5, when discussing GPM.)

(b) The user does not know whether or not to use double-length arithmetic. A macro is therefore used to declare the attributes of variables.

(c) Two slightly incompatible compilers exist for the base language. Macros can be defined to correspond to all the features that may vary.

At any one time, all the macros have a fixed replacement text and hence all the details are fixed. However, when he wishes to change a detail, the user simply needs to redefine the corresponding macro, rather than to search laboriously through his program identifying all the places where changes have to be made. (Of course if changing a detail only necessitates a single change to a program, the value of macros is more questionable.)

This use of macros to allow a fixed element of a base language to vary is called *delayed binding*, because the binding of a value to the fixed element is delayed until the last possible moment. Although delayed binding often applies to the values of numerical constants (as in example (a) above), its use can be extended to any element of the base language (as examples (b) and (c) illustrate).

Language extension

When talking about the use of macros to extend a programming language —particularly a high-level language—there is a potential confusion of function, which is made worse by a loose usage of terminology in the literature.

Almost every programming language has some built-in features that allow the user to extend the language. For example several high-level languages allow the user to define data structures, and these may be regarded as new data types which are expressed in terms of existing ones. Recently there has been a trend to design languages with a high degree of built-in extensibility and these are called 'extensible languages'. The built-in extensibility might be implemented, partially at least, by the use of macros but the macros need to be integrated into the base language compiler. This subject is discussed in the next chapter.

The situation under discussion here is a different type of language extension in that a macro processor extends a base language by pre-processing the input to it. The compiler for the base language is treated as a black box, not to be tampered with. This is the most common application of macros, and the reader is no doubt familiar with many macro packages that extend languages. Most extensions are built on assembly language, partly because it is here that the need for extension is greatest and partly because macro-assemblers are widely available and over the years a good deal of expertise in their use has grown up.

There are additional reasons why macro extensions of high-level languages have been under-exploited. There is a syntax problem. High-level languages have relatively complex and distinctive syntaxes—an ALGOL program looks nothing like a FORTRAN program, an APL program or a BASIC program—and if macro extensions are to fit in naturally with the rest of the language, these must have a similar syntax to the base language. Not many macro processors are capable of achieving this.

The use of macros may also be hampered by the fundamental limitation of pre-processors that they can only extend a language in terms of itself.

Nevertheless there remain many possible macro extensions of high-level languages that can be exploited, and there may well be a lot of activity in this direction in the future. Among the published descriptions of existing applications are papers by P. Brown (1972c) and by Lindstrom (1973). The former describes how the BASIC language was extended to include character manipulation and stacking facilities, which were lacking in the implementation concerned. The latter describes how extra control facilities, including coroutines, were added to the LISP language. This is an interesting piece of work, as most pre-processors deal with data manipulation facilities rather than the flow of control through the program.

Manipulation of data

In the applications mentioned so far, it has been assumed that the macros are operating on computer programs. Macros can, however, be used just as well on computer data. All computer data is expressed in some kind of language, although the language may be a relatively trivial one. The language may, for instance, have the single rule that data is a sequence of decimal integers separated by commas. 'Data languages' may usefully be subjected to language bending, delayed binding and language extension. This applies particularly if the data is structured in some way. The example of Fletcher's pentomino macros, quoted in Chapter 1.1, showed how macros could map a tree structure into a computer program, and therefore represented an instance of a translation from a data language to a programming language. Even for non-structured data, macros can perform such useful operations as checking that numbers are within certain ranges or converting identifiers to numbers (e.g. MALE to 1).

All in all, therefore, this reinforces the widely held view that computer programs and computer data should not be regarded as disparate entities.

Standardization

This discussion of the use of macros to add flexibility to languages will conclude by considering an application that may combine language bending, delayed binding and language extension. It concerns the standardization of programming languages.

Everyone is in favour of standardization. The trouble is that we all think of it in terms of everyone else changing to our methods and styles rather than we ourselves giving ground to others. Moreover, if people do agree on a standard, this might take several years to disseminate and implement and may have become obsolete in the meantime.

One way of allowing local variations to a standard without prejudicing the value of the standard is to make use of macros. This is done by insisting that all local variations should be mappable by macros into the standard language, so that a standard form of any program can easily be generated if it is required at some later date. This is not a complete solution to the problem, however, since it constrains the local variations to be of a type that macros can implement, but it does allow some degree of escape from the straitjacket of a standard and this can be of immense value.

An example could arise in a country where English was not the native language. Most programming languages use English keywords (IF, BEGIN, DECLARE, etc.), but the use of macros could permit local words to be used instead. Programs could still be exchanged with other installations by converting them into the English form. In fact, macros might even be used in the reverse direction to convert programs in English, received from other places, into the equivalent in the native language. This would, however, require the use of a free-mode macro processor.

Text generation

A rather different application is in generating relatively large pieces of repetitive text. The letter-writing macros of Chapter 1.1 provide an example of this; here some paragraphs that are repeated in several different letters are invoked by a short macro call. The term 'shorthand notation' is used to describe applications such as this.

Macro-time looping statements often come in useful for text generation. Occasionally it is required to repeat something several times, and a macro-time loop can save the original writer a lot of trouble. A macro could easily generate 500 lines of

I MUST NOT TALK IN CLASS

or, for more modern and perverse schoolboys,

I MUST NOT WASTE COMPUTER TIME

More often, however, there is some variation in the repeated material. This may occur in the initial value of some built-in table for the computer. It is hard to give a convincing example without going into a lot of detail, but the sort of table envisaged is one of 100 lines of form

$$DC \quad 3, x, 6, LABx$$

with x going from 1 to 100.

Another form of text generation is conditional generation. This is where material is included in some text only if some macro-time variable is set in a certain way. A popular use of this is for controlling the inclusion of optional printing statements in a program. During debugging runs one needs a lot of output statements in a program to show what is going on. When the program is working these should be omitted, but they may need to be resurrected at a later stage if the program goes wrong again. The best way of implementing this facility is by putting it under the control of one or more macro-time variables, whose values can be changed as circumstances warrant.

A second application of conditional generation is for configuring programs to work on different types of hardware. A routine might be included in the program, for example, only if the hardware lacked a floating-point facility.

Free-mode macro processors

We will now move on to consider some applications that are only open to macro processors that work in free-mode. These applications are all concerned with changing some text that already exists.

Many of the applications mentioned so far have been concerned with adding flexibility to a program. The program writer thinks ahead and ensures that it will be possible to adjust his program if circumstances change. Unfortunately, no programmer can foresee all the likely future changes to his program, and some programmers make no effort at all in this direction. Anyone who has any experience of computers must have come across a host of programs which, although no functional change is required, need to be altered as a result of a change of hardware, an increase in the size of the data to be manipulated or a new compiler coming into operation.

The changes required in programs under these circumstances are not isolated ones but *systematic* ones. Every occurrence of a given type of statement or every occurrence of a given variable needs to be systematically changed throughout a program, or, more often, throughout a large number of programs. This is called *systematic editing*, and is a very different kind of editing from that employed during the debugging stages of a program, when a number of isolated, unrelated corrections need to be made. Some examples of the use of systematic editing have already been presented, when ML/I and the macro processor for PL/I were being described.

It should not be inferred that macros can provide a complete solution to the problem of translating from one language to another. Language translation, whether for programming languages or natural languages, requires intelligence and it would be naive to suppose that a macro processor which cloddishly goes through replacing one string or pattern by another could achieve an adequate translation.

In the case of programming languages, a good deal of syntactic analysis may be necessary to identify the patterns to be replaced. For example, consider a problem that often arises in converting FORTRAN programs. In standard FORTRAN, expressions used as array subscripts have a restricted form whereas many local FORTRANs allow any expression to be used as an array subscript. A program to convert from extended FORTRAN to standard FORTRAN would have to recognize all expressions which occurred as array subscripts and which were more complex than standard FORTRAN allows. This requires two capabilities:

(a) to recognize the context of an array subscript;
(b) to recognize expressions that were more complicated than a given form.

Few macro processors could do either.

Moreover this example illustrates another translation problem, namely that the output might require reordering. The example requires text of form

.... A *(complicated expression)* ...

(where A is the name of an array) to be converted to something like

ITEMP = *complicated expression*
... A(ITEMP) ...

In other words the *complicated expression* needs to be extracted from the statement in which it occurs.

Nonetheless, although some of these translation problems may require a tool that is sharper than an ordinary macro processor, they can still be solved mechanically. There exist more difficult translation problems, which require a knowledge of how the program works, at least if an efficent translation is to be achieved. This may necessitate a human intelligence or certainly a form of artificial intelligence that is at the frontier of current research. It is particularly hard to translate efficiently between low-level programming languages by mechanized means because of the large amount of detail in programs, some of which may be necessary and some coincidental. Questions that might arise are:

(a) Do these variables have to be stored contiguously?
(b) Does this variable have to occupy a full 16 bits?
(c) This instruction sets some condition bits. Are they used?

Similar problems arise, albeit less frequently, with high-level languages. Side effects on subroutine calls are typically a thorny problem.

However, we are being too gloomy. Translation from one language to another by means of systematic editing has been a popular and successful use of free-mode macro processors. In most cases the two languages have been very close to one another, normally two dialects of the same language, or, at the assembly language level, languages for two very similar types of computer. Nevertheless useful translations have been achieved between apparently different languages. A case in point is between a derivative of the JOSS language and BASIC. Macros were successful here because, although two languages are distinctly different in their syntax, the syntax of both is simple and both languages have similar semantics.

To summarize, macros can translate between languages when it is possible to define the translation by some simple mechanical rules. Otherwise macros can aid the human translator by making routine changes that the human would find irksome.

Summary of uses

A consistent pattern emerges when one considers the uses of macro processors. Macros can exploit an application to a useful degree, but not as far as one would like. The limitation is because the macro processor is tacked on to a system (e.g. a compiler) and does not completely understand or control what is going on inside the system. Therefore there are limitations in the way it can affect the system. One answer is to integrate the macro processor more closely in the system and this is what the next chapter is about. Another answer is for an operating system to be organized so that the macro processor appears to be an I/O device. Thus the macro processor, rather than, say, the card reader might be made the input device to a program, and, similarly, programs might send their output to be post-processed by the macro processor. This should apply to the operating system itself, which should allow the macro processor to process its commands and its messages. In this situation, although the macro processor is not integrated with any particular program, it can have a reasonable control of what is going on. As Mandil (1972) says, when describing his work of this nature, the macro processor acts as a front-end to the system.

Even so, these answers are palliatives rather than complete solutions. The best view is to accept that the capabilities of macro processors are not boundless, and to try to make them do well what they can do.

A computer's software can be viewed thus. The compilers are the power tools. They do fixed jobs quickly and well, but cannot easily be adapted to do new jobs. A macro processor provides the hand tools. These are adaptable and simple to use, and they can be employed for a wide variety of relatively small jobs. The two kinds of tools are complementary. Makers of hand tools have plenty of scope for introducing new designs without trying to make their tools ape power tools.

Chapter 1.10

Compiler-integrated Macros

Introduction

In the late fifties and early sixties, almost every worker in computer science was designing his own high-level programming language. Those languages that worked were often imposed on users so that everyone at the University of Chew Magna and North Somerset was using the CHEWSOM language (or perhaps CHEWGOL, the local variant of Algol) and everyone at the Amalgamated Widget Company was using the AMWIG language. These days have passed, and, leaving aside special applications, a relatively small set of programming languages account for most programs. The CHEWSOM language and its contemporaries have been forgotten, their only influence on future languages being that maybe some of their features have inspired similar features in the current widely-used languages. It was not necessarily the best languages that survived—CHEWSOM might well have been 'better' than FORTRAN—but those supported by commercial and political forces.

The field of compiler-integrated macros appears currently to be in the same state as programming languages in the late fifties. In fact the situation is, if anything, worse as there is no sign of an emerging FORTRAN or ALGOL, and, what is more, few of the products of the research workers are actually used by anyone else.

As with many other aspects of macros, terminology is loose and diverse. One common synonym for compiler-integrated macros is *definition(al) facilities*. Moreover, the term *extensible language* is frequently used to describe a language whose compiler contains macro facilities. Sometimes this term is used to include pre-processing macro facilities. Occasionally it means almost nothing: an author says his language is extensible because he thinks, probably wrongly, that its compiler has been written in such a clear and well organized manner that any fool could modify it. A search of the literature for references to extensible languages will throw up a huge number of papers. Perhaps the best starting point for a study of the subject would be the Proceedings of Symposia on Extensible Languages held at Boston in 1969 and Grenoble in 1971. These are published as two issues of *SIGPLAN Notices*, one in August 1969 and the other in December 1971. The latter features no less than twenty-nine papers, mostly describing individual extensible languages. Whether this plethora of information makes the reader much the wiser is perhaps questionable. As one of the attendees of the 1969 conference said in the discussion at the end : 'I thought I understood extensible languages before I came here'. However there is some wheat among the chaff.

All this makes the subject hard to write about. If I really knew how to design an extensible language I would have done it, just as, if a racing correspondent knew what horse would win, he would be backing horses rather than writing about them.

The discussion will therefore concentrate on guidelines, and only one project will be described in any kind of detail. Most of the material that follows is concerned with high-level programming languages, but there are sections at the end describing assemblers and job control languages.

Attractions

The attractions of extensible languages are obvious. It is a very common occurrence that when one has a problem to solve on the computer, be it a big problem or a small one, there is no suitable language available. One therefore has to tailor one's solution to the language available, and this leads to programs that are inefficient and hard to understand. Efforts to solve this problem by designing a single all-embracing language have been at best partially successful. It is clear, therefore, that a really good extensible language would find favour in the market place.

Cheatham's categorization

Cheatham (1966) has written an excellent survey of how macros can be integrated into high-level languages. He distinguishes four types of macro :

(1) Text macros. These are the ordinary pre-processing macros that are the subject of most of this Part of the book.

(2) and (3) Syntactic macros. These are macros that are expanded during the syntax analysis phase of a compiler. There are two types, which Cheatham calls MACROs and SMACROs.

(4) Computation macros. These are macros that are expanded during some later stage of the compilation process, the most obvious time being during code generation.

Of the two types of syntactic macro, MACROs are similar to GPM macros. In particular they are called with a warning character at the front.

The only difference is that arguments, instead of being arbitrary string as in GPM, have a specified syntactic type. An example of a declaration of a MACRO is

> LET N BE INTEGER-EXPRESSION
> MACRO MATRIX(N) MEANS 'ARRAY(1:N,1:N)'

where INTEGER-EXPRESSION is a predefined syntactic type. A call of this MACRO would be

$$\%MATRIX(25)$$

(where $\%$ is the warning character), and this would generate

$$ARRAY(1:25,1:25)$$

There are two advantages of specifying that an argument should be of a given syntactic type. Firstly, if an incorrect argument is supplied, this can be detected immediately and the error message can be expressed in terms of the macro (e.g. ILLEGAL MATRIX SIZE). (Without syntax checking the error would not be detected until a later stage of the compilation process, when the macro had vanished.) Secondly, calls such as

$$\%MATRIX((6+7))$$

would be correctly analysed, and in particular the parentheses would be correctly matched. (If arguments are treated as arbitrary strings the *first* closing parenthesis might be taken as the closing delimiter of the MATRIX macro thus making the argument "(6 + 7".)

One could postulate an equivalent of the MACRO facility that did not need the warning character, i.e. worked in free-mode rather than warning-mode. We discussed the pros and cons of free-mode in Chapter 1.6. The main disadvantage is that every occurrence of the word MATRIX in the source text would be taken as a call of the MATRIX macro, and this might be undesirable. Cheatham's SMACROs get around this difficulty by specifying the syntactic context in which the macro is to occur. In the case of the MATRIX macro this would be as the attribute of a declaration. The SMACRO would be declared thus

> LET N BE INTEGER-EXPRESSION
> SMACRO MATRIX(N) AS ATTRIBUTE
> MEANS 'ARRAY(1:N,1:N)'

It would then be called in a context such as

$$DECLARE \ X \ MATRIX(25)...$$

SMACROs therefore provide all the notational advantages of free-mode recognition of macro calls without the dangers found in corresponding pre-processing free-mode macros.

The last type of macro, the computation macro, is best illustrated, not by an example from Cheatham's paper, but by the macro facility in the MAD language (Arden, Galler and Graham, 1969).

The MAD definitional facility

A definitional facility was added to the MAD compiler for the IBM 7090 computer in 1963, and was almost certainly the first realization of computation macros. For many years it remained as one of those things which the programming fraternity knew about but for which no readily available published description existed. This deficiency was not remedied until 1969.

The MAD definitional facility is relatively simple, even crude, but has the great merits of effectiveness and field-proven serviceability. It is designed for the sole purpose of introducing new data types and operators into arithmetic expressions. The key to any scheme such as this, which opens up a compiler so that it can be changed by a user, is that the workings of the compiler must be organized in an easily comprehensible, extensible and modifiable form. Normally, the best way of doing this is to design the compiler so that its workings are controlled by a set of tables. This is, indeed, a popular way of writing compilers, even if considerations of extensibility are not paramount, and there are well known techniques for making both the syntactical analysis and code generation phases of a compiler 'table-driven'.

The MAD compiler uses these table-driven methods, and there exist statements in the MAD language which allow a user to specify modifications to the tables. The names of operators are stored in the *operator table*. To define a new operator the user must specify its name, whether it is unary or binary, and its precedence. The precedence is defined in relation to some existing operator. Note that this is all that is said about the syntax of the operator.

A typical statement to define a new operator would be

DEFINE BINARY OPERATOR .MINE., PRECEDENCE SAME AS +

This defines a binary operator called .MINE. whose precedence is the same as the addition operator. On encountering such a statement the compiler would modify its tables accordingly. The modification would apply just to the current program that the compiler was processing.

One of the characteristics that distinguish high-level languages from assembly languages is the concept of data type. High-level languages usually provide *polymorphic* operators, i.e. operators that can work on a variety of data types. For example the addition operator may be such that the user can write

$$A + B$$

irrespective of the attributes of A and B. They may, for example, be fixed-point or floating-point, single-length or double-length, and so on. Moreover, A and B may even have differing attributes. Clearly the machine code that the compiler will generate for the addition operator will vary according to the attributes of its operands, but the user does not need to know about this. (This point has previously been discussed, in the context of a macro-assembler, in Chapter 1.3.) A further advantage of the use of data types is that the operands of an operator can be examined, and, if their data type is unsuitable, the error can be pointed out to the user at compile-time. An example of this would be an attempt to use a program label as an operand to a multiply operator. (A few high-level languages, designed for skilled programmers, forgo such checking because it may be restrictive, but we are not concerned with these.)

Hence when an operator for a high-level language is defined, the data type of the operands and of the result of the operation must be specified. For polymorphic operators there may be several possible operand types.

MAD allows for polymorphic operators. It also permits the user to define new data types, which can be used as operands of either new or built-in operators. There are five built-in data types and the user can define up to three more.

The data types—they are called 'modes' in MAD—are represented by integers in the range 0 to 7. A typical declaration of the data types associated with an operator would be

MODE STRUCTURE 2 = 1 .MINE. 1

which would mean that the .MINE. operator worked on two operands of data type 1 and produced a result of data type 2. If .MINE. were polymorphic there would also be MODE STRUCTURE declarations for other data types that it worked on. Each declaration is followed by the replacement text of the macro, i.e. the sequence of machine instructions that is to replace it. Macro-time conditional statements may be placed within the instructions in order that the instructions may be varied to suit the context. For example it is possible to test if a given machine register is in use and, if so, to generate a machine instruction to store its contents in a temporary variable before re-using it.

Not only can new operators be defined in MAD, but built-in ones can be re-defined or extended to cater for new data types. All this is accomplished by simple adjustments to the tables.

If one is to introduce new data types, one needs to be able to declare variables of that data type. In MAD this is simple as each type is represented by an integer and this integer is used in the declaration. If a more mnemonic form of declaration is needed, a name can be used to stand for the integer. Obviously, declaring a data item to be of type 'COMPLEX' is clearer than declaring it to be of type '6'.

Critique of the MAD definitional facility

In their paper on MAD, Arden, Galler and Graham describe some of its limitations that experience has shown up. Some are simple to remedy, like the need for more powerful macro-time statements, but others are more fundamental. One such problem is that few compilers are *completely* table-driven. There are always a few features that are treated in an exceptional way, and therefore cannot be changed or extended by adjustments to the tables. The reasons why features may be specially singled out are diverse; typical causes are inhomogeneity in the source language syntax, the need to produce optimized object code or the need to make the compiler run faster. MAD suffers from a few of these problems.

An obvious limitation to the MAD definitional facility is that it is confined to operators within arithmetic expressions, and cannot be used, for example, to introduce new statements into the language. The authors point out, however, that their scheme could be extended to cover other syntactic classes provided that the base language was a *full precedence* language, i.e. a language where the syntax of a construction could be defined exclusively by its precedence relative to other constructions.

One could add that a further limitation of the scheme is that it is tailored for a language with a relatively small number of data types. Obviously the eight possible data types could be extended to, say, sixteen, but indefinite extension in this direction would lead to tables becoming excessively large. More powerful and more general tools would be needed.

The reason why the MAD definitional facility has been so successful, however, is probably *because* of these limitations. The limitations make the facility simple enough to be usable.

Summary of features

We have examined the MAD macro facility in some detail because it is relatively simple but it contains, in rudimentary form at least, all the facilities needed to extend a language. These can be summarized as
(a) Specification of syntax for new operators.
(b) Declaration of new data types. It should be possible to declare both variables and constants.

(c) Extension and modification of existing operators (including I/O operators and control operators).

(d) Polymorphic operators.

(e) Powerful macro-time facilities for defining replacement text. It seems that the requirements for compiler-integrated macros are very similar to pre-processing macros. It may be possible to add power to the macro-time facilities by allowing them to make use of some of the routines built into the compiler.

(f) Interaction with environment. When generating replacement text for one syntactic form it is necessary to interact with the replacement text of adjacent syntactic forms (e.g. to examine how machine registers are used). Similarly at the syntactic analysis stage it may be desirable to examine the context in order to adjust the parsing in some way.

We will not examine any other extensible language in such detail. For a comprehensive description of a scheme for syntactic macros the reader should consult a book by Galler and Perlis (1970). Other illuminating papers include those by Irons (1970) and Molnar (1971). The latter describes the SEL language, which is set at a low level and can run on a small computer, thus making it different in nature from most other extensible languages.

In addition to Cheatham, Solntseff (1972) has produced a classification scheme for compiler-dependent macros; this involves more subdivisions than Cheatham's. His paper has the great merit of including details of many individual extensible languages and how they fit into the classification.

A completely extensible language

A good way of understanding the advantages and limitations of a technical development is to speculate what would happen if it was exploited to the ultimate. We will therefore do this to extensible languages and postulate a language which is completely extensible. This language is called ELASTIC and has the property that every facet of it can be extended or changed by a user during the compilation of his program. The following are therefore some of the things that could be done with ELASTIC.

(a) New scope rules could be introduced. Most languages have a statically nested block structure to define scope. In ELASTIC one could define disjoint blocks that partially overlapped one another (provided that logically consistent semantics could be defined for this situation) or even dynamic scope rules. New declarations could be created at run-time, perhaps read as input, and new blocks could be created dynamically.

(b) The user could define new ways of aggregating data, such as triangular arrays or even stacks of dynamically changing data types.

(c) New run-time interrupts, like the PL/I ON conditions, could be added.

(d) Error diagnostics could be modified.

(e) New naming conventions could be introduced. In ELASTIC, variable names would not have to be identifiers.

(f) Multiprogramming could be provided.

(g) The extension facilities themselves could be modified and extended.

Obviously this list could be extended *ad infinitum*. ELASTIC could be moulded to provide the function of any existing language, be it PL/I or SNOBOL, a macro-assembler or a text editor.

Clearly, ELASTIC, the final goal of the language extender, is impossible to realize. The reason is quite fundamental. Since nothing is fixed about ELASTIC, there is nothing to build upon. Using ELASTIC to build a compiler is exactly equivalent to building the compiler from scratch.

The lesson to be learned is this. Since full extensibility is a self defeating goal, any scheme for extensibility must be limited in its scope. When designing an extensible language, one should provide a relatively small subset of features and extensions should be restricted to fit in naturally with what is there already.

Design aims

Given these constraints, what extensions should be provided and how should they be designed?

A point to be emphasized is one that was made in the previous chapter. This is that high-level languages already contain a degree of built-in extensibility. The concept of a subroutine allows the user to define new statements in terms of existing ones, and functions allow new operators to be defined. Furthermore many languages cater for data structures, thus permitting the user to design new data types in terms of existing ones. However, these two facilities have their limitations. Firstly, they provide no way of extending the notation (syntax) of the language or bending it towards a particular type of use. Secondly, the execution of a function or subroutine call is very slow in many languages and even relatively complicated operations are best done by in-line code. Thirdly, there is the question, which we have mentioned already, of error checking. A compiler should produce an error message if an operator is applied to an incompatible data type, e.g. subtraction is applied to a file name, and this indeed happens for built-in data types. Assume, however, that two new data types, complex and double-length, are added to a language, each being represented by a data structure consisting of a pair of numbers. If a function is designed to work on a complex number and is inadvertently supplied with a double-length number instead, then no error can be detected as these two data structures look the same. Similarly no polymorphic operators can be designed to work on both complex and double-length data. In order to differentiate data types one needs the extra facility of 'tagging', i.e. being able to say that one pair of numbers has the tag 'complex' whereas another has the tag 'double-length'.

Hence user-defined functions, subroutines and data structures give only limited extensibility. They need to be supplemented by mechanisms to provide the following three properties:

(a) improved or adaptable notation,
(b) improved efficiency,
(c) improved error checking.

To achieve these aims, the extensibility mechanisms must be compile-time replacement facilities rather than run-time replacement facilities.

Note that improved function, i.e. being able to do something one could not do before, need not be a design goal. Indeed if the extension facility only permits the base language to be extended in terms of itself it is impossible to achieve improved function.

A fourth design aim, which is concerned with how extensibility features are provided rather than what they can achieve, should be added to the three above. The fourth is that the extensibility features *must be easy to use*. It is failure to achieve this aim, more than anything else, that has upset most extensibility projects. It is too much to expect, perhaps, that every single user should be able to design his own extensions to a language, but the extensibility mechanisms should be sufficiently simple for any systems programmer to employ them.

It must be recognized that people who *specify* extensions will often get them wrong. Definitions of syntax might, for example, be circular or inconsistent. There must therefore be good diagnostics at two levels, firstly for wrongly specified extensions and secondly for incorrect use of extended facilities.

Changing the compiler

One way of extending a language is to get one's hands on its compiler and change this. Certainly if the compiler is written in a modular, table-driven form and is encoded in a high-level language, or, better still, is implemented using a compiler-compiler, this may be quite easy to do. We will call such a compiler an *adaptable compiler*. However, there is a difference between an adaptable compiler and a proper extensible language. For a language to be genuinely extensible it must be possible for a programmer to include statements within his program that specify the extensions used by that program in the same way as he might define, say, a subroutine to be used by the program. (One might even have extensions local to a restricted part of a program.) The extensions may well be included from a library, just as subroutines may be, but the important point is that the extensions are specified within the program as an integral part of it.

It is wrong to conclude, however, that extensible languages completely encompass all the merits of adaptable compilers. Scowen (1971) has argued that adaptable compilers have many merits. One is that they provide more scope for making changes, and a second is that they are more efficient.

Conclusion on extensible languages

In summarizing extensible languages one cannot do better than to quote from Standish's (1971) paper that considers why his own extensible language fell short of its design goals. He says: '*You can't state something simple to an unknowledgeable mechanical recipient and expect it to alter its behaviour in major ways*'.

Further compiler-dependent macros

This chapter will conclude by discussing two special cases of compiler-integrated macros. One is concerned with a compiler for a low-level language, i.e. an assembler, and the other is concerned with a compiler that runs exclusively in interpretive mode. In the latter case the discussion concentrates on interpreters for job control languages, since this is such a fruitful field for the use of macros.

Meta-assemblers

Ferguson (1966) introduced the idea of the *meta-assembler*. Meta-assemblers are generalized macro-assemblers that can process the assembly language of (almost) any computer. The input to a meta-assembler is a program in assembly language and the output is the equivalent program in binary or in loader code. The mapping from input form to output form is done by a set of macro definitions. To create an assembler for a machine M, one simply writes a set of macro definitions corresponding to the instruction and data formats of M.

From the macro point of view, the interesting point about meta-assemblers is that macro processing is deeply embedded in the assembly process—indeed it defines the assembly process. This is in contrast to the traditional assembly process where macro processing is normally a separate activity, which precedes assembly. The relationship of meta-assembler macros to an assembler is, in fact, roughly equivalent to the relationship of the MAD definitional facility to its compiler. Each allows macro activity at the lowest practical level.

A second interesting point (though it is not related to compiler-integrated macros) is that Ferguson's meta-assembler macros can be used within the operands to instructions. These macros are called *functions*, and return a numerical value. It is a defect of most macro-assemblers that macros correspond to complete statements and cannot be used within other statements. There seems no good reason why. The only difference between functions in an ordinary macro-assembler from those in a meta-assembler would be that they would return character strings rather than numbers as their values.

Job control language macros and subroutines

In job control languages for operating systems it often happens that a particular sequence of commands is frequently repeated, the only variation being in one or more parameters, e.g. the names of files. A typical command sequence might be:

COPY CARD DECK TO DISC FILE x
ASSEMBLE x SENDING OUTPUT TO WORKFILE 1
LINKEDIT WORKFILE 1 SENDING OUTPUT TO WORKFILE 2
RUN WORKFILE 2

(Most real job control languages are verbose, and the above sequence of commands is likely in practice to take ten lines rather than four lines.) It is unlikely that such a command sequence would be repeated within a single job, but it is very likely that the sequence would be used in a large number of different jobs, each with a separate name substituted for the parameter x. It is useful, therefore, to store the sequence in a library under a suitable name, ASSRUN say, so that any job which wants to use the commands can accomplish it in a single line, such as

CALL ASSRUN(FILENAME)

where FILENAME is the argument that is to be substituted for the parameter x.

Many operating systems support such a facility, two examples being ICL's GEORGE 3 and IBM's JCL/360. (For a fuller discussion see Barron and Jackson (1972).) In GEORGE 3 the facility is called 'macro commands' and in JCL/360 it is called 'catalogued procedures'. The remarkable thing about the terminology used is that the same mechanism is regarded in one instance as a macro facility and in the other as a subroutine facility. We said in Chapter 1.1 that subroutines and macros were totally separate entities and we implied that no intelligent person could possibly confuse the two. The question arises as to who is being unintelligent, the GEORGE 3 people, the JCL/360 people or ourselves.

To find the answer (and the reader will get no prizes for guessing that the answer will *not* be that we ourselves have been unintelligent) it is best to go back to the criterion we have for distinguishing a macro from a subroutine. This is that a macro is a replacement facility that operates at macro-time (i.e. at or before compile-time) whereas a subroutine is a replacement facility that operates at run-time. If a language is executed purely interpretively and a macro facility is integrated with the interpreter, then macro-time and run-time are simultaneous and hence it may be arbitrary whether a replacement facility is considered to be a macro or a subroutine. This is just the situation with GEORGE 3 and JCL/360. (Note that this only arises with pure interpreters. Most so-called interpreters actually contain a compiling phase in which source programs are pre-processed in some way; hence macros and subroutines can be differentiated.)

Thus the answer to our question as to who was unintelligent is 'no-one'. A happy ending, if not a surprising one.

Part 2

SOFTWARE PORTABILITY

Chapter 2.1

Use of Macros for Software Writing

Introduction

This Part of the book is devoted to a pressing problem in computer software. This is that a huge amount of time and effort is spent in converting software from one computer to another, or in implementing identical pieces of software on different computers. This is not a problem that will ever be completely solved; it will always be a non-trivial matter to transfer software efficiently from computer to computer, and some individual pieces of software may always need to be rewritten for each environment. Nevertheless many effective techniques have been developed and have drastically reduced the transfer costs within certain areas. These techniques are discussed and compared in this Part of the book. Each has its own relative merits; some methods are cheap, others efficient, others wide ranging. A primary aim of our discussion is to present some approximate numerical measures by which to characterize these various techniques, so that an implementor can select the method most nearly meeting his needs. The implementor's position should be like someone buying binoculars, who can choose 7 × 50 glasses if he wants good light or 10 × 40 if magnification is more important.

Characteristics of software

We will discuss in this chapter some problems concerned with the implementation of software. The term 'software' tends to be used loosely; we use the term to mean an algorithm for implementing a programming aid, not the programming aid itself. Thus an Algol compiler is an example of software, but the Algol language is not.

Broadly speaking, the characteristics that distinguish software from ordinary computer programs are

(a) Software is heavily used and therefore needs to be encoded as efficiently as possible.

(b) Software is mainly concerned with non-numerical operations such as manipulating bits, characters and data structures. Even the compiler for a language for numerical working, such as FORTRAN, will consist mainly of non-numerical operations.

(c) Software should be written by experienced programmers.

(d) Software is likely to be used over a period of years and needs changing in response to user requirements.

(e) Software is costly to implement since it requires a good deal of time from expensive systems programmers.

Much software in the past has been encoded in assembly language. In cases where the software is potentially machine-independent, this has the obvious disadvantage that the software is unnecessarily tied to one machine, and an implementation for subsequent machines will be very expensive. We will discuss this in more detail in subsequent sections.

Assembly language macros

If one is forced to write in assembly language, macros can certainly help. Firstly they can be used to build up languages which are tailored to the task in hand and which map into assembly language, thus removing some of the tedium and opaqueness of assembly language coding. Secondly, and more importantly, macros can lessen the danger of future changes necessitating a major rewrite of the software. Let us show an example of this. We will assume that the software manipulates a dictionary in which each entry contains a field called the 'size field'. It is possible for the programmer to write a set of macros for accessing the size field. One macro, for example, might take the form

LOADSIZE   X

where X pointed at the requisite dictionary entry. This macro would map into instructions to add the necessary offset to X and then to extract the size field, perhaps using masking and shifting. A second macro, STORESIZE, say, would be needed for storing into the size field. These macros have obvious merits of conciseness and simplicity, but an even greater benefit might arise if, at a later date in the development of the software, the dictionary format was changed. The size field might then be at a different offset and consist of a different number of bits, and it is even possible that the nature of its contents might be changed, for example it might contain the size minus one instead of the true size. Such changes are a notorious problem in software development, as they often force the programmer to check all his program laboriously and change those parts that access the dictionary. In our example, however, this problem is avoided. A change in dictionary format only necessitates a simple change to the replacement text of the macros LOADSIZE, STORESIZE, etc.

If software is encoded in a high-level language, macros can also help. Here a free-mode macro processor may have an important role in making systematic changes to the high-level language program when using it on a new machine.

There is, however, a use of macro processors that is even more important and far reaching. This is the use of macro processors to provide a middle way between encoding software in a pre-defined machine-independent high-level language and encoding it in a machine-dependent language.

Portability

Assume some software S, which is machine-independent in nature, is to be implemented on several machines. We will use the term *object machine* for a machine on which software is to be implemented. We are not concerned with the design of the algorithm that S represents, but with the problems of implementing it, i.e. in obtaining an encoding of S in the order code of each of the object machines. Our starting point is therefore a correct machine-independent algorithm; this can be an idea in someone's head or it can be described in words and symbols or a general flow-chart—the initial form is immaterial. In comparing the methods of implementing S on a set of object machines there are four main factors to be assessed. These are as follows.

(a) The cost of the implementation on the first object machine.
(b) The cost of implementations on subsequent object machines. We will call this the *portability cost*.
(c) The *range*, i.e. the number of different object machines that S can be implemented on at the cost given in (b).
(d) The efficiency of the implementations.

The costs mentioned in (a) and (b) can be measured in man hours of programming time. A program is said to be *portable* if, given an implementation on one machine, it is relatively easy to obtain an implementation on another, i.e. if the program can be carried around from machine to machine. We will attempt to quantify this by using such concepts as the portability cost.

One way of implementing S on all the object machines is to encode it directly in the assembly language of each machine. In this case the cost of all implementations will be potentially the same (though there may be variations due to the 'nastiness' and 'niceness' of order codes). In practice the first implementation might have an added overhead because S will turn out to have some logical bugs in it. However since we are solely concerned with problems of encoding S this aspect is irrelevant—in fact our basic assumption was the somewhat unreal one that S was correct. The efficiency of the implementations coded directly in assembly language should be unsurpassable by any other method, and the range is unrestricted—the technique will work for all object machines. We will take this method of implementation as a yardstick to measure the others. Taking each of the four factors in turn, we will define the *initial cost factor* of a given implementation method as the percentage given by

$$\frac{\text{Cost of first implementation by given method}}{\text{Cost of an implementation by direct coding in assembly language}} \times 100$$

and the *portability cost factor* as the percentage

$$\frac{\text{Cost of subsequent implementations by given method}}{\text{Cost of an implementation by direct coding in assembly language}} \times 100$$

The *portability limitation factor* is defined as the percentage of computer designs for which the method fails. This measure is therefore an estimate of the flexibility of the method. In fixing the value of the portability limitation factor, it is assumed that all computers are equal, and the fact that some markets may be currently dominated by models from one manufacturer is ignored. Lastly, the *inefficiency factor* is defined as the percentage inefficiency in speed and size of an implementation compared with an assembly language one. (For the sake of argument we will take the average of the speed inefficiency and the size inefficiency.)

We therefore have a quadruple of numbers to measure an implementation method. We will represent the quadruple in the form (*Cost N1% then N2% failing N3% Inefficiency N4%*) where $N1$, $N2$, $N3$ and $N4$ are the initial cost factor, the portability cost factor, the portability limitation factor and the inefficiency factor, respectively. The quadruple for implementation by assembly language is therefore (*Cost 100% then 100% failing 0% Inefficiency 0%*). The four measures have each been designed so that the lower each number the better. Obviously it would be impossible to obtain completely accurate values of all these numbers—indeed the choice of value may be a subject of much argument—but it is possible to quote 'ball park' values and these can usefully help to identify the differences in various implementation methods.

Let us first assume that S is a numerical algorithm and it is encoded in FORTRAN. In this case the initial cost factor could be said to be 40%, i.e. it is $2\frac{1}{2}$ times as quick to write a program in FORTRAN as in assembly language. (Doubtless almost every reader will quarrel with this, some saying a factor of 20% would be better, others saying they can work as quickly in assembly language as FORTRAN, others saying it all depends. We will, however, proceed undaunted.) FORTRAN is a machine-independent language (indeed the widespread use of FORTRAN almost forces hardware designers to produce machines capable of processing it) and so the portability cost factor of a FORTRAN program is nice and small, say 5%. Ideally it should be almost zero but there always seem to be problems in transferring programs between machines even if they are in standard FORTRAN. One problem is that the permissible sizes of quantities varies between FORTRAN compilers, and hence machine-dependence can creep into a FORTRAN program. FORTRAN compilers exist for most computers so we can say the portability limitation factor is only 5%. Lastly most FORTRAN compilers produce good code for numerical operations—some even claim to do better than a human coder could reasonably expect to do—so we can safely put the inefficiency factor at 10%. We therefore have a quadruple (*Cost* 40% *then* 5% *failing* 5% *Inefficiency* 10%) compared with the assembly language norm of (*Cost* 100% *then* 100% *failing* 0% *Inefficiency* 0%). For those machines without FORTRAN compilers the algorithm could be encoded in assembly language or some similar language. (Although we judge the method to fail if the object machine has no FORTRAN compiler, it might be economic, if the algorithm or algorithms to be implemented are very large, to write a FORTRAN compiler specially.) In any case, the portability limitation factor, being small, is not an important defect or limitation in this method. All in all, therefore, using FORTRAN to encode a numerical algorithm gives as good a set of figures as one could expect short of implementing software by waving a magic wand. Similar figures would apply to the other well-known high-level languages for encoding numerical algorithms, and to COBOL for data processing algorithms.

Unfortunately, as we have said, software is very seldom numerical in nature. It is usually possible to encode non-numerical algorithms in FORTRAN but the quadruple would be a much less favourable one, say (*Cost* 60% *then* 10% *failing* 10% *Inefficiency* 100%). In particular the inefficiency factor can deteriorate considerably, a rough estimate of it being 100%, i.e. the final program might be twice as large as it need be and take twice as long to run. In addition, more machine-dependence is likely to creep into the FORTRAN program, particularly if attempts are made to pack more than one item of data into a word. There are several widely used high-level languages with better non-numerical facilities than FORTRAN. PL/I, for example, aims to cover this field, but it is not widely available and the code produced, by most current PL/I implementations at least, tends to be worse than FORTRAN. The quadruple for PL/I might be (*Cost* 40% *then* 10% *failing* 60% *Inefficiency* 150%) though the last two figures might improve in the future.

There do exist high-level languages which are specially designed for software writing. (The interested reader should refer to the October 1971 issue of *SIGPLAN Notices*.) These range from the thousands of examples of languages of the 'my-private-language-that-is-better-than-anyone-else's' variety to comparatively widely accepted languages such as BCPL (Richards, 1969). The quadruple for BCPL might be something like (*Cost* 40% *then* 10% *failing* 50% *Inefficiency* 75%) and BCPL would be a good choice for software writing in cases where a largish inefficiency factor is not a crucial disadvantage. Indeed the BCPL compiler itself is relatively easy to implement so the portability limitation factor is not as bad as it looks.

It has proved extremely difficult to design any high-level language which can be used to encode non-numerical algorithms with a high efficiency, in spite of the success with numerical algorithms. The main reason for this difference between numerical and non-numerical algorithms is that numerical algorithms can be efficiently represented using a few primitive operations (addition, multiplication, etc.) that are available on almost all computers, whereas machines differ widely in the way they manipulate characters and data structures, and it is certainly not possible to distil a set of common primitive operations that would be universally efficient. Indeed there is a large body of opinion that thinks that if software is to be encoded in a fixed high-level language, the best choice is a language specially tailored for a particular machine architecture. Examples are BLISS (Wulf, Russell and Habermann, 1971) and, at a lower level, PL360 (Wirth, 1968). Such languages, however, are less useful when portability is an object.

Descriptive languages

A solution to the problem of combining efficiency with portability is not to attempt to encode software in a pre-defined high-level language, but rather to start from the other end and design a special-purpose language for implementing each piece of software. We will call such a language a *descriptive language* of the software, and will use the symbology DL(S) to represent a descriptive language of some software S. A descriptive language should be designed to have, as its primitive operations, exactly those primitive operations that the software it describes needs. Thus if S uses stacks, then the primitive operations of DL(S) should include stacking operations, and if S happens to spend much of its time manipulating data structures that consist of a character followed by a pointer followed by a digit, then DL(S) should contain primitive operations to define and manipulate these specialized data structures. The use of a descriptive language has two main advantages: firstly that DL(S), if well designed, should make the encoding of S exceptionally easy, and secondly that implementations of S should be efficient. The efficiency results from the primitives of DL(S) being just the primitives that S needs. It is not hard to write a translator that maps a set of primitive operations into efficient code but it is hard to generate efficient code for all possible combinations of primitive operations. When a pre-defined high-level language is used for encoding software it is very unlikely that the primitive operations and primitive data types provided in the language will be exactly those that the software needs, and hence it is necessary to represent the primitive elements of the software (e.g. stacking or the character–pointer–digit data structures mentioned earlier) in terms of combinations of the primitives offered by the high-level language. This is a big source of inefficiency. A second source may be the non-use of some of the facilities that the high-level language provides, for example one might pay a price for such features as recursion, dynamic sizes of data structures or dynamic limits on looping statements even if one does not use these features.

The descriptive language approach to software writing can be summarized by saying that, in order to gain efficiency, one tailors the software-writing language to the software rather than vice-versa. Special-purpose languages are more efficient, within their limited domain, than general-purpose ones.

There is, of course, a catch. If one uses FORTRAN one can take advantage of all the FORTRAN compilers that exist in the world, whereas if one creates a descriptive language one needs to write a translator for the descriptive language for each object machine. Unless this can be done relatively easily the whole idea is a practical write-off. One answer lies in the use of a macro processor. The task of implementing a special-purpose language to be used by experienced programmers is precisely what macro processors should be good at. Given their advantage of flexibility, they are just the tool for the job. Macro processors, however, tend to be fussy about the syntax they will accept, and therefore a descriptive language should be designed with this consideration to the fore. The descriptive language designer may have a single macro processor in mind—it must, of course, be a macro processor that is capable of generating any assembly language—or he may design the syntax to be acceptable to a range of macro processors. We will assume for the moment that the former applies but will discuss the advantages of the latter approach later.

To show an example of how the macro processor would be used we will assume the descriptive language requires the statements STACK and UNSTACK. These might be written in the form

> STACK   *argument*
> UNSTACK   *argument*

and, for each implementation, macros would be written to map these statements into the appropriate assembly language instructions. If the macro processor in the mind of the descriptive language designer was, say, GPM, then he would use the syntax §STACK, *argument*; rather than that shown above.

The work needed to produce an implementation is not great. All that is needed is a set of macros corresponding to the statement types in the descriptive language. There may also be a need for macros corresponding to other syntactic types, for example variables, constants or blocks, but, unless the descriptive language is exceptionally complicated, these should be easy to write. If variable names in the descriptive language are identifiers, for example, these can be carried over into most assembly languages without change and no mapping macros are therefore needed for these except in rare cases. Since software writers are, one hopes, experienced programmers, they should have no problem writing, debugging and using macros.

This technique will be called a *DLIMP*, which is an abbreviation for *D*escriptive *L*anguage *I*mplemented by *M*acro *P*rocessor. The quadruple for software implemented by a DLIMP might be (*Cost* 175% *then* 15% *failing* 10% *Inefficiency* 10%). This is worthy of further explanation.

The initial cost factor is very high. This is because a descriptive language needs to be designed and to be documented for further use. The portability costs are, however, cheap. My own experience has been that a DLIMP is marginally worth while if only two implementations are required and thereafter the pay-off increases dramatically. The portability limitation factor is small. This is because the macro processor need not run on the same machine as the software is to be implemented on. Thus if, say, GPM is the macro processor to be used, any implementation of GPM can perform the mapping. If GPM is already available on the object machine this is an advantage but the lack of it would not be a serious inconvenience. The limitation on portability arises only if a descriptive language is unsuitable for some object machines. Finally the object of the exercise, to achieve efficiency, can be, and has been measured to be, achieved.

The quadruples, approximate though they undoubtedly are, highlight the fundamental differences between implementation methods, and show the relative merits of each. No implementation method is 'better' than all the others, and the implementor selects his method according to how he rates the importance of the four factors. Cost versus efficiency is normally the crucial question. A DLIMP is best at the end of the spectrum where a high initial cost factor is acceptable to achieve good efficiency and portability; at other points in the spectrum BCPL or FORTRAN may be the best choice. It would be nice to find a 'universal implementation method' that is best over the whole spectrum, but unfortunately one rarely gets something for nothing in this world, and any new improved software implementation method that claims to give a dramatic improvement in one or more of the factors without degrading the others either represents an unusual stroke of genius or an example of over-selling.

Machine-dependent features

It is an oversimplification to pretend that the way a piece of software works is either totally machine-independent or totally machine-dependent.

Almost all software contains both facets. We will therefore separate the two and assume that software consists of some MI-logic (machine-independent logic) and some MD-logic (machine-dependent logic). An exercise in portability is only worthwhile if the MI-logic is large. The MD-logic, by its nature, needs to be coded by hand for each object machine. Fortunately, for a good deal of software, the MI-logic can be considered to be at least ten times as big as the MD-logic.

Typical routines that might be placed in the MD-logic of any software might be a hashing algorithm, a conversion routine from internal numerical form (e.g. two's complement binary) to external character form (e.g. ASCII code), initialization routines (borrowing resources from the operating system) and perhaps I/O routines. The way these routines are encoded depends either on the way data is represented on the object machine or on the nature of its operating system.

There are two possible ways of dealing with the interface between the MI-logic and the MD-logic. One is by means of subroutine calls or direct GOTO statements. The other is to disguise the existence of the MD-logic by introducing high-level statements in the MI-logic to perform the machine-dependent operations. Thus there might be a statement

$$\text{HASH} \quad X$$

meaning apply the hashing algorithm to X, leaving the nature of this algorithm to the designer of the mapping macro. Since the implementor would presumably map this into a call of a special hand-coded subroutine, the difference between the two ways of dealing with the interface is more apparent than real.

Like most concepts in the field of portability, the ideas of 'machine-dependence' and 'machine-independence' cannot be precisely defined and there is certainly no exact dividing line between the two. The test for deciding if an algorithm is machine-independent is the subjective one 'Is the algorithm a sensible way of doing things on almost all current and likely future production computers?'. Nevertheless even with this unsatisfactory subjective definition, there is a good measure of agreement among practitioners on what sort of features are and are not machine-independent, so the dividing line does not vary grossly.

levels of language

It is an interesting question as to how high-level a descriptive language might be. Should it contain statements such as

$$\text{IF } X + Y = Z \text{ THEN SET } P = Q$$

or should it consist of a series of equivalent low-level statements such as

```
          LOAD      X
          ADD       Y
          COMPARE   Z
          GONE      LAB1
          LOAD      Q
          STORE     P
LAB1   ...
```

The higher-level form is more readable, but it would be a comparatively hard job for a macro processor to map it into assembly language. Implementing software encoded in such a language might have a portability cost of 20–30%. The low-level form has the advantage of simplicity and its portability cost might be 10% or lower, but how machine-independent is it? It is making certain assumptions about the structure of the object computer.

In the design of descriptive languages, the higher the level the more machine-independent the language is, but the harder it is to implement. The higher you fly in a balloon the more towns you can see, but the longer it takes to land at any of them.

In an extreme case, a descriptive language for a compiler could consist of only two statements

COMPILE

RUN

but it would be some job to map them into assembly language.

A case study has been published (Brown, P., 1972b) which compares the results achieved for implementations of the same software using a high-level descriptive language and a low-level descriptive language. In this case the portability cost for the low-level language was found to be cheaper than for the high-level language by a factor of four, but the inefficiency of the low-level language was on average about 5% worse. This difference in efficiency is worthy of illustration, as superficially one might expect the low-level language to give the better efficiency. The reason that this is not so is that the design for a low-level language makes a number of assumptions about the structure of the object machine. Thus the descriptive language, LOWL, which was the low-level language used in the study, involved the use of three pseudo-registers. On any one implementation, these were mapped either into real registers or, if the object machine lacked suitable available registers, into storage locations. This use of pseudo-registers may or may not be an efficient way to use a given object machine. With a high-level descriptive language no assumptions are made about register structure and hence there is more scope for the implementor to write mapping macros that fully exploit the register structure of the object machine.

A second source of inefficiency with low-level descriptive languages is that it is harder to take advantage of specialized machine instructions. Assume, for example, that an object machine has an instruction which decrements a storage location by one. In a high-level descriptive language this might be easy to exploit, the mapping macros would simply need to recognize a pattern such as

$$\text{SET } X = X - 1$$

The corresponding low-level statements might be

```
LOAD    X
SUBL    1
STORE   X
```

which would span three macro calls. With most macro processors it is comparatively hard to recognize such patterns and take action accordingly.

Nevertheless, if the low-level DLIMP takes one month where a high-level DLIMP might take four months, one can argue that the low-level implementor can spend the three months he has saved in improving the efficiency of his implementation. He should easily make up his loss of 5% in that time.

The conclusions of the case study are that a low-level descriptive language is usually the better choice, but it is valuable to have a high-level one in reserve to cater for unusual object machines—the Burroughs B6700 was a case in point—and to provide a more readable program. This leads to the possible use of a hierarchy of descriptive languages. This idea emanated from Poole and we will consider it further when we have described his work.

Attempting the impossible

There are those who argue that true portability is impossible (Warshall, 1972). However high one sets the level of the descriptive language there will always be computers (real or imaginary) for which this is unsuitable. For example, although our two-statement compiler description COMPILE, RUN certainly does not impose great restrictions on the structure of the compiler—the computer could, for example, be an interpreter, in which case COMPILE would be null—it does specify that compiling should come before running. There may be machines built where this is undesirable, as it may be better for the two activities to be interleaved in some way.

The argument is, of course, correct. It must be impossible to achieve portability over all current machines and all that can be imagined in the future. The best one can do is to achieve portability over most of the computers that are in current production, and to have sufficient flexibility in design to adapt to future needs.

Fortunately this is one of the rare cases where the problem in theory is worse than it is in practice. In practice, it is true that, although computers differ in details (such as the way they manipulate characters), the fundamental design principles have remained static, and most newly introduced computers continue to have the traditional Von Neumann architecture. Successful computer manufacturers have to be conservative, because users, who mostly have a huge investment in traditional techniques, are conservative. Hence if we ascend in our balloon in order to look down on all computer designs we do not have to go very high, because instead of being scattered widely over the countryside all the designs are collected together in one small area.

More serious problems of portability tend to occur when the software depends on the characteristics of peripheral devices, as these tend to vary more widely. We will discuss this aspect in more detail in the next chapter, after we have considered some of the practical examples of portable software.

Effects of computer networks

It is unlikely that the need to transfer programs between machines will ever be totally eliminated. However the recent development of networks of different computers linked together will help to alleviate the problem. In such networks the user of one of the machines has, in principle, access to all the others. Hence if some software is available on one machine in the network it is generally much easier to use this software via the network than to try to implement it on the home machine. Indeed this is a central purpose of the networks. The problem of portability is therefore bypassed, though the networks have some compensating problems such as administration, communication and documentation.

The time may come when most computers are connected to some network, though it is hard to imagine that each computer in the world will have easy access to every other computer in the world. Even if only small networks become common, each computer should still have access to a wide range of software and the need for portability will be diminished, since it only arises when one network wants a program that another has, rather than when one computer wants a program that another has. In the ultimate case of a global (or interplanetary?) network, the only need for programs to be transferred is when a machine has become obsolete and is due to be replaced on the network.

It may be useful to consider the public telephone network as a parallel (although it is, of course, dangerous to assume that computer networks will develop in an exactly similar way). Almost all the telephones of the world are linked together though mutual access between two telephones is only convenient and cheap if they are relatively close. 'Programs' such as 'recipe of the day' tend to be duplicated on a regional basis, as it is expensive and slow, for example, for a London user to make use of the 'recipe of the day' service in Sydney, Australia.

Emulation

Another hardware development that has a considerable effect on the transfer of software is the *emulation* feature. This is a feature whereby one computer may be made to perform exactly like another one. From the software point of view the machine is identical to the one it is emulating and hence, provided that emulation is efficient, the need to transfer programs is eliminated. Emulation has been used extensively in running IBM 1401 programs on IBM System/360 computers. Recently there has been a trend in minicomputer design towards machines with a variable microprogram, thus making it relatively easy for one machine to emulate almost any other.

From the viewpoint of efficiency, emulation is much preferable to *simulation* whereby software is written to simulate one computer on another.

Chapter 2.2

Some Practitioners of DLIMPs

We will now consider some practical examples of software portability using DLIMPs.

Wilkes' work

A good, easy to read, account of an exercise in portability is given by Wilkes (1964). Wilkes' paper is concerned with a simple list processing language called WISP. There are two aspects of the paper that are of relevance to portability; firstly the way WISP is transferred between machines and secondly the so-called 'bootstrapping' technique. We will consider these in turn.

WISP is implemented by a macro processor specially designed for the purpose. A set of built-in macros maps WISP programs into assembly language and the programs are then assembled and run. The user views the whole system as a 'black box'. (The user therefore does not know he is using a macro processor and indeed the macro processor is not even credited with a name in Wilkes' paper.) The use of WISP on a machine M is illustrated by Figure 2.2A.

The WISP language was designed to act both as a simple general-purpose list processing language and as a descriptive language for the macro processor which is used to implement WISP. The macro processor was therefore encoded in WISP, and, when this was fed to the WISP compiler in the way shown in Figure 2.2A, the macro processor generated a new implementation of itself. This is a specialized example of a DLIMP, where the software being implemented and the software doing the implementing are the same. Such DLIMPs are not things to be thought about at the end of a long day, as, although the concepts are simple, it requires clear thinking to avoid confusion between the dual roles of the software concerned.

When WISP is to be moved to a new computer, the ordinary DLIMP mechanisms are employed. If we assume an implementation exists on a machine M and a new implementation of WISP is required for machine N,

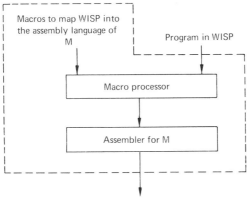

Program in order code of M

Fig. 2.2A. Compilation of a WISP program. The user regards what is inside the dotted line as the WISP compiler

the macros are recoded to map into the assembly language of N rather than M, and the encoding of the macro processor in WISP is mapped by these macros into the assembly language of N. This is illustrated in Figure 2.2B.

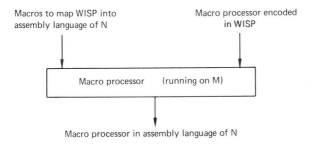

Fig. 2.2B. Use of WISP on machine M to implement WISP on machine N

The output from this process is a macro processor that will run on machine N and if this is coupled with the macros to map WISP into the assembly language of N it forms a WISP compiler for N.

The second interesting aspect of Wilkes' paper is the use of bootstrapping. To start with, we will describe the use of bootstrapping to develop a compiler for a single computer, and will then extend the description to cover portability. When one computer is involved, a bootstrapping process works as follows.

(a) A language X is designed and a compiler written for X.
(b) A new language SUPERX is designed and its compiler written in X, and so the old compiler is used to produce the new one.

(c) A new language EXTRASUPERX is designed and its compiler written in SUPERX. . . .

This has since become a very fashionable exercise. In most cases the language X is a subset of SUPERX which in turn is a subset of EXTRASUPERX, and so each step in the process generates a more powerful version of the same language. Hence the name 'bootstrapping', which refers to the apparent similarity of the process to the task of pulling oneself up by one's own bootstraps. There is actually no logical need for X,SUPERX, etc., to be closely related as languages.

Bootstrapping is splendid fun, and it also has serious uses that may be exploited. The language X can be made a simple one, so that its compiler is very small and easy to implement. Since the entire family of SUPERX, EXTRASUPERX, etc. is based on the compiler for X, if a compiler for X is written for another machine then the entire family will work on the new machine. (Wilkes did not do his machine transfer in this way, however, as the ultimate in his family was a macro processor that itself was a good tool for portability.)

The bootstrapping technique also has the advantage that it fits naturally with the way programming languages are developed. A language designer produces a language X. After X has been in use for a while, the language designer thinks up some improvements and designs SUPERX. He thinks X is such a good language even without the improvements that he will write the compiler for SUPERX in it. In this way a bootstrapping process may evolve naturally, with no pre-planning of such an exercise.

On a superficial analysis, bootstrapping may appear to have the disadvantage of compounding inefficiencies. If the compiler for X is 20% inefficient and the compiler for SUPERX is also 20% inefficient, then the compiler for EXTRASUPERX would appear to be 44% inefficient, exactly as a 20% rate of compound interest works out at 44% after two years. This is wrong. A careful analysis shows that there are two kinds of inefficiency.

(a) A compiler may run more slowly than it needs to.
(b) A compiler may compile into inefficient code.

Inefficiencies of type (a) in one generation in no way affect the next. Inefficiencies of type (b) in one generation lead to inefficiencies of type (a) in the next, which in turn disappear in the following generation. Hence all such inefficiencies work themselves out of the system in two generations.

A more serious objection to bootstrapping is that the family of languages may suffer from inbreeding. Assume, for example, that the language X has no facility for floating-point working. Since a compiler for a language containing floating-point operations must itself contain some floating-point operations (if they can be avoided in the translation phases of the compiler, they will still almost certainly be needed for the run-time routines), it is impossible to build floating-point operations into any successors of X. (In practice implementors usually cheat by adding some extra machine code subroutines or the like.)

It is unfortunately a very common occurrence that a language designer develops a language X, and then cannot persuade anyone else to use it. The only use he can find for X is as a language for writing the compiler for SUPERX. Bootstrapping is then fun and nothing more.

The work of Poole and Waite

Poole and Waite, with their co-workers, have been one of the most active teams in the field of software portability. They have produced many papers on the subject, including a good overall summary and analysis (Newey, Poole and Waite, 1972). The essence of their work is that they have combined a DLIMP with a bootstrap. They use the term 'abstract machine' instead of 'descriptive language', but these two apparently different concepts are in fact the same. The rationale behind 'abstract machine' is that the operations provided in a descriptive language can be viewed as the order code of an imaginary machine that is independent of all real machines.

In a normal DLIMP a macro processor on machine M is used to produce software for machine N. M and N may well be different, and certainly will be when the software to be mapped is the macro processor itself. This may be an advantage; if N is a new machine still under design or has no software for some other reason, then it is useful to use another machine to get the software for N off the ground. However if N is an established computer there are disadvantages due to communication problems, particularly if it is the people at the place where machine N is located who are producing the implementation. If you are in California trying to implement, say, WISP, it is difficult to use an implementation of WISP on a machine in England to produce the implementation, even with the cooperation of someone at the English end.

Poole and Waite (Waite 1970a, 1970b) solve this problem in the following way. They have designed an ultra simple macro processor called SIMCMP. This can be implemented easily on any machine. SIMCMP is encoded in FORTRAN and it should be possible to compile this directly on most object machines. If FORTRAN is not available on the object machine, the logic of SIMCMP is so simple that it is easy to recode it in whatever other language is available. There is therefore no absolute dependence on FORTRAN. When SIMCMP is running, it is used to implement a more powerful macro processor, called STAGE2, that can be used for all subsequent mappings. The logic of STAGE2 is encoded in a simple descriptive language called FLUB which SIMCMP can map into the assembly language of the object machine. If efficiency is important, the implementation of STAGE2 resulting from this can then be used to remap FLUB to produce a more efficient implementation of itself. The advantage of this remap is that STAGE2 contains conditional facilities and can thus be used to produce a more optimized mapping of FLUB than SIMCMP can.

It can be misleading to talk of time scales for such operations as these as there may be a big difference between getting a working implementation of a piece of software and producing a polished product that is fit for others to use. However, as a guide, Poole and Waite quote a man week as the effort required to implement STAGE2 on a new machine, though some implementors have, of course, taken rather longer than this.

As a result of its ease of implementation, STAGE2 is running on at least twenty-five different types of machine. Moreover, two other major pieces of software, a text editor called MITEM and a BASIC interpreter, have been encoded in descriptive languages based on STAGE2 and implemented on several machines. The MITEM text editor, in particular, contains some interesting features that illustrate the flexibility of DLIMPs. MITEM contains a large range of features over and above the ordinary simple replacement, insertion and deletion facilities found in all text editors. This may be fine for a large computer, but when MITEM is implemented on a small computer the extra features may make it too big to fit. To solve this problem, MITEM has been divided into six versions, MITEM6 being the complete system and MITEM1 the smallest viable subset. An implementor can choose which version or versions he wants. He might for example decide to implement MITEM3 for everyday use and MITEM6 to be kept in reserve for really tough text manipulation problems. The logical description of MITEM, which is encoded in a descriptive language called TEXED, contains statements such as

"Omit this routine if the version number < 4"

or

"Include this statement only if the version number is 2"

On each mapping the version number is placed in a STAGE2 global variable, and STAGE2 is made to select just those parts of the logic that are needed for the version concerned. Similar mechanisms are also used to control various options that are available within versions. Altogether, this is a very useful technique.

With these facilities, the algorithm that represents the workings of MITEM is not only portable, but is also *adaptable*, i.e. the algorithm itself can be changed to fit different objectives. The adaptability of MITEM involves making several different subset levels available, but one can have adaptability without any variation in the overall function of an algorithm. In solving a sorting problem, for example, the choice of the best method depends on how much fast storage is available. A sorting algorithm could be made adaptable so that it could be mapped into the best algorithm for any given set of circumstances. Similarly a translating algorithm may best be performed in several passes under some circumstances and in a single pass under others, and adaptability is clearly useful in this respect. One can summarize by saying that adaptability is certainly a desirable property to add to portability, and some of its uses still remain to be investigated and exploited. To a certain extent adaptability is related to the level of language. All other things being equal, an algorithm expressed in a high-level language is more adaptable than one expressed in full detail in a low-level language. Wirth (1970) points out that the use of the hierarchical programming technique called 'structured programming' aids adaptability. However, at any one level of language the technique of Poole and Waite can improve adaptability to make it as good as a much higher level of language.

STAGE2, MITEM and the BASIC interpreter have all been implemented using radically different descriptive languages, and a merit of the survey paper by Newey, Poole and Waite is that it describes all three descriptive languages and indicates the good and bad features of each. All three languages are set at a fairly low level and most of their problems emanate from the constraints they place on the way the object machine should work. For example AIM1, the descriptive language for the BASIC interpreter, forces the object machine to perform all its arithmetic using a push-down stack. This is not a good way of working on a large number of object machines, particularly as the stack usually only contains two elements and hence the fact that it is a stack is not greatly exploited by the BASIC interpreter. The authors' conclusion is that the design of a descriptive language is a difficult software engineering problem, and it requires a good degree of practice and experience (and luck) to arrive at a good design.

A further idea to emanate from the Poole and Waite stable is the use of partial interpretation. We will first explain how descriptive languages can be interpreted at run time, and will then explain how partial interpretation works.

Instead of translating a descriptive language into machine code, it is possible to write an interpreter for the descriptive language that will run on the object machine. The end result will be a program that will run rather slowly but may occupy less storage than a directly translated version. For example assume that a descriptive language contains fifty different statement types, one of which has the form

$$\text{STACK} \quad variable$$

If this is to be interpreted it can be mapped into a 6-bit operation code (to cover the fifty alternatives) followed by an operand field. If there are, say, 100 different variables that can be directly addressed then seven bits need to be reserved for the operand field, thus making thirteen bits in all. Since 13-bit entities are not conveniently manipulated on many computers the instruction length might be padded out, say to sixteen bits. These instructions would then be executed at run time by the interpreter. If the STACK statement was translated rather than interpreted it might occupy something like 32–64 bits, even if the statement was implemented by a subroutine call. Thus if a program is mapped into interpretive code it can be made considerably smaller, even allowing for the added overhead of the interpreter.

It is well known that most programs, when run, spend 90% of the time executing 10% of the instructions. In fact in any one run of a program 50% of its instructions may never be executed at all. It is evident therefore that if a program written in a descriptive language is mapped so that the most heavily used 10% is translated directly into machine code and the remaining 90% is interpreted, then the program will not run much more slowly than a version that was totally translated into machine code, but would be nearly as concise as a fully interpretive version. This technique of partial interpretation is, therefore, a compromise that retains the best features of both worlds. A DLIMP is such a flexible method of software implementation that it is possible to vary the degree of interpretation at will. For example the program might be first translated into purely interpretive code and tested in this form. Selected parts might then be mapped into machine code when experience of use showed which parts were the most frequently used. In this second mapping each macro would have two alternative forms, and a global macro variable would be used as an on/off switch to determine whether each macro was to map into interpretive code or compiled code.

DLIMPs to implement SNOBOL4

By far the most powerful and complex programming language to have been implemented by a DLIMP is SNOBOL4, the text processing language. This project is described in a book by Griswold (1972), which goes into considerable detail and gives a very good insight into the work. The portable implementation of SNOBOL4 is a SNOBOL4 interpreter rather than a SNOBOL4 compiler, though it does contain a translating phase which converts the source program into a form than can conveniently be interpreted. The size of the SNOBOL4 system can be gauged by the fact that the instructions and built-in tables that implement it on an IBM System /360 occupy about 100,000 bytes. In addition, big work areas are required. (The main reason for this large size is not that there are defects in the implementation mechanism, but that SNOBOL4 is inherently complex.)

The descriptive language of SNOBOL4 is called SIL and contains 130 different types of statement. In addition, each implementation requires some complex I/O routines that are based on FORTRAN. The idea is that an implementation of SNOBOL4 should share the I/O modules with the FORTRAN compiler on the object machine.

An implementation of SNOBOL4 using SIL takes 3–12 man months. Although this is a relatively long time, it represents a good portability cost factor (say 10–15%) given the size and complexity of SNOBOL4. From tests made on one implementation, that on the IBM System /360, Griswold estimates the inefficiency factor at about 20%. The portability limitation factor is relatively high, since the portable version of SNOBOL4 is only suitable for running on big machines.

SNOBOL4 is a widely used language and almost all the implementations have been performed by DLIMPs. This has been a great advantage to the SNOBOL4 designers since all these implementations support an identical language, using the same well-tried translator and interpreter. Hence the problems of incompatibility that have beset almost all other programming languages have been largely avoided.

One of the features of SIL that improves portability is that its syntax has been designed to be mappable by any macro-assembler. (It may be necessary to perform minor changes of character representations, etc.) As well as being mappable by macro-assemblers, SIL should also be mappable by most free-mode general-purpose macro processors and even by using text processing languages. This generality is accomplished simply by sticking to the most commonly used format of a macro call, namely a macro name (which is an identifier) followed by an argument list separated by commas. Macro calls are one to a line and can optionally be labelled.

The generality of SIL means that the implementor can select any suitable macro processor that is conveniently available to him, and he would have a good chance of finding one at his own installation. There are therefore two possible ways of allowing the implementor to do all his work on his local machine. Firstly, there is the STAGE2 approach, which relies on a particular macro processor but provides an easy way of bootstrapping it to the object machine. Secondly, there is the SIL approach, which removes the dependence on one particular macro process. (It cannot be guaranteed, of course, that the SIL implementor will always find a suitable mapping tool locally, but it is usually the case in practice. If not, he could bootstrap STAGE2 and use this to perform the mapping!)

Brown's work

I have also been active in this field, using ML/I as a tool for portability.

Work started with the development of a language called, simply, L (Brown, P., 1969), which is a descriptive language for ML/I itself. The distinguishing feature of L is that it is set at a higher level than any of the other descriptive languages that have been developed. L contains four different data types, elaborate arithmetic expressions, constructions nested within one another, a kind of block structuring and several different statement formats. The data types are character, number (integer), pointer and switch, the last being bit patterns that are used as masks and are subject to logical operations. All variables are declared but to obviate the need for ML/I to maintain a dictionary of variables and their data types, names of variables are chosen so that the data type is manifest from the name. The scheme is, in fact, that the last two letters of the name give its data type in the following way

> PT means pointer,
> CH means character,
> SW means switch,
> anything else means number.

A potential problem arises because different implementations may use varying numbers of storage units for the different data types. Thus a word machine may store each data type in one word but a byte machine might store an item of character data in one byte and a pointer in four bytes. Consider the following situation: a pointer and three characters have just been placed on the top of a stack and it is desired to increase the stack pointer, STAKPT, accordingly. This cannot be achieved by

$$\text{SET STAKPT} = \text{STAKPT} + 4$$

as it will not work for a byte machine. The solution in L to this problem is to have a macro, called OF, which contains as its argument an arithmetic expression involving the following possible submacros

> LPT   the number of storage units occupied by a pointer,
> LCH   the number of storage units occupied by a character,
> LSW   the number of storage units occupied by a switch,
> LNM   the number of storage units occupied by a number.

Thus the statement to update STAKPT would be written

$$\text{SET STAKPT} = \text{STAKPT} + \text{OF(LPT} + 3*\text{LCH)}$$

The submacros are defined appropriately for each implementation—for a word machine they might all have the value one, whereas for a byte machine LPT and LNM might have the value 4. The OF macro is then defined to generate the appropriate constant. Hence OF(LPT + 3*LCH) might be four for a word machine and seven for a byte machine.

The following sample of L should give the reader a hint of its flavour.

```
// SAMPLE PROGRAM TO SHOW SYNTAX OF L //
IF COPYSW = TRUE THEN
    SET   IND(STAKPT)NM = IND(LAST + OF(LNM))
                                    NM + LASTPT − LENGTH
    IF STAKPT − FIRSTPT GR STSIZE THEN GO TO ERSO
```

```
      STACK  XPT + OF(3*LNM + 2*LCH) (PT) XSW (SW)
      END
      [LABEL] SET COUNT, NOCHAR = 0
      CHAIN FROM HEADPT EXIT LAB3
         IF  IND(CHANPT + OF(LPT))CH = X' THEN  SET
                                                   COUNT = COUNT + 1
         SET  NOCHAR + NOCHAR + 1
      ENDCH
      CALL  INCHAR  (NOCHAR – COUNT)NM
```

The reader is not expected to understand the full details of this—indeed the program does not do anything in particular—but he should, perhaps, look at the statement forms and consider the problems of mapping. The following points may be of interest.

(a) The macro IND(. . .). . . represents indirect addressing. The last two letters give the type of the indirectly addressed data. Thus IND(XPT)CH means the CHaracter pointed at by XPT.

(b) Arithmetic expressions may occur in many places, for example in an assignment, CALL or IF statement and within the IND macro.

(c) Data types are indicated in all possible places. For example the two letters following an argument of the CALL statement give the data type of the argument, and each argument of STACK is followed by the data type in parentheses.

(d) CHAIN is a statement like the FOR statement found in most languages except that it follows down a chain rather than through a sequence of values. ENDCH indicates the end of the scope of the CHAIN statement, and CHANPT points to each element on the chain in turn.

(e) TRUE is a macro that defines the constant representing the logical value 'true'.

(f) There are also L statements of a kind not shown in the above example. These declare variables and define built-in constants and tables.

We have already discussed the advantages of high-level languages such as L, namely the readability, high degree of machine-independence, and scope for efficient implementation, and the disadvantage of a relatively large portability cost.

One subsidiary aim of L was that, should there happen to be a suitable high-level language available on the object machine, it should be possible to map into this rather than into assembly language. This has been done three times, the object languages being PL/I, Burroughs Extended Algol and BCPL. The mappings were easy to do, but the efficiency of the final product was only good in one of the three cases. Since efficiency is one of the most important advantages of a DLIMP, the other two implementations contained an element of throwing away the baby with the bathwater.

Because of the heavy portability cost of L, it was decided to supplement it by a low-level language called LOWL. LOWL is fully described in Part 3, and we will confine ourselves at this stage to mentioning one important feature. This is the concept of *supplementary arguments*. To improve portability several LOWL statements contain supplementary arguments which convey extra information about the statement. For example the GOTO statement has one supplementary argument which says how far away the designated label is. This argument is ignored on most mappings, but some object machines have special instructions for jumps over short distances, and these can make use of the supplementary argument.

Hierarchy

The languages L and LOWL are an example of the concept of a hierarchy of descriptive languages which has been suggested by Poole (1971). L has been mapped by macros into LOWL so an implementor can choose whether to take the L or the LOWL version of the program he wants to implement, bearing in mind the advantages and disadvantages of each. The hierarchy that L and LOWL form could be carried further in both directions. One could design an even lower-level language than LOWL, called, say, LEASTL, and make LEASTL the ultimate in ease of portability, with all other factors such as readability and efficiency disregarded. If LOWL was then mapped into LEASTL, the implementor whose first requirement was a low portability cost would implement his software via LEASTL. He could then at a later stage improve efficiency by doing a mapping using one of the languages higher in the hierarchy. Indeed the macro processor that was to do the mapping might first be implemented on the object machine using LEASTL, thus gaining the convenience of performing all subsequent mappings using only the object machine. This is exactly how Poole and Waite use SIMCMP to implement STAGE2.

Similarly, at the other end of the hierarchy, higher-level languages might be developed. It is doubtful if any language higher than L would be used to actually implement software on an object machine because of the massive job of mapping it. The merits of such languages would be that they would be easy to write programs in. There are many proponents of the method of program writing called 'structured programming'. The method is to write a program by describing it in very general terms at first, and then gradually refining this by filling in details at successively lower levels. Hierarchies of descriptive languages would be a means of realizing this.

Poole adds further variety to his hierarchies by proposing a tree structure. In our example we might have several languages mapping into LEASTL and perhaps even several languages mapping into LOWL and L. A possible hierarchy is shown in Figure 2.2C.

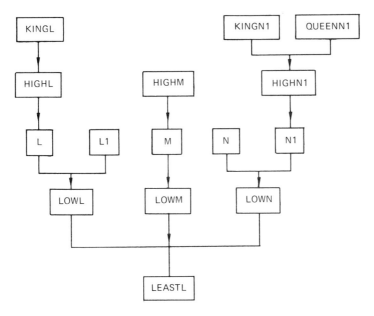

Fig. 2.2C. A possible hierarchy of descriptive languages. An arrow indicates that one descriptive language can be mapped into another

(A similar picture arises with ordinary programming languages, where assembly language is at the bottom of the hierarchy and several high-level languages map into this, perhaps through an intermediate language. In turn, other languages might map into the high-level languages. In this case the mappings between languages are usually performed by compilers.)

It would also be possible to build a hierarchy of descriptive languages using FORTRAN as a base, relying on the wide availability of FORTRAN to achieve portability. This would be a short cut to the creation of relatively high-level descriptive languages but the efficiency of implementation would not be good unless the languages were numerical in nature. Finally one might merge a hierarchy based on FORTRAN with one based on a very low-level assembly language, thus giving any implementor an exceptionally wide choice of implementation techniques.

It is time to put our feet back on the ground. We estimated the initial cost factor of a DLIMP to be 175%. If, instead of one descriptive language, a hierarchy is to be provided, each language requiring design, documentation, and testing of programs in it, the initial costs will be enormous, even though the hierarchy would not, of course, be developed all at once, but would tend to evolve in time as new languages were fitted into it. I can only quote from personal experience that I find a hierarchy of only two languages, L and LOWL, a big headache in maintenance of programs, documentation, etc.

To summarize, hierarchies can allow the implementor some freedom of movement on the cost/efficiency spectrum, but the cost to the provider of the software may be high. There is the danger that the set-up will become so complicated that the implementor will feel like a complete novice being sat in the pilot's seat of an aircraft and being told that it is easy to fly (using automatic pilot, etc.) once he has learnt which of the 465 lights and knobs is which.

Limitations

Most, if not all, of the DLIMPs described in this chapter have been successful in implementing software cheaply and efficiently, and a DLIMP can be judged to be a viable and attactive software implementation method. There are, however, some limitations on the kind of software that can be implemented by a DLIMP. Clearly a DLIMP, or for that matter any other aid to portability, is useless if the software to be implemented is largely machine-dependent in its very nature. In this respect it is interesting to speculate to what extent an operating system can be made portable. An operating system is concerned closely with the management of input/output devices and this is an area which has traditionally been regarded as machine-dependent. (The designers of Algol 60, for instance, did not even think it desirable to specify machine-independent statements for reading numbers, etc., from I/O devices, let alone actually controlling the devices.) Why are routines for using and controlling I/O devices considered to be machine-dependent whereas routines using other computing facilities are considered to be machine-independent? The answers may come from a combination of the following points:

(a) Computers vary considerably in the way they control I/O devices.
(b) The nature of I/O devices is changing continually.
(c) There are a large number of physical constraints and parameters concerned with I/O devices, e.g. block size, packing density, character code, and these intimately affect the way routines to control the devices are written.
(d) Control of I/O devices may involve timing constraints, and programming languages for expressing such constraints are not well developed.

As time goes by some of these problems may cease to apply or may be solved by hardware or software developments.

There is a good deal more to an operating system than the control of I/O devices. Some of the other aspects, such as the interpretation and execution of job control commands, are much more machine-independent. It may therefore be a fruitful exercise to apply portability aids to operating systems, though the best results one should expect to achieve might be a portability cost factor of 50% with a portability limitation factor of the same order.

Another type of software that contains definite machine-dependent parts is the compiler, since a compiler translates into the order code of the machine on which it runs. Thus if one took a compiler that translated FORTRAN into IBM System /360 order code, and somehow translated the compiler into CDC 6600 order code, one would end up with a compiler that ran on the CDC 6600 but produced code that needed to be run on an IBM System /360. To make the compiler produce code for a new machine one needs extra mechanisms built into the portability process. Moreover the nature of certain parts of the compiler, such as those parts that deal with machine code optimization, need to be changed. We will discuss this in the next chapter. Fortunately interpreters or hybrid compiler/interpreters that translate into reverse Polish notation and execute this, do not present any special portability problems, and can be implemented by ordinary DLIMPs (e.g. SNOBOL4).

Other limitations on portability arise from the relative size of the software compared with the storage available on the object machine. Computer manufacturers with ranges of compatible machines usually write compilers of completely separate designs for different machine sizes. There may be one team developing a small FORTRAN compiler and one team developing a large FORTRAN compiler with little communication between the two teams. If there are two software designs for different sizes of the same hardware, how can one hope to achieve one machine-independent design that will suit all hardware? The answer is that when software gets large one cannot hope to achieve machine-independence over all machines; one can, however, aim to be machine-independent over machines of a roughly similar size. Even this can be a great advantage since big software means big costs, and so each machine that can be covered by the same software design is worth comparatively more. (It would be an interesting research topic to find out whether it was really necessary to have a different software design for small and large machines in the same family. To what extent can the adaptability techniques used by Poole and Waite to produce various versions of MITEM solve this problem?)

Planning a DLIMP

Portability is not free. If software is to be implemented in a portable way then the planners must allow for the extra time and cost of the first implementation. All too often this is not done. Worse still, portability may come as an afterthought when the software has already been implemented on one machine in a machine-dependent way.

Practitioners would all agree that the most difficult and vital aspect of a DLIMP is designing the descriptive language. It is this that makes the initial cost factor of a DLIMP of the order of 175%. There are basically two approches to the selection of a descriptive language: to adapt an existing descriptive language—more about this later—or to design a new one. We will assume the latter approach is taken. In this case, the design of the descriptive language should proceed hand in hand with the design of the software, each helping to illuminate the other. The quest is to find the best set of primitive operations for describing the software. A descriptive language is likely to evolve gradually, typically in the following way. A Mark 1 descriptive language is designed, and part of the software is encoded in this. This exercise might show that the software is better written using slightly different primitives. Possibly some of the data types may need changing as well. This leads to a Mark 2 descriptive language, and so on, the process becoming one of gradual refinement. At some stage in this process, macros are written to map the descriptive language into the assembly language of the machine for which the first implementation is required.

It is important that a descriptive language be made as flexible as possible, since it is never possible to foresee which machines the software will be implemented on in the future. A portability exercise is rarely of the form: software S is to be implemented on machines M1, M2, M3 and M4 and that is that. Rather the software is implemented on one machine and then someone else says he would like an implementation for his machine. In later years one of the original machines might be replaced by a new machine and an implementation might be required for the new machine. This new machine would quite likely not have been in existence at the time the descriptive language was designed. Hence the need for extreme flexibility to cater for such future contingencies.

It is a great aid to flexibility if the macro processor used to effect a DLIMP works in free-mode. This increases the chances of being able to cater for maverick object machines and assembly languages. As an example of the latter, assume that names in a descriptive language are identifiers of up to six characters. On most mappings these names can be left unchanged but some assembly languages require numerical or semi-numerical labels and some only accept five character names. On mappings into such assembly languages, all the label names need to be changed and a free-mode macro processor could do this automatically. Typically it might be achieved as follows. A pre-pass examines all label declarations, and outputs for each label a macro definition to replace the label name by the form required by the assembler. If, for example, the assembler required a label name to consist of the letter L followed by a number, the output from the pre-pass might look like this

Define   BEGIN   as   L1
Define   NEXT   as   L2
Define   STKERR   as   L3
etc.

These macro definitions would then be combined with the rest of the mapping macros for the descriptive language on a subsequent pass through the macro processor.

The point to be emphasized is that a free-mode macro processor does not fix in advance what is a macro and what is not, in other words which parts of the descriptive language are to be changed on a mapping and which parts are not. This point is really worth sledgehammering home. Anyone who has been engaged in any exercise in portability knows that it is not so much the overall organization of such a project that causes the problems. Instead it is a wealth of apparently trivial details such as assembler label formats. Many well planned projects have failed because of such problems. A flexible tool that can solve at least some of them is therefore invaluable.

Good and bad object machines

The variation in the inefficiency factor of a DLIMP can be considerable. In an analysis of DLIMPs that mapped the ML/I macro processor to various object machines using the L descriptive language it was found that the inefficiencies typically varied in the range 7 to 20 % with one catastrophe at 40 % and one triumph at 3 %.

The efficient implementations all corresponded to simple machines with concise order codes. The inefficient implementations arose on machines with complicated order codes where almost every operation could be performed in several different ways, the simple way not necessarily being the best. It is often said that there are three numbers in computing: 0, 1 and infinity. Machines with N general-purpose registers where N is not one of these three magic numbers present problems to software implementors. This was certainly borne out by the results of the DLIMPs, and similar conclusions would no doubt come if a study was made of, for example, the code FORTRAN compiled for various machines.

It is a problem of human nature that no-one likes to design something simple and conventional, and simple computers, like simple programming languages, are not as common as they should be. It is therefore pleasing to learn that in the design of one modern computer, the MU5 at Manchester University, there is just one general-purpose register because this is what the software designers asked for. It is unreasonable to expect hardware designers to take special account of the problems of DLIMPs, but similar problems apply to all artificially generated code, and it is surely time that machines designed for the tricky assembly language programmer became a thing of the past. Unfortunately the increasing cheapness of computer logic makes such machines easier to produce.

Chapter 2.3

Making Compilers Portable

Compilers are probably the most important components of software, and we will, in this chapter, examine some of the problems in making them portable.

UNCOL

One of the earliest ideas to ease the portability problems of compilers was that of UNCOL (Mock *et al*, 1958; Steel, 1961). UNCOL was to be a universal low-level machine-independent language that all compilers were to translate into. For each object machine a translator was to be written which would convert UNCOL to the order code of that machine. Thus if there were m languages to be implemented on each of n machines, it would be necessary to write $m + n$ translators (i.e. m translators to translate each language to UNCOL and n further translators to translate UNCOL to each machine code). To implement each language directly on every machine would take $m \times n$ translators and each of these would be at least as much work as any of the translators in the UNCOL method. Since m and n are in practice very large the UNCOL method sounds extremely attractive. Unfortunately the concept was never realized, because the universally accepted standard low-level machine-independent language suitable as a target for all compilers was never agreed upon. It was really too much to hope for. If UNCOL had been supported by powerful interests it might have been possible to enforce it. However the compilers generated by the UNCOL method would have had a high inefficiency factor, since the UNCOL language would be a gate through which every translator would need to pass, irrespective of whether the gate was on the direct path between the starting point of the translation (a high-level language) and the goal (the order code of the object machine). A second problem with an UNCOL language would be obsolescence. In a developing field like computer science, the value of any standard quickly gets eroded as better ways are found of doing things. Nevertheless UNCOL makes a pleasant dream. Imagine that UNCOL compilers for PL/I, ALGOL 68,

APL, SNOBOL4, etc., are freely available. Each of these compilers translates into UNCOL and is itself written in UNCOL. One gets a new machine. All that one needs to do to implement all these compilers is to write an UNCOL translator for the machine. The UNCOL language would be the key to all the treasures of the programming language universe.

Writing a compiler in the language it compiles

A second, and more successful, method of aiding portability is encoding the compiler in the language it compiles, for example writing a FORTRAN compiler in FORTRAN. Such a compiler is called a *self-compiling compiler*. It is also an idea which has been known for a relatively long time. There is a 1960 paper (Masterson) that describes the method and how it was used to implement the NELIAC language.

The method is as follows. Assume the compiler for a language X is to be made portable. The compiler is designed so that the parts that generate machine code are, as far as possible, separated from the remaining parts, i.e. there is a single 'code generation module' which generates machine code from some internal machine-independent form. The remaining, machine-independent, parts of the compiler are coded in the language X. The first implementation of the compiler presents a problem, since there is no existing compiler for X. It can be resolved either by translating the compiler from X to machine code by hand or by using a bootstrapping technique like that of Wilkes. The latter is more appealing. The former is dull but probably the quicker method.

Given an implementation on one machine, M say, the job of deriving an implementation on a second machine N is relatively easy. We will call the existing compiler the *XM* compiler. The first task towards deriving an XN compiler is to change the code generation module of the XM compiler so that it translates into the order code of machine N instead of machine M. One then has a hybrid compiler that runs on machine M but produces code for machine N. We will call this the *XMN* compiler. The description of the machine-independent parts of the compiler, which are encoded in the language X, are then fed to the XMN compiler. The output is then a version of the compiler that will run on machine N. If this is combined with the code generation module which produced code for N, then the result is a fully fledged XN compiler.

The code generation module for machine N may be a slight difficulty on this process, since it is first used on machine M as part of the XMN compiler and then on machine N as part of the XN compiler. It is therefore best encoded in some machine-independent way, or at least in a form that is acceptable to both of machines M and N. It may be that the code generation module is simply a set of tables, in which case the problem is minimal. It is, however, more likely to be an algorithm that needs to be expressed in some programming language. The obvious choice is the language X, thus adding further spice to the process. Figure 2.3A shows an implementation performed in this way. Note that all the work is done on machine M.

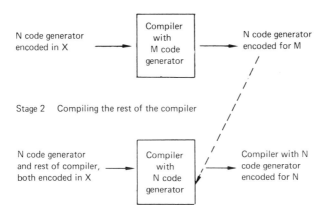

Stage 1   Compiling the code generator

Stage 2   Compiling the rest of the compiler

Fig. 2.3A. Implementing a self-compiling compiler for a language X by using a compiler on machine M to produce a compiler for machine N

The great problem with self-compiling compilers is that not many languages are really suitable for writing their own compiler in. Is, for example, COBOL the best language for a COBOL compiler and SNOBOL4 the best language for a SNOBOL4 compiler? Probably not. Certainly if a language has no character manipulation facilities it cannot possibly be self-compiling since the syntax analysis phases of the compiler will be impossible to encode.

The portability for a self-compiling compiler would be approximately (*Cost* 175% *then* 20% *failing* 10% *Inefficiency* 20–1000%). The initial cost is high because of the overhead of designing and documenting the code generation module.

Note that self-compiling is a method that can only be applied to compilers. The corresponding concept of a self-interpreting interpreter is useless for portability.

The portability of BCPL

BCPL is a language that has a self-compiling compiler that has been implemented widely (Richards, 1971). Since BCPL is a language designed specially for software writing, it should indeed be a suitable language for encoding its own compiler.

The BCPL compiler has a rigid interface between the code-generation module and the rest of the compiler. The compiler translates into a machine-independent low-level language called OCODE. The code-generation module then acts as a second phase of the compiler, and translates OCODE into the object code of the required object machine. At first sight OCODE might appear to be a realization of the UNCOL concept, but this is not so. OCODE acts as an intermediate stage between BCPL and all object machines, and was designed specially for the BCPL compiler. The UNCOL concept, on the other hand, envisages an intermediate language between *all* high-level languages and all object machines. OCODE is, in fact, very similar in nature to some of the low-level descriptive languages used in DLIMPs.

The implementor of BCPL is supplied with the BCPL compiler in OCODE, and is free to write the OCODE translator for his object machine in any way he likes. This translator is used first to translate the BCPL compiler and then acts as a second phase to the BCPL compiler when it runs on the object machine. There are many alternative ways of writing the translator. One is to write it in BCPL, which has the advantage of extra flexibility and portability but the possible disadvantage that it necessitates access to an existing BCPL compiler to produce the new one. A second way is to make a macro processor perform the translation, thus making the implementation of BCPL similar to a DLIMP. The code generation module would simply be a macro processor with a set of built-in macros. This has advantages in ease and simplicity, but the serious disadvantage that, since the code generation module and hence the macro processor forms part of the final production compiler, it may, as a result, be slow. It is another instance of the common occurrence that a general-purpose tool, in this case the macro processor, is slower than a special-purpose one, in this case a handwritten OCODE translator. (Note that this disadvantage of a DLIMP only applies when a compiler is being implemented. In other cases, once the software has been implemented it runs entirely independently of the macro processor used to implement it.) The third way to implement the OCODE translator is to write the translator in the most suitable language available on the object machine. In this case the work can be done entirely on the object machine in the way shown in Figure 2.3B.

BCPL actually makes provision for the implementor to adopt a hybrid between the first and third ways. An ultra-low-level language called INTCODE has been designed, and the BCPL compiler has been made available in this language. It is a relatively trivial matter for the implementor to write a crude translator that will run on his object machine and will translate INTCODE into the order code of the object machine. He can use this to produce a crude BCPL compiler that will run on the object machine. This is therefore exactly equivalent to the third way described above, but is a much simpler task because of the elementary nature of INTCODE. Given this

Stage 1   Translating the compiler

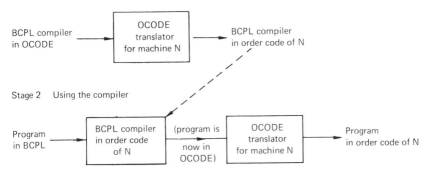

Stage 2   Using the compiler

Fig. 2.3B. Implementation of a BCPL compiler on machine N

crude BCPL compiler that runs on the object machine, the implementor can then implement a better BCPL compiler using the first way described above, i.e. writing the OCODE translator in BCPL. This hybrid method combines the advantages of writing the OCODE translator in BCPL and performing all the work on the object machine. It is, in fact, an example of a simple two-level hierarchy.

The portability of ALTRAN-F

ALTRAN-F is a FORTRAN-like language designed for manipulating symbolic algebra. The ALTRAN-F compiler translates into FORTRAN rather than into machine code, and therefore does not have the problems of a machine-dependent code generation module. The compiler has been made portable by encoding it in standard FORTRAN extended by macro facilities (Brown, W., 1969). The macro processor used to extend FORTRAN is called M^6, and is a simple macro processor with the normal facilities for macro replacement. M^6 is itself made portable by encoding it in standard FORTRAN. The purpose of the macro extensions to FORTRAN is to gain increased machine-independence. The M^6 macros which map the extended FORTRAN into standard FORTRAN can be rewritten for each implementation of ALTRAN-F, and allow the implementor to fix how certain features are best represented in the FORTRAN that is available on his object machine. One macro, for example, fixes how many characters are to be packed into a word.

The use of the macro processor therefore removes the machine-dependence that can occur in FORTRAN programs and this should improve the portability factor, though there is the added overhead of implementing the macro processor. The inefficiency factor should also be lessened as the implementor can to some extent tailor data representations to fit his machine.

What the macros cannot do, however, is to remove any inefficiencies caused because FORTRAN is an unsuitable language for encoding the software concerned.

Secret systems

Many software houses and computer manufacturers have their own languages for encoding software. Some of these languages have compilers that contain a variable code generation module, thus allowing programs to be compiled for a variety of machines. Others compile into a fixed object code, which can be interpreted on any required machine. The object of these devices is not so much to make the compiler portable, because the compiler itself is not released to customers, but to make programs written in its source language portable. Unfortunately, these compilers and languages are generally kept more or less secret, for commercial reasons, so there is little that can be said about them. One may speculate, on the assumption that there is nothing new under the sun, that all these systems are based on the techniques described already, but one may be horribly wrong.

Chapter 2.4

Families of Descriptive Languages

If one examines different descriptive languages, it turns out that many of them share similar features, though each also contains some individualistic features. In this chapter we will examine how this overlap between descriptive languages can be exploited.

If I may quote from my own experience, after ML/I itself had been made portable (using the L language), it was desired to make a further piece of software, which was called ALGEBRA, portable. The full details of ALGEBRA need not concern us yet; it is sufficient to know that it is a program for students and research workers in Boolean Algebra and other forms of logic. It is best used conversationally.

When the design of the descriptive language for ALGEBRA began, it soon became clear that it could share many features with L, in spite of the apparent difference in nature between ALGEBRA and ML/I. This state of affairs turned out to be a good illustration of the concepts of *outer syntax* and *inner syntax* described by Wilkes (1968).

Outer and inner syntax

Wilkes pointed out that a programming language can be divided into two parts:

(i) *The outer syntax.* This consists of those language features that are independent of the data being manipulated.
(ii) *The inner syntax.* This consists of those language features concerned with the manipulation and declaration of data.

Thus, for example, a GOTO statement would belong to the outer syntax, whereas expressions would belong to the inner syntax. It is possible to design a language with a fixed outer syntax but with a range of possible inner syntaxes, each oriented towards a different application area. There might be one inner syntax for numerical problems, one for list processing and perhaps a highly specialized one for dealing with a particular kind of hospital record.

Since all these different languages can share the same outer syntax there are considerable potential economies in implementation and documentation.

An approximately similar situation arises with descriptive languages. There exists a set of features that are needed by most or all descriptive languages, but each descriptive language needs its own supplementary features tailored to the application in hand. Experience shows, however, that the dividing line between outer syntax and inner syntax need not be as Wilkes propounds. Features concerned with the flow of control through a program need not belong to the outer syntax. For example, ML/I needs recursion whereas ALGEBRA does not. Some other software might need coroutines. Hence recursive subroutines might well be placed in the inner syntax tailored to the application in hand. Conversely, operations for manipulating integers and perhaps characters can be placed in the outer syntax since almost every descriptive language will need them.

Although the concepts of outer syntax and inner syntax fit descriptive languages very well, the terms themselves do not. Semantics are more important then syntax and there is no obvious way of remembering which part is inner and which outer. We shall therefore use the terms 'kernel' and 'extensions' instead of 'outer syntax' and 'inner syntax'.

The dividing line between the kernel and the extensions of a descriptive language has a good deal of arbitrariness in it. One could specify, as an acceptance level for inclusion in the kernel, that a feature was to be needed in $n\%$ of descriptive languages where n could reasonably be given any value between 50 and 95. It is, of course, unreal to think of the universe of descriptive languages. One can confine one's attention to a family of descriptive languages that are likely to be of immediate need. Clearly, the smaller such a family is, the larger the kernel of common features.

The 'cost' of placing a facility in the kernel is that it will be necessary for each implementor to write a macro to map that feature into his object language, irrespective of whether it happens to be used in the software he is implementing. It would be possible for each piece of software to have an associated list of the features actually used, but this further level of complication might well be considered an undesirable extra burden.

If we adopt the use of kernels and extensions it is worth examining how this affects our original ideas concerning the purpose of descriptive languages. We said originally that there were two choices for software-writing languages:

(a) encoding the software in a pre-defined language,
(b) designing a language specially for encoding each piece of software.

We decided that (b) had many advantages. We have now taken a step towards a middle course between the two. It is amusing to note that those people who prefer approach (a) are wanting extensible programming languages to write their software in. If such extensible language becomes universally available and proves efficient, we will be able to shake hands with our opposite numbers when we meet in the middle.

The LOWL family of languages

The LOWL language, which holds the stage throughout most of Part 3 of this book, is an example of a language with a kernel and some extensions. A family containing four pieces of software has been implemented using LOWL, and each requires different extensions. The members of the family are:

(a) The ALGEBRA program, which has been mentioned already.
(b) UNRAVEL, a system for putting intelligence into core dumps.
(c) The ML/I macro processor.
(d) An implementation of SCAN, a simple conversational language for text analysis.

To give an idea of the relative sizes of the kernel and extensions of LOWL, the kernel of LOWL contains fifty-nine different kinds of statement (of which any one member of the family uses about fifty), and the extensions for the pieces of software (a) to (d) above contain two, four, seven and seventeen extra statements, respectively. (This is actually an over-simplified measure of the relative sizes of the kernel and extensions as LOWL contains constructions other than statements, and these are also amplified in some of the extensions. However, such complications have marginal effect.) The kinds of feature supplied by the LOWL extensions are extra input/output streams, new forms of data declarations (relative pointers and hash chains for ML/I), a recursive subroutine, and extra multiply and divide operations. The reason why SCAN requires seventeen extra statements is that it 'compiles' its source program into a sequence of Reverse Polish pseudo-instructions. These pseudo-instructions effectively form an extra data type, and special statements are needed to manipulate this data type.

Even with SCAN, however, the extensions are much less than the kernel, and this applies *a fortiori* to the rest of the family. Hence if one member of the family has already been implemented on a machine then the work necessary to implement any other member is at least halved, since the only work to be done is to write macros for the necessary extensions and encode the MD-logic. Taken as a whole, therefore, the family has an excellent portability factor, and this is a good justification for the method. (There is a minor defect in that, if only one member of the family is to be implemented, this member might not use all the features of the kernel of LOWL and some of the mapping macros dutifully written by the implementor would not be used.)

The LOWL family, however, presents an untypically rosy picture of the closeness of families. It would certainly be wrong to assume that any four pieces of software could be grouped together in a family using a descriptive language with a large common kernel. The four pieces of software encoded in LOWL, although superficially different from one another, are actually rather similar in nature. All are exclusively concerned with logically simple manipulations of integers and characters, and all have simple input/output requirements. If the family was increased, for example, by the inclusion of an editing program this would certainly necessitate extensions for further input/output facilities. Nevertheless the editor would otherwise fit in well as, in common with the rest of the family, it only needs simple character and numerical operations. A sine/cosine routine, on the other hand, would be a total misfit, since it is almost totally concerned with floating-point manipulations. It would use little of the kernel of LOWL and would necessitate massive extensions. It would therefore do better to set up house on its own and hope that it might become the basis of a second family.

Part 3

A PORTABILITY PROJECT

Chapter 3.1

Description of the Project

This Part of the book describes in complete detail how a given piece of portable software can be implemented. The reader can approach this material in two alternative ways. Firstly, he may regard it in the same way as the other Parts of the book, in other words simply as reading matter. In particular he may have read Part 2, which deals with concepts in general terms, and may be interested in finding out exactly how these concepts are applied, or, more selectively, how some specific details are treated. Secondly, he may feel that he would like to implement some portable software for himself in order to gain a true understanding of the problems involved. This Part of the book provides him with such a project. If the reader has sufficient time available the second approach is recommended, and the reader will therefore be henceforth called 'the implementor'.

The project is to implement a piece of portable software called ALGEBRA on a machine of the implementor's own choice using a technique called a DLIMP with a simple descriptive language called LOWL. The implementor who has read Part 2 should be familiar with what this entails, but, for the reader who has not, the basic mechanisms are explained in the next section.

Outline of the project

A DLIMP is a *descriptive language implemented by macro processor*, and is a means of making software portable.

The project to be undertaken deals with a descriptive language called LOWL. A program in LOWL can be regarded as a sequence of machine-independent macro calls. To implement LOWL on a given machine (the *object machine*) a set of macros is written to map LOWL statements into the assembly language of that machine. The macros are called *mapping macros* for LOWL. LOWL is sufficiently simple for almost any macro processor to be chosen to perform the mapping. (In fact the choice is even wider as one mapping, at least, has not used a macro processor at all, but has employed a text processing language.) If there is a macro assembler available on the object machine this may well be the best choice. The choice of macro processor, like the choice of object machine, is for the implementor to make. In some cases it may be necessary to write a simple pre-pass to convert LOWL programs into a suitable format and character set for the macro-processor to be used. This is discussed further in Chapter 3.3.

To quote a simple example of a mapping macro, one LOWL statement has the form

$$AAV \quad V$$

where V is a variable name. This statement means Add to the A register a Variable. On the object machine the equivalent instruction might be ADD, and in this case, the mapping macro for the AAV statement might map into

$$ADD \quad V$$

Not all the macros will be as simple as this, of course. The implementor might do well at this stage to glance ahead to the LOWL listing of ALGEBRA in Chapter 3.8 in order to gain an impression of what a LOWL program looks like and what mapping macros need to be written.

It is not an absolute requirement that LOWL be mapped into the assembly language of the object machine; instead it can be mapped into any language that is available. However the whole design of LOWL is geared to assembly language mapping and a mapping into a higher-level language is likely to lose much in efficiency.

Several pieces of software have been encoded in LOWL, but this project is concerned with only one of these, a program called ALGEBRA. ALGEBRA is a package for students and research workers in Boolean Algebra and other kinds of logic. It is described in detail in Chapter 3.2.

LOWL consists of a *kernel*, which is used by all the software encoded in it, together with extensions oriented towards each individual piece of software. We are interested here only in the extensions needed for the ALGEBRA program, which are trivial.

Even if it is largely machine-independent, every piece of software contains a few parts that are machine-dependent and therefore need to be coded by hand for each implementation. Hence we divide software into two parts, the MI-logic (*m*achine-*i*ndependent part of the logic), which is encoded in LOWL and mapped by a macro processor for each object machine, and the MD-logic (*m*achine-*d*ependent part of the logic), which is described in words rather than by means of LOWL statements and which needs to be recoded by hand for each implementation.

The choice of example

The reason why the ALGEBRA system was selected as the subject of this portability project is that it is reasonably small, and its action, as the user sees it, is simple to describe and understand. It is the kind of system one can demonstrate to a user in five minutes and then leave him to use it for himself. Once implemented, it should be a useful system to have available, although its clientele is somewhat specialized. A more general piece of software, like a text editor, may have more potential users than ALGEBRA, but most installations already have a text editor and do not want a different one.

ALGEBRA consists of about nine hundred LOWL statements, and it is felt that anything smaller than this would not provide a fair experience of the merits and demerits of portability. A piece of software that could be described in a hundred or two LOWL statements would be simple to implement by any method and the effort of making it portable would not be worth while. A better evaluation of portability could probably be derived from implementing something bigger than ALGEBRA but problems would arise, as far as this book is concerned, because of the bulk of the material to be presented, particularly the listings. Actually the bigger the software the more worthwhile portability is, because the amount of work in implementing portable software increases only slightly as the size of the software increases. The selection of ALGEBRA was therefore a compromise.

Tasks to be performed

We will assume the implementor has selected an object machine O, which has an assembler called ASSO, and has chosen the macro processor to perform the mapping. We will call the macro processor MACWILLING and assume that it runs on a machine M. (M may well be the same as O, and if ASSO is a macro-assembler then ASSO might act as MACWILLING.) The procedure for implementing some software S on machine O using ASSO and MACWILLING is given in Figure 3.1A.

The output from this procedure, which is a version of the software encoded in the order code of machine O, is then run and tested on machine O.

The implementor's first job is to write the mapping macros. He will doubtless make some mistakes in these, so the macros will need testing before they are used to map ALGEBRA. For this purpose a *LOWL kernel test program* called LOWLTEST is provided. It is described in Chapters 3.5 and 3.6. LOWLTEST tests the execution of all the statements in the kernel of LOWL and, as far as possible, prints a meaningful error message if anything goes wrong. LOWLTEST is mapped by performing the procedure shown in Figure 3.1A with LOWLTEST substituted for 'software S'. The MD-logic of LOWLTEST consists of a few short routines which are simple to encode. The output from the mapping of LOWLTEST is run on machine O, and if this produces error messages, the macros need to be corrected and the procedure repeated until the errors have been eliminated.

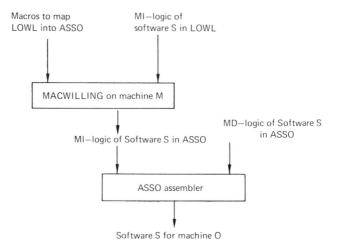

Fig. 3.1A. Procedure for implementing on a machine O some software S encoded in LOWL

Now the stage is set for the mapping of ALGEBRA itself. The implementor needs to write mapping macros for the two LOWL extensions that ALGEBRA needs. (There is no explicit test program for these.) The MD-logic of ALGEBRA is then written and the mapping procedure shown in Figure 3.1A is repeated with ALGEBRA as the software S. The result is an implementation of ALGEBRA for machine O. This can be tested using the test data given in Chapter 3.9. If there are errors these will be either due to errors in the MD-logic or due to errors in the mapping macros for the LOWL extensions for ALGEBRA. (It is also possible that there are still errors in the mapping macros for the kernel of LOWL. No test program can cover *all* possible variations and combinations of LOWL statements and LOWLTEST must therefore have its blind spots.) Full details of the MD-logic of ALGE-BRA and the LOWL extensions it requires are given in Chapter 3.7.

In summary, therefore, the order of action is as follows.

(0) If necessary, write a pre-pass to convert LOWL programs to a suitable format and character set.
(1) Write mapping macros for the kernel of LOWL.
(2) Map LOWLTEST using these.
(3) Run LOWLTEST. If there are bugs correct the macros and repeat.
(4) Write mapping macros for LOWL extensions for ALGEBRA, and encode MD-logic of ALGEBRA.
(5) Map ALGEBRA.
(6) Test ALGEBRA using the given test data.

Time scales

Before going into action, the implementor would almost certainly like to be given some idea of time scales. He would like to know whether he can write the whole thing on the back of an envelope or whether to make the project his life's work. The answer is, of course, that it all depends. However, we can usefully say that if the implementor

(a) has had experience of writing MACWILLING macros, and
(b) knows the machine O and its assembly language

then, given reasonable machine access, he should be able to have ALGEBRA working in one or two man weeks. Further factors that affect the time scale are the degree of optimization attempted, and the quality of ASSO. If, for example, ASSO required all names to consist of two letters and all constants to be written in binary, the implementor should dig trenches and prepare for a long battle.

The amount of machine time needed is an even more variable factor. To give some sort of guide, a mapping of ALGEBRA might take two or three minutes of CPU time on a batch processing machine with a two microsecond store. The entire project might take half an hour of CPU time.

Another thing the implementor would like to know in advance is what he is implementing. We will, therefore, describe in the next chapter exactly what ALGEBRA does.

Chapter 3.2

The ALGEBRA System

The ALGEBRA system (Brown and Lowe, 1971) allows the user to declare a set of objects and then to define a number of operators that can be applied to these objects. The objects are called *values*. Once the operators and values have been defined, the user can investigate their properties by evaluating expressions involving variables, operators and values. ALGEBRA is best used in a conversational manner.

The main usage of ALGEBRA has been by students and research workers investigating logics. Students have used it to learn Boolean Algebra. At a single session on a console they can get a real feel for Boolean operators and may even get as far as 'discovering' theorems for themselves. Research workers have used ALGEBRA for more complicated logics.

The use of ALGEBRA is, however, by no means restricted to logic, and users have thought out all kinds of novel applications to exploit its generality. One frivolous illustration of this would be to define four football teams as the values with V (for versus) as an operator. The value of X V Y would be defined as the team which, in the view of the user, would win when team X played at home to team Y. Thus the value of SOUTHAMPTON V CHELSEA could be defined as SOUTHAMPTON. The results of knock-out competitions could be calculated by evaluating expressions such as

(ARSENAL V LEEDS) V (CHELSEA V SOUTHAMPTON)

To carry the nonsense further another operator VN (versus on neutral ground) could be introduced to increase the possible combinations.

The exact workings of ALGEBRA are best introduced by an example. We will show how it might be used at a conversational computer console to simulate Boolean Algebra. In this example there are two values, TRUE and FALSE, and the operators are the well-known Boolean operators 'implies' and 'not'. The underlined parts are typed by the computer and the remainder by the console user. A commentary appears to the right of the example. It is reprinted with permission from the *Bulletin of the Institute of Mathematics and its Applications*, 1971, **7**, pp. 320–322.

Introductory example

VALUES = TRUE FALSE	Declare values.
OPERATOR –	Define an operator. This is the operator 'not', which is represented by a minus sign.
UNARY OR BINARY = UNARY	
PRECEDENCE = 100	See below for meaning of this.
– TRUE = FALSE	⎰ Define meaning of 'not' for
– FALSE = TRUE	⎱ all possible values.
OPERATOR HOOK	Define another operator. This is the operator 'implies', which is represented by the symbol 'HOOK'.
UNARY OR BINARY = BINARY	
PRECEDENCE = 50	Precedence has been specified as less than that of 'not'. This means that if 'implies' and 'not' are used in the same expression, then 'not' is done first, i.e.

$-A$ HOOK B
is taken as
$(-A)$ HOOK B
and not as
$-(A$ HOOK $B)$

TRUE HOOK TRUE = TRUE	
TRUE HOOK FALSE = FALSE	
FALSE HOOK TRUE = TRUE	
FALSE HOOK FALSE = TRUE	

Now that the operators and values have been defined, it is possible to evaluate expressions involving them. Any symbol in an expression that has not been defined as a value or an operator is taken as a variable and is enumerated for all possible values. The TABLE statement illustrates this.

TABLE A HOOK $-$ (A HOOK B)

A	B	: VALUE	
TRUE	TRUE	: FALSE	⎫ This entire table is typed out by
TRUE	FALSE	: TRUE	⎪ the computer. The last column is
FALSE	TRUE	: TRUE	⎬ the value of the expression for
FALSE	FALSE	: TRUE	⎪ the given values of the variables
			⎭ A and B.

TABLE −(P HOOK Q) HOOK(P HOOK −Q)

P	Q	: VALUE
TRUE	TRUE	: TRUE
TRUE	FALSE	: TRUE
FALSE	TRUE	: TRUE
FALSE	FALSE	: TRUE

Table typed by the computer.

The TRY statement is an abbreviated form of the TABLE statement, e.g.

TRY A HOOK −(A HOOK B)
IS A CONTINGENCY

This means that the value of the expression depends on the values of its variables.

TRY −(P HOOK Q) HOOK (P HOOK −Q)
= TRUE

This means that the expression has the same value, TRUE, for all values of its variables.

Definitions

The above example shows enough of ALGEBRA to allow the average person to use the system for himself. The remainder of this chapter explains more exactly the concepts that the example has illustrated. As likely as not the average user of ALGEBRA would not need to read this information, except perhaps to clear up a specific query, but it is, of course, necessary to have an exact specification of the system.

The fundamental units in ALGEBRA are symbols, expressions and statements, and these will now be described.

Symbols

A *symbol* is used to represent the name of a value, operator or variable. A symbol must be either

(a) a *name symbol*, which is a sequence of one or more letters or digits. The sequence may be arbitrarily long and all characters are significant, but symbols will be truncated to six characters if they appear in tables; or

(b) a *punctuation symbol*, which is a single character that is *not* any of the following: a letter, a digit, a comma, a tab, a space, a semi-colon, a left parenthesis, a right parenthesis or the newline character.

For example the following are legitimate symbols:

ABLE,A,1,12A3, + ,/,.,VERYLONGNAME

and the following are *not*:

$$A \quad B,P,J,B.,(,A +$$

Expressions

An *expression* is a series of operators with values or variables as operands. Any symbol that is not the name of an existing operator or value can be used as the name of a variable.

(To be precise the syntax of an expression is, in Backus Normal Form:

⟨expression⟩:: = ⟨expression⟩⟨binary operator⟩⟨expression⟩|
⟨unary operator⟩⟨expression⟩|(⟨expression⟩)|⟨variable⟩|⟨value⟩

where ⟨unary operator⟩ etc. are all symbols.)

During the evaluation of an expression, operators of highest precedence are performed first. Subject to this, operators are evaluated from left to right. Parentheses can be used to override precedence and redundant pairs of parentheses are permissible.

Thus if ' + ' and '*' are binary operators and '*' has the higher precedence then:

$$A + B*C \quad \text{is taken as} \quad A + (B*C)$$
$$A + B + C \quad \text{is taken as} \quad (A + B) + C$$
$$A*B + C*D \quad \text{is taken as} \quad (A*B) + (C*D)$$
$$A*(B + C)*D \quad \text{is taken as} \quad (A*(B + C))*D$$

The choice of precedence for operators is a matter of convention and no fixed rules can be stated save that unary operators should normally be given higher precedence than binary operators.

Statements

Each line of data fed to **ALGEBRA** must be a *statement*. There are four kinds of statement: the **OPERATOR** statement, the **TABLE** statement, the **TRY** statement and the null statement. The first symbol on a line identifies what statement it is.

A comment may be appended to any statement. The comment must be preceded by a semicolon, e.g.

OPERATOR + ; THIS IS THE 'OR' OPERATOR

If two adjacent name symbols occur within a statement, they must be separated by one or more spaces, commas or tabs. Redundant commas, tabs and spaces are ignored. Thus

TRY (A,, + B,) : XXX

is equivalent to

$$TRY(A + B)$$

but

$$TRY \ A \ AND \ B$$

is not the same as

$$TRY \ AANDB$$

Similar formatting rules apply to the answers to the questions asked by ALGEBRA, i.e. these may also contain redundant spaces, tabs and commas, and they may also have comments appended to them.

Declaration of values

When ALGEBRA is initially entered it asks the question

$$VALUES =$$

At this point the user types a list of different symbols, separated by spaces, commas and/or tabs. These symbols are used thereafter as the value names. They cannot be changed without starting again from scratch.

Note that it is possible to define any number of value names. For example ALGEBRA has proved useful in examining three-valued logics.

After the values have been declared, ALGEBRA proceeds to execute the sequence of statements fed to it. The four different kinds of statement are described below:

The null statement

Null statements are completely ignored and can be used to place comments, for example

$$;TRY \ DE \ MORGAN'S \ LAW$$

The OPERATOR statement

Syntax: OPERATOR *symbol*

Any symbol that is not the name of a value may be used as the name of an operator. If the operator·symbol being defined is the same as an existing operator then, provided the OPERATOR statement is completed without error, the new definition overrides the old. Operators can therefore be redefined. OPERATOR statements need not necessarily be at the start of the data: it is quite legal to add new operators at any time during the use of ALGEBRA.

The OPERATOR statement is followed by a series of questions. The first question is

$$UNARY \ OR \ BINARY =$$

and the answer must be either 'UNARY' or 'BINARY'. The second question is

$$PRECEDENCE =$$

and the answer must be an integer in the range [0,999]. The magnitude of the integer does not matter in itself—it is its magnitude relative to the precedence of other operators that counts. For example a precedence of one is the same as a precedence of 998 if the only other operator has precedence 999.

After the above two questions have been answered, the user is asked to define the value of the operator for all possible values of its operands. This is done by asking a series of questions of the form

$$var \ 1 \ symbol \ var \ 1 =$$

$$var \ 1 \ symbol \ var \ 2 =$$

$$\vdots$$

$$var \ 2 \ symbol \ var \ 1 =$$

$$\vdots$$

where *var 1* is the first value defined in the answer to the

$$VALUES =$$

question, *var 2* is the second, and so on. For a unary operator the above questions are abbreviated, as shown in the introductor example.

If the answer to any of the above questions is incorrect, then the message

$$EH$$

is output and the question is repeated.

In some uses of ALGEBRA the user may wish to define operators that are undefined for certain values. This can be done, albeit rather tediously, by including an extra value, called UNDEF say, in the list of values.

The TABLE statement

Syntax: TABLE *expression*

A table is output of the values of the expression for all possible values of its variables. The expression must include at least one variable. There is no upper limit on the permitted number of variables in the expression, but if the size of the rows of the table exceeds the width of a line the format of the table is upset.

The TRY statement

Syntax: TRY *expression*

If the expression has the same value, V say, for all possible values of its variables, then the result

$$= V$$

is given; otherwise the result

IS A CONTINGENCY

is given.

Abbreviations

Statements are, in fact, identified only by the first two characters of the initial symbol on a line. Thus OPERATOR may be written OP (or even OPZQP). The same applies to the answers to the 'UNARY OR BINARY =' question.

User-defined symbols, however, cannot be abbreviated. Thus, for example, if IMPOSSIBLE is chosen as a value name this must be spelt out in full every time it is used.

Errors

All errors are diagnosed and give rise to a message, which should be self-explanatory. Errors in answers to questions cause the question to be repeated. Errors in statements cause the current one to be abandoned and the next to be taken. The only exception to this is the error that arises when all available storage has been used up; this causes the run to be abandoned.

Chapter 3.3

The Kernel of LOWL

This chapter gives a complete description of the kernel of LOWL, and acts as a User's Manual for the LOWL language.

Statement formats

Statements in LOWL are written one to a line and each consists of a mnemonic operation code followed by a number of arguments separated by commas. Operation codes are represented by names that are sequences of up to five letters. Each operation code has a fixed number of arguments, some operation codes having no arguments at all. Arguments that are literal character strings (e.g. text to be printed, comments) are enclosed in quotes. No argument is ever null; instead the letter X is often used to indicate that a certain argument is not applicable in a given case. The argument list consists of not more than fifty characters. The operation code is preceded by a tab character and, if it has any arguments, it is also followed by a tab. (These tabs may be replaced by spaces if the implementor thinks this is more convenient.) Statements may optionally be preceded by a label, which is an identifier of not more than six characters enclosed in square brackets and occurs at the very start of a line. Blank lines are used to improve layout.

The following are examples of LOWL statements

```
          NB        'THESE ARE LOWL STATEMENTS'
[ENDSTR]  LBV       IDPT
          BMOVE
          SUBR      CHEKID,X,1
          MESS      'ERROR - - STACK OVERFLOW'
```

Extensions to LOWL follow the same form as statements in the kernel.

The LOWL statement format has been found acceptable to most macro processors. The fact that each type of statement has a fixed number of arguments and no argument is ever null helps considerably. There are, however, usually a few problems of which the following are typical:

(a) The square brackets round labels are unacceptable. Since label names are usually unaltered on a mapping it is usually sufficient simply to remove the square brackets on a pre-pass.

(b) Arguments enclosed in quotes cause problems, particularly when the argument itself involves a comma, for example

$$\text{MESS 'TYPE YOUR NAME,AGE AND SEX'}$$

Here the entire text in quotes is a single argument, not two arguments separated by commas. Solutions to this problem vary according to the macro processor used.

(c) In general each macro call occupies one line, but there exists one possible exception to this. Certain constants which occur as arguments to other macros may themselves need to be mapped as macros. For example in

$$\text{CCN   NLREP}$$

NLREP stands for the internal code for newline, and in

$$\text{LAL   OF}(2*\text{LNM}+\text{LCH})$$

the argument is the value of twice the length of a number (LNM) plus the length of a character (LCH). (See the full description of the OF macro later.) Fortunately most assemblers have their own mechanism for dealing with such named constants, even when addition and multiplication are involved, so this problem can be solved without the use of macros.

A possible pre-pass algorithm

Because of the type of problem described above, it may be necessary to make certain systematic replacements of characters and symbols in order to make LOWL suitable for MACWILLING. This will apply particularly if MACWILLING is a macro-assembler, since these tend to be inflexible about the formats they will accept. Almost certainly the syntax of labels would require changing and quite likely the OF macro as well. Most machines possess editors or string manipulation languages that are capable of replacing every occurrence of one string by another one. If such software is available to him the implementor need not read the rest of this section. If it is not, it will be necessary to write a special pre-pass program to make the replacements. Such programs should be trivial in nature, but 'trivial' programs often take a long time to get right, and 'ten-minute jobs' become ten-hour jobs. Because of this, a possible form of a pre-pass algorithm is shown below. It has been tested in practice and its use may save the implementor a few debugging runs. The algorithm is expressed using a few elementary operations that should be readily convertible into whatever high-level language or assembly language is being used for encoding the pre-pass.

	comment Possible form of a program to adapt character representations, etc., in LOWL to local needs; Set OFSW, QSW = 0;
[LOOP]	Input a character into CHAR, stopping if end of data;
[TEST]	*comment* Test for unique individual characters to be changed, e.g.:;

        If CHAR is "[" then go to LBRAC;
        If CHAR is " < " then go to LESS;
        If CHAR is a tab then go to TAB;
        etc.

        comment   To test for quotes, distinguishing opening ones from closing ones::
        If CHAR is not a quote then go to TRYOF;
        Set QSW = 1 − QSW;
        If QSW = 1 then go to OPENQ;
        Go to CLOSEQ;

[TRYOF]   *comment*   To recognize the OF macro and its closing parenthesis: (It is assumed that the argument of the OF macro is to remain unchanged.);
        If CHAR is not the letter "O" then go to TRYRP;
        Input a character into CHAR;
        If CHAR is not "F" then Output "O" and go to TEST;
        Input a character into CHAR;
        If CHAR is not "(" then Output "O", Output "F" and go to TEST;
        Set OFSW = 1 and go to OFMAC;

[TRYRP]   If CHAR is ")" and OFSW is 1 then set OFSW to zero and go to ENDOF;
        comment   Finally, for characters that do not need changing:;
        Output CHAR and go to LOOP;
        comment   At labels LBRAC, LESS, TAB, OPENQ, CLOSEQ, OFMAC and ENDOF, output whatever is to replace the given characters and return to LOOP;

The nature of test data to verify that the algorithm works will depend on what is being changed. The following might be some useful test cases.

```
[LABEL]   LAV    ABC,X
          LAM    OF(LCH + LNM)
          LAL    OF(2*LNM)
          CCL    ')'
          CCL    '<'
```

```
[LAB2]    MESS   'ERRORS(S)'
          NB     'ENDS IN O'
          NB     'ENDS IN OF'
          CCL    '('
```

Supplementary arguments

Some LOWL statements have what are called *supplementary arguments*. These are used to convey extra information about the statement, which may be used on some mappings. For example a branching statement might be written

GO   PIG,130,E,X

This means branch to label PIG. There are three supplementary arguments. The first of these says that the label PIG is 130 LOWL statements after the current statement. The E means the branch jumps out of a subroutine and the final X means that it is not a special case (e.g., it is not part of an array of jumps forming a multi-way switch). Most mappings of LOWL would ignore all the three supplementary arguments.

Character set

The character set used in the kernel of LOWL consists of:

(a) the upper-case letters A to Z,
(b) the digits 0 to 9,
(c) the following punctuation characters: comma, plus, minus, divide, asterisk, colon, quote, greater than, less than, left square bracket, right square bracket, left parenthesis, right parenthesis, equals, dollar sign (used to signify newline in messages), space and tab (used for layout purposes).

Data types

There are two data types: character and numerical. An item of character data can be any single character in the character set for the implementation; an item of numerical data is an integer or a pointer. The implementor chooses how these should be represented on the object machine. On many machines both will be chosen to correspond to a word and there will be no need to differentiate the two data types. There will be some space savings if character data can be stored in a smaller unit of storage than a word, but this should be done only if the smaller unit is directly addressable (i.e. if no packing, unpacking or masking is necessary when characters are manipulated). Some object machines may require data alignment; this is discussed further at the end of this chapter.

The character code in which the object software is to work may be chosen by the implementor. Most machines have their own preferred internal code, but if there is any choice in the matter it is best to select a code such that the 3 classes

(a) letters
(b) digits
(c) others

can be simply and quickly differentiated.

Operations on numerical data always yield integer results and hence there are no floating point operations. No allowance has been made in LOWL for integer overflow and the best action is to ignore it if it occurs.

Constants

Several LOWL statements have constants as arguments. Constants may be numerical constants or character constants.

Numerical constants are represented as decimal integers or by a call of the OF macro. Before describing the OF macro it is necessary to define its submacros, which are machine-dependent constants that define how data is represented on the object machine. They are as follows:

LCH   the number of storage units occupied by an item of character data.

LNM   the number of storage units occupied by an item of numerical data.

LICH   = 1/LCH

(Another way of looking at these is that LCH and LNM are the amounts a stack pointer would be increased to stack items of character and numerical data, respectively.) On a word machine LCH and LNM would both be one; on a byte machine LCH might be one and LNM four. Some extensions of LOWL use extra submacros.

LICH is only used in the context

MULTL   OF(LICH)

which means multiply by LICH. In most implementations LCH and LICH will both be one, but if LCH is greater than one then LICH will not be an integer. The problem is best solved by turning multiplication by LICH into division by LCH, thus eliminating LICH altogether.

The OF macro takes the form OF (*argument*) where *argument* is one of the following

(a) $N*S+S$
(b) $N*S-S$

(c) $N * S$

(d) $S + S$

(e) $S - S$

(f) S

Here N stands for any positive integer, S for any of the submacros, and an asterisk represents multiplication. Examples of the OF macro are therefore OF(3*LNM + LCH), OF(LNM − LCH) and OF(LCH), and an example of its use within a statement is

BUMP   STAKPT, OF(LNM + LCH)

The result of the OF macro will never be negative, assuming that LNM is not less than LCH.

(If it happens that ML/I is the macro processor being used to effect the mapping then the mapping macros for OF might take the following form

```
MCDEF   LNM AS 4
MCDEF   LCH AS 1
MCDEF   LICH AS 1
MCDEF   OF WITHS ( ) AS ⟨%%A1..⟩
```

In ML/I %A1. inserts argument one whereas a % sign on its own evaluates an arithmetic expression. If the argument was, for example, LNM + 2*LCH then the replacement text of OF would be equivalent to %4 + 2*1., which would yield the result 6.)

There is a facility for 'manifest' numerical constants, i.e. numerical constants represented by names. The purpose of manifest constants is simply to make programs easier to understand. For example if the code 4 were being used to mean 'black', then the statement CAL BLACK is easier to understand than CAL 4. In the former case the name BLACK needs to be declared to be identical to 4 and this is done by the IDENT statement, which has the form

IDENT   name, decimal integer constant

for example IDENT BLACK,4. IDENT statements occur within the declarative statements at the start of a program, and always come before any usage of the name being defined. When a mapping is performed IDENT statements may either be made to perform an explicit replacement of the name by its value, or, perhaps better, to map into a directive in the object assembly language that accomplishes the same effect.

Whether generated by the OF macro or not, almost all numerical constants are small. Few pieces of software encoded in LOWL contain constants larger than 100.

A character constant in the kernel of LOWL is represented by a literal character within quotes (e.g. 'P' '+') or, for some special characters, by a name. In the latter case the name is one of the following

NLREP   meaning newline (i.e. the character denoting the end of a line).
SPREP   meaning space.
TABREP   meaning tab.
QUTREP   meaning a double-quote sign ('').

(In addition, some further names are used in certain LOWL extensions.) Values corresponding to suitable internal codes for the object machine should be assigned to these names either by means of macro mapping, or, better, by 'EQUATE' statements in the object machine's assembler. (Such 'EQUATE' statements might also profitably be used to supply values for LNM, LCH and LICH, thus adding flexibility to the final object code.)

Registers

Almost all statements in LOWL involve at most one storage address, and all assignments, comparisons and arithmetic operations are done via registers. There are notionally three registers as follows

A   is the numerical accumulator,
B   is the index register,
C   is the character register.

However no two of these registers are ever used simultaneously and it is possible to represent all three by the same physical register. The only merit in making them different is a gain in efficiency. In particular the LAM and LCM statements (q.v.) may be faster if B is different from A and C, and, on implementations where character and numerical data is different, character operations may be faster if C is different from A. (On one LOWL implementation C was dispensed with altogether, and all character operations were performed by storage-to-storage instructions.) Since the registers are never used simultaneously any operation on one register may clobber any of the others. Moreover most of the LOWL statements that do not explicitly set registers may use the registers as workspace. The table at the end of this chapter gives a list of such statements.

All statements that use the A or B registers have numerical operands and all statements that use the C register have a single character as operand.

Names and scope

The names of all variables, labels, constants and subroutines consist of an identifier (i.e. a letter followed by a sequence of letters and/or digits) of up to six characters, e.g. SUM, BC3, STKARG, GL13. No names have local meanings; the meaning is always global to the entire MI-logic.

Variables

All variables are numerical. Each variable is declared by one of the following statements

DCL   *name*
EQU   *name1, name2*

The EQU statement means that *name1* can share the same storage as the previously declared variable called *name2*. It is not, however, imperative that the two be made the same and EQU may be treated as if it had been

DCL   *name1*

if this is easier to map.

Variables do not need to be given any special initial values.

Ambitious implementors for object machines with some spare registers may choose to maintain some variables in registers rather than in storage. However, some blocks of variables need to be stored contiguously, either because they are subjected to block moves or to indexing instructions, and none of these variables should be placed in registers (unless all variables can be stored in registers). If such blocks exist, the relevant declarations are enclosed between the comments 'THE FOLLOWING MUST BE STORED CONTIGUOUSLY' and 'END OF CONTIGUOUS BLOCK OF VARI-ABLES'.

Table items

Most of the software encoded in LOWL requires certain fixed tables. There is a set of statements in the kernel of LOWL for defining table items. These statements may be labelled, in the same way as program statements may be labelled.

Table items are never changed. They may therefore be placed in read-only storage, and in a multi-access environment the same tables may be shared by all users.

All table items should be stored contiguously, in the order in which they are defined. Table items are always addressed indirectly by means of pointers (see the LAA statement).

Statements

We are now ready to enumerate the statements that make up the kernel of LOWL. The following notation is used to describe arguments to statements.

(a) *V* means a variable name.

(b) *N* means a non-negative decimal integer constant (possibly represented by a name).

(c) *OF* means a call of the OF macro.

(d) *N–OF* means either *N* or *OF*.

(e) *table label* means a label attached to a table item.

(f) *charname* means one of the names representing literal character constants (e.g. NLREP).

(g) *character* means a single character.

(h) *characters* means a string of one or more characters.

(i) $\left\{ \begin{array}{c} A \\ B \end{array} \right\}$ means either *A* or *B*.

Statements for defining table items

The following are the statements used for defining table items:

(a) CON $\left\{ \begin{array}{c} N–OF \\ –N–OF \end{array} \right\}$

defines an item consisting of the single numerical constant represented by the argument. A minus sign indicates a negative constant.

(b) NCH *charname*

defines an item consisting of the single character named by the argument.

(c) STR *'characters'*

defines an item consisting of the string of characters within the quote signs. (This string must be represented by one character per character data storage unit, e.g. if character data is stored in words then the string should be represented one character to a word.)

Load statements

Three of the load statements shown below have a subsidiary argument that can be R or X. In these cases R means that the load instruction is redundant if compare statements and the conditional branching statements GOEQ, GONE, GOGE, GOGR, GOLE, GOLT do not clobber the register being loaded, e.g.

```
LAV     ABC,X
CAL     6
GOGR    LAB3,...
LAV     ABC,R
```

The complete list of load statements is as follows.

LAV   *V*, $\left\{ \begin{array}{c} R \\ X \end{array} \right\}$ Load A with value of *V*.

LBV	V	Load B with value of V.
LAL	$N-OF$	Load A with literal value $N-OF$.
LCN	*charname*	Load C with literal named character.
LAM	$N-OF$	Derive the pointer given by adding $N-OF$ to the contents of B, and load A with the value pointed at by this (i.e. load A modified).
LCM	$N-OF$	As LAM, but load a character into C.
LAI	$V, \begin{Bmatrix} R \\ X \end{Bmatrix}$	Load A with value pointed at by V.
LCI	$V, \begin{Bmatrix} R \\ X \end{Bmatrix}$	Load C with character pointed at by V.
LAA	V, D	Load A with the address of variable V.
LAA	*table label*, C	Load A with the address of the table label. (In most implementations this will be identical to the preceding statement.)

Store statements

STV	$V, \begin{Bmatrix} P \\ X \end{Bmatrix}$	Store A in V.
STI	$V, \begin{Bmatrix} P \\ X \end{Bmatrix}$	Store A in address pointed at by V.
CLEAR	V	Set value of V to zero. (This may clobber A.)

In the first two cases, the second argument specifies whether A needs to be preserved: P means A must be preserved; X means it need not be. (On a two-address machine it is possible to implement a load statement followed by a store statement without passing through A, provided that A does not need to be preserved after the store statement.)

Arithmetic and logical statements

AAV	V	Add value of V to A.
ABV	V	Add value of V to B.
AAL	$N-OF$	Add literal value $N-OF$ to A.
SAV	V	Subtract value of V from A.
SBV	V	Subtract value of V from B.
SAL	$N-OF$	Subtract literal value $N-OF$ from A.
SBL	$N-OF$	Subtract literal value $N-OF$ from B.
MULTL	$N-OF$	Multiply A by literal value $N-OF$ (which might be one). In no case is the value $N-OF$ very large and multiplication can, if desired, be performed by repeated additions.

BUMP	*V, N–OF*	Increase value of *V* by literal value *N–OF*. (This may clobber A.)
ANDV	*V*	AND A with value of *V*.
ANDL	*N*	AND A with literal value *N*.

Compare statements

These statements compare A or C with an operand. Each is always followed immediately by a conditional jump statement. Compare statements may clobber registers and hence may be implemented as subtract instructions. The subsidiary argument to the CAV and CAI statements specifies whether the items to be compared are addresses (A) or signed integers (X). In the latter case either of the values to be compared may be positive or negative. (Some machines, for example the PDP-11, use the first bit as a sign bit for numerical values but not for addresses. For most machines, however, there is no difference.) If two addresses are compared these may be addresses of variables, table labels, or stack items (see later). Both addresses will always be of the same nature, so there are, for example, no comparisons between stack addresses and addresses of table labels.

CAV	$V, \begin{Bmatrix} X \\ A \end{Bmatrix}$	Compare A with value of *V*.
CAL	*N–OF*	Compare A with literal value *N–OF*.
CCL	'*character*'	Compare C with given character.
CCN	*charname*	Compare C with named character.
CAI	$V, \begin{Bmatrix} X \\ A \end{Bmatrix}$	Compare A with value pointed at by *V*.
CCI	*V*	Compare C with character pointed at by *V*.

In the case of the CAL statement, the argument may be zero. On some machines, comparing with zero is a redundant operation and the implementor may decide to eliminate such statements. If he does, he should, however, bear in mind that CAL 0 may be the very first instruction in a subroutine (meaning test if the parameter is zero—see later). Because of this possible optimization, no load statements immediately before a CAL 0 have the subsidiary argument R.

Subroutines

A subroutine in LOWL may be called from anywhere, including from within another subroutine. However no subroutines are recursive. There may be at most one parameter, which, if it exists, is always numerical, is always passed in the A register, and should always be stored in the variable PARNM. (In Algol 60 terms, parameters are always called by value.)

Some subroutines have multiple exits. In this case exit 1 is a normal return to the point of call, exit 2 returns to the point of call but skips over the next LOWL statement, exit 3 skips two LOWL statements, and so on. The LOWL statements thus skipped over are always GO statements with a special subsidiary argument (q.v.). Subroutines in the MI-logic never return a value in a register.

Before defining the statements for subroutine linkage it is best to show an example. Assume the subroutine FACT calculates the factorial of its parameter and places the result in VALUE. If the parameter is negative it uses exit one and in normal cases it uses exit two. The calling sequence for FACT might be

```
          LAV       ARG,X
          GOSUB     FACT,...
          GO        ERROR,...
```

and the declaration might be

```
          SUBR      FACT,PARNM,2
          LAL       1
          STV       VALUE,X
          LAV       PARNM,X
          CAL       0
          GOGR      FCT1, 1,X,X
          EXIT      1,FACT
[FCT1]      .
            .
          STV       VALUE,X
          EXIT      2,FACT
```

The declaration of a subroutine may come before or after the first call of the subroutine.

As can be seen from the example, subroutines are declared by a LOWL statement of form

$$\text{SUBR} \quad \textit{subroutine name,} \left\{ \begin{array}{c} \text{PARNM} \\ \text{X} \end{array} \right\}, N$$

where the second argument is X if there is no parameter. The third argument gives the number of exits. The SUBR statement should be mapped into code to place A in PARNM if there is a parameter and store the return link. If there is a parameter it should remain in A, i.e. the action of setting PARNM and preserving the link should not clobber A. The code would normally be labelled with the subroutine name so that the GOSUB statements can reference it.

Since there is no recursion, each subroutine may preserve its link in a fixed variable unique to that subroutine. Alternatively subroutine links can be stored in a stack (though *not* the stack used by the MI-logic). Such a stack need only have room for a dozen items since this is the maximum depth of subroutine nesting.

The statement to return from a subroutine takes the form

$$\text{EXIT} \quad N, \textit{subroutine name}$$

where N is the number of the exit to be taken.

Subroutines are called by the statement

$$\text{GOSUB} \quad \textit{subroutine name,} \quad \begin{Bmatrix} \textit{distance} \\ \text{X} \end{Bmatrix}$$

A call may reference a routine in the MD-logic, in which case the second argument is X. Otherwise the second argument gives the number of LOWL statements between the call and the subroutine declaration. The distance is negative if the declaration precedes the call.

(The purpose of giving the distance is to allow optimization on machines with special instructions for short-distance jumps. The distance does not include LOWL statements that are comments, and is measured from the statement following the given one—i.e. the following statement is at distance 0 and a statement is at distance -1 from itself. When LOWL is mapped into another language, distances will change unless the mapping is one-to-one. However the distance in terms of LOWL statements will still usually be a useful approximation.)

The GOADD statement

The statement

$$\text{GOADD} \quad V$$

is a multi-way branch statement. It is always followed immediately by a series of unconditional GO statements. If the value of V is zero the first such GO is executed; if the value of V is one the second GO is executed, and so on.

Branching statements

LOWL contains both conditional and unconditional branching statements. The former always immediately follow a compare statement. Any conditional branching statement may clobber any register, but an unconditional branch must leave the registers unchanged. There are no branches into a subroutine from outside, but there are branches out of subroutines to the main logic (i.e. those parts of the logic not within a subroutine). If subroutine return links are being stored on a stack, these branches may cause problems, so there is a special statement of form

CSS

(which means *clear subroutine stack*) to alleviate this situation. CSS statements appear after each label in the main logic that is referenced from within a subroutine. On implementations which do not use a stack for return links, the CSS statement will, of course, be mapped into a null instruction.

All branching statements have a set of four arguments called a *label spec*, which takes the following form:

Argument 1 name of designated label.
Argument 2 distance of designated label (as for second argument to GOSUB).
Argument 3 $\begin{cases} \text{E if the branch goes out of a subroutine.} \\ \text{X otherwise.} \end{cases}$
Argument 4 $\begin{cases} \text{C if the branch is an exit following a GOSUB statement.} \\ \text{T if the branch is one of a sequence following a GOADD} \\ \quad\text{statement.} \\ \text{X otherwise.} \end{cases}$

(The purpose of argument 4 is that if it is not X the branch must be mapped into an instruction of a standard form; this may be significant on a machine with different lengths of jump instruction.)

The full list of branching statements is as follows:

GO   unconditional branch.
GOEQ   branch if equal.
GONE   branch if not equal.
GOGE   branch if greater than or equal (i.e. if A is greater than or equal to the compared operand).
GOGR   branch if greater than.
GOLE   branch if less than or equal.
GOLT   branch if less than.

There are, in addition, two statements which test the C register. These do not follow compare statements but rather they follow a statement that loads the C register. The statements are

GOPC   branch if character in C is a punctuation character, i.e. not a letter or digit.
GOND   branch if character in C is not a digit. If it is a digit, load the A register with the value of the digit (i.e. if C contained the value 23, which happened to be the internal code of the digit 3, then A should be set to the value 3).

The following example illustrates the use of label specs.

```
         SUBR    SHOW,X,1
         LAV     PIG,X
         CAV     COW,X
         GOEQ    SAME,3,X,X
         GOSUB   INVERT, – 620
         GO      SAME,1,X,C
         GO      OUT,516,E,X
[SAME]   EXIT    1,SHOW
```

Stacking and block moving statements

All software encoded in LOWL uses a double stack within a single contiguous block of storage. If this block of storage runs from, say, addresses 2000 to 6000 the stacks might look like this

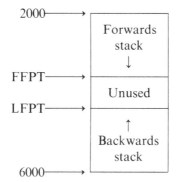

In particular the variable FFPT points at the first free location of the forwards stack and LFPT points at the last location in use on the backwards stack. Stacks are initialized by routines in the MD-logic.

There are four statements in LOWL concerned with stacking. These are

FSTK   stack A on forwards stack.
BSTK   stack A on backwards stack.
CFSTK   stack C on forwards stack.
UNSTK *V*   unstack number at top of backwards stack and put it in *V*.

In terms of other LOWL statements the action of these is as follows:

```
FSTK    STI     FFPT,X
        LAV     FFPT,X
        AAL     OF(LNM)
        STV     FFPT,P
        CAV     LFPT,A
```

	GOGE	ERLSO,...	(ERLSO is the label of the code that deals with stack overflow. It is present in every MI-logic.)

....

CFSTK	as FSTK except that C is stored and FFPT is incremented by OF(LCH).

....

BSTK	preserve A	
	LAV	LFPT,X
	SAL	OF(LNM)
	STV	LFPT,X
	restore A	
	STI	LFPT,X
	LAV	FFPT,X
	CAV	LFPT,A
	GOGE	ERLSO,...

....

UNSTK	LAI	LFPT,X
	STV	*V*,X
	BUMP	LFPT,OF(LNM)

On most mappings of LOWL these rather clumsy instruction sequences can be improved upon; indeed the very purpose of the stacking statements is to permit the use of specially optimized code.

There are two 'block moving' statements for moving blocks of contiguous locations to and from positions in the stacks. In each case SRCPT points at the start of the source field, DSTPT to the start of the destination field and A contains the length of the fields (which exceeds zero). The statements are

FMOVE   perform forwards move.
BMOVE   perform backwards move.

Each should perform a character-by-character move from source to destination. FMOVE should start with the first character and end with the last and BMOVE should do the reverse. The effect only differs, of course, when the two fields overlap.

I/O statements

Almost all I/O in LOWL is performed through machine-dependent subroutines. There is just one statement in the kernel of LOWL which deals with I/O and this has the form

MESS   *'characters'*

The MESS statement means output the given message, which may be an error message or an informatory message. The output device will normally be a lineprinter or an on-line console. Each character of the message stands for itself except for a dollar sign, which means a newline. Thus

MESS 'ONE$TWO$$THREE'
MESS 'FOUR'

should produce the output

ONE
TWO

THREEFOUR

The way the message is represented and stored is entirely up to the implementor. If it is possible to pack the message this should be done.

Although all the other I/O routines belong to the MD-logic it is worth noting a few general points. Most messages contain some variable information, for example

IDENTIFIER ... IN LINE ... NOT DECLARED

The fixed parts are generated by MESS statements and, because of variations in character sets, the variable parts are generated by MD-logic subroutines. The output from the two is therefore interspersed. Because the variable information is indeterminate in length as well as in form, lines may be arbitrarily long. The identifier name in the above message might, for example, be one character or a hundred characters. Hence both the MESS routine and the associated MD-logic subroutines may, in some implementations, need to check for overflow of the output buffer.

Most LOWL software caters for two output streams: the *message stream* described above and *results stream*, which is used for the main results. In all cases the logic is defined so that the two may or may not go to the same physical device. Two possible situations are, for example, messages going to a console and results to a disc file, or both messages and results being interspersed on a lineprinter listing.

Comment and layout statements

Comments in LOWL are written

NB *'characters'*

There are two other layout statements, namely

PRGST *'characters'*

which occurs once, at the very start of the MI-logic, the *characters* giving the program name, and

PRGEN

which occurs at the end. PRGST and PRGEN will probably map into null instructions on most implementations. Neither NB, PRGST nor PRGEN is ever labelled.

The MI-logic is always organized so that the variable declarations come first, the table items (if any) come second and the executable statements come last. The first table item, if one exists, is labelled TABFST and the first executable statement is labelled BEGIN. The overall layout of the MI-logic is therefore

> PRGST *'characters'*
> declarations of variables (and any manifest constants)
> [TABFST] table items
> [BEGIN] executable statements
> PRGEN

Uniqueness of names

All variable names, constant names, labels, subroutine names and statement names in LOWL are unique. Thus, for example, GO, being a statement name is never used as the name of anything else and all occurrences of GO can be taken as a call of the mapping macro for the GO statement unless the GO occurs in string quotes, e.g.

MESS 'ILLEGAL GO TO'

Interface with the MD-logic

The MD-logic consists of some initialization code together with a set of subroutines. The initialization code is entered before the MI-logic. When the MD-logic has performed the necessary initialization it branches to the label BEGIN in the MI-logic, which then takes control. Communication with the MD-logic is then by means of subroutine calls. At the end of execution, either by natural termination or because of a fatal error such as stack overflow, the MI-logic calls the MD-logic subroutine MDQUIT, which performs the final tidying up.

All subroutines in the MD-logic have names beginning with the letters MD. These subroutines may clobber registers, but should not, except where otherwise stated, change the values of any MI-logic variables.

The nature of the initialization code varies according to the software concerned, but always includes the following tasks, which are called the *common initialization code*.

(1) Reserve an area of contiguous storage for the stacks. A suitable size for this depends on the nature of the software being implemented, but clearly the bigger the better. The software must not be entered with a stack smaller than two words, and for most software the practical minimum is about fifty words. FFPT should be set to point to the start of this area and LFPT should be set to point immediately beyond the end.

(2) Perform any necessary I/O initialization.

(3) If the GOSUB statement is being implemented using a stack then initialize the stack.

(4) Print an introductory message if desired (e.g. "SUPERSYS VERSION 1 ENTERED").

(5) Branch to the label BEGIN in the MI-logic.

All initialization in the MI-logic is performed dynamically (i.e. by means of explicit assignments rather than by preset initial values) so that the software can be re-used without being reloaded. Ideally the MD-logic initialization should be performed in the same way.

The duties of the MDQUIT subroutine are to close all I/O (there might be incomplete lines in output buffers), to release resources (e.g. storage areas 'borrowed' from the operating system) and to quit. (MDQUIT does not return to its point of call in the MI-logic.) The way MDQUIT is encoded depends, of course, on the software being implemented.

Alignment

On implementations where LNM and LCH are unequal it may be necessary to consider the question of data alignment. Implementors without alignment problems can skip this section—all they need to do is to map the ALIGN statement into a null instruction.

We will discuss alignment problems with reference to a specific example. Assume that the object machine works in units of words, each word being divided into four bytes. An item of character data occupies one byte and an item of numeric data four bytes. Problems may arise in a table of data when, for example, a single character is followed by a number. (These may occur as table items or as dynamically created data on a stack.) One way of storing such data is to place the character in the first byte of one word and the number in the next three bytes of that word and the first byte of the next word. However some object machines cannot directly address numbers that straddle word boundaries. Hence LOWL statements that address numbers indirectly, such as LAI, would need to be mapped into instructions to assemble the number into a word before loading it. Similarly for statements to store indirectly addressed numbers. This may be very slow and cumbersome.

To combat this problem LOWL provides a statement called ALIGN, which has no arguments. This can be used to force numerical data to be aligned to any desired boundary. Taking the example of the number following a single character, the number could be stored in the next word following the word containing the character, the last three bytes of the latter being unused. This might eliminate addressing problems.

The following are the rules for the implementor to follow, depending on whether he wants his data aligned or not.

Unaligned data. The ALIGN statement is mapped into a null instruction. Statements for defining numerical table items (e.g. a CON statement) are *not* aligned but follow immediately after the preceding table item.

Aligned data. The ALIGN statement is mapped into instructions to align the contents of the A register up to the desired boundary. Statements defining numerical table items are aligned to the same boundary, as are the initial values of FFPT and LFPT together with any numerical pointers created by the MD-logic. (When alignment is performed no special markers need be put in the unused portions of words. Software written in LOWL always works with the true lengths of character strings and never looks at padding beyond the end.) Given this alignment, the implementor can always assume that, when a number is to be addressed indirectly, the requisite pointer is correctly aligned. This applies for example to statements such as LAI, LAM, STI, FSTK, UNSTK and to pointers supplied as arguments to MD-logic routines. He can thus forget about alignment problems when mapping such statements.

In either situation, variable declarations created by DEC or EQU statements should be aligned to the boundary most convenient for direct addressing.

Summary of LOWL

To summarize, the basic elements in the kernel of LOWL are as follows:

Data types	Character (single character), number (may be integer value or pointer).
Variables	Represented by identifiers. No character variables.
Constants	Numerical: decimal integer or call of OF macro. Character: single character in quotes or name.
Registers	Three: A, B and C.
Labels	Represented by identifiers. Enclosed in square brackets where placed.
Subroutines	Names are identifiers. At most one argument.

The following is a complete list of the statements in the kernel of LOWL. Those marked with an asterisk may clobber any of the registers.

DCL	*V*	declare variable.
EQU	*V, V*	equate two variables.
IDENT	*V, decimal integer*	equate name to integer.

CON	$S/B \begin{Bmatrix} N\text{--}OF \\ \overline{-N\text{--}OF} \end{Bmatrix}$	numerical constant.
NCH	*charname*	character constant.
STR	*'characters'*	character string constant.
LAV	$V, \begin{Bmatrix} R \\ X \end{Bmatrix}$	load A with variable.
LBV	*V*	load B with variable.
LAL	*N--OF*	load A with literal.
LCN	*charname*	load C with named character.
LAM	*N--OF*	load A modified.
LCM	*N--OF*	load C modified.
LAI	$V, \begin{Bmatrix} R \\ X \end{Bmatrix}$	load A indirect.
LCI	$V, \begin{Bmatrix} R \\ X \end{Bmatrix}$	load C indirect.
LAA	$\begin{Bmatrix} V, D \\ \textit{table label}, C \end{Bmatrix}$	load A with address.
STV	$V, \begin{Bmatrix} P \\ X \end{Bmatrix}$	store A in variable.
STI	$V, \begin{Bmatrix} P \\ X \end{Bmatrix}$	store A indirectly in variable.
*CLEAR	*V*	set variable to zero.
AAV	*V*	add to A a variable.
ABV	*V*	add to B a variable.
AAL	*N--OF*	add to A a literal.
SAV	*V*	subtract from A a variable.
SBV	*V*	subtract from B a variable.
SAL	*N--OF*	subtract from A a literal.
SBL	*N--OF*	subtract from B a literal.
MULTL	*N--OF*	multiply A by a literal.
*BUMP	*V, N--OF*	increase a variable.
ANDV	*V*	'and' A with a variable.
ANDL	*N*	'and' A with a literal.
*CAV	$V, \begin{Bmatrix} X \\ A \end{Bmatrix}$	compare A with variable.
*CAL	*N--OF*	compare A with literal.
*CCL	*'character'*	compare C with literal.
*CCN	*charname*	compare C with named character.
*CAI	$V, \begin{Bmatrix} X \\ A \end{Bmatrix}$	compare A indirect.

*CCI	V		compare C indirect.
SUBR	subroutine name, $\left\{ \begin{array}{c} \text{PARNM} \\ \text{X} \end{array} \right\}$,N		declare subroutine.
*EXIT	N, subroutine name		exit from subroutine.
GOSUB	subroutine name, $\left\{ \begin{array}{c} \text{distance} \\ \text{X} \end{array} \right\}$		call subroutine.
*GOADD	V		multi-way branch.
*CSS			clear subroutine stack (if any).
GO	label spec		unconditional branch.
*GOEQ	label spec		branch if equal.
*GONE	label spec		branch if not equal.
*GOGE	label spec		branch if greater than or equal.
*GOGR	label spec		branch if greater than.
*GOLE	label spec		branch if less than or equal.
*GOLT	label spec		branch if less than.
*GOPC	label spec		branch if C is a punctuation character.
*GOND	label spec		branch if C is not a digit. Otherwise put value in A.
*FSTK			stack A on forwards stack.
*BSTK			stack A on backwards stack.
*CFSTK			stack C on forwards stack.
*UNSTK	V		unstack from backwards stack.
*FMOVE			forwards block move.
*BMOVE			backwards block move.
*MESS	'characters'		output a message.
NB	'characters'		comment.
PRGST	'characters'		start of logic.
PRGEN			end of logic.
ALIGN			align A up to next boundary.

A mapping of LOWL simply requires mapping macros for each of the above statements plus possible subsidiary macros to deal with labels and constants.

Chapter 3.4

Mapping and Documentation

Some of the attributes that mark the professional software writer from the playboy are

(a) His software is completely tested.
(b) His software is completely documented.
(c) His software is easy to use and operate. In particular the operating system interface is smooth.
(d) The implementation process is adaptable to future changes.
(e) The implementation process is sufficiently well documented for someone else to take it over at any time.

A person who thinks he has completed an implementation when the software has been coded up and a few test cases run can be equated with a man who thinks he has overcome all the problems of marriage when he has finished his speech at the wedding reception.

The purpose of this chapter is to cover (b), (d) and (e) of the above points. Of the other two points, point (a) is covered by LOWLTEST and the test data for the software to be implemented, and point (c) largely by the way the MD-logic is encoded. The implementor might add a further point to the above list.

(f) He expects others to adopt the same professional standards.

He should therefore feel free to hit back and point out errors and inadequacies in LOWL itself, its documentation or the software issued in it.

The mapping

The most important point about a mapping is that it should not be regarded as a one-off job. Several pieces of software have been encoded in LOWL, and, although the immediate aim may be to implement only one of these, others may be implemented at a later date. It may even be that the implementor himself, after seeing the software in use for a while, may design his own extensions to it. In this case he would do well to make his changes to the LOWL encoding of the software and remap this, thus retaining portability. Since his mapping macros might be re-used, perhaps by someone else, the implementor should write them in a well organized and well documented manner.

An extension of this point is that LOWL itself might be developed and improved. In particular, subsidiary arguments might be added to some existing LOWL statements. If at all possible, mapping macros should be written so that if an extra subsidiary argument is added to the end of the argument list, this should not affect the working of the macro. To take an explicit example of this that arose in the past, the CAV statement in LOWL was originally written in the form

$$CAV \quad V$$

It subsequently became clear that, for at least one object machine, it would be useful to know whether V was an address or simply a number. Hence a subsidiary argument was added, the CAV statement being written

$$CAV \quad V, A$$

or

$$CAV \quad V, X$$

depending on whether V was an address or not. All previous mappings of LOWL were not interested in this argument, and, since the mapping macros had been written to allow for extra redundant arguments, these mappings still worked although LOWL had been changed. The point is this: it is not worth taking a lot of trouble to make mapping macros allow for extra arguments, but if they have this property naturally—as is the case for most macro-assembler macros—then it is foolish to do anything to destroy it (like assuming that a certain argument is the last argument). Since flexibility is the key factor in portability projects it is certainly an advantage to be able to make slight changes to descriptive languages painlessly.

Common mapping problems

It may be worth bringing the implementor's attention to two rather mundane problems which, nevertheless, cause difficulties on many mappings.

One problem concerns arguments that are character strings, particularly arguments to the MESS and STR statements. These strings are literals and should not be subject to macro replacement (except perhaps the $ which stands for a newline in the MESS statement). Moreover, spaces within these character strings are significant, including any that occur at the beginning and end.

Character strings provide the only instance in LOWL where spaces occur within arguments. Tabs never occur within arguments but are used to separate the statement name from the first argument. These tabs (which may be represented by spaces) do not, of course, count as part of the first argument. The amount of difficulty presented by spaces and tabs varies between macro processors. However it is often necessary to plan carefully the layout of the output from a macro processor and where spaces and tabs are to appear in it.

A further problem concerns potential recursion. It may happen for example, that the object machine has an instruction called GO and the GO statement of LOWL will map into this (although the argument structure will almost certainly be different in the two cases). The replacement text of the GO statement will then involve a GO instruction. Many macro processors, unless told otherwise, would treat this GO instruction as a recursive call of the GO macro.

Some mapping macros

This section contains some samples of mapping macros. Unfortunately it is necessary, when showing examples, to fix on one macro processor, and in this case ML/I has been chosen. It is hoped, however, that the macros will still provide some useful insight for all implementors, although they most likely will not be using ML/I as the mapping tool and will be unfamiliar with ML/I notation.

When using ML/I it is convenient to perform the minor systematic editing on LOWL at the same time as the macros are mapped, thus eliminating a pre-pass. Assuming, for example, that the square brackets round labels were to be deleted, this would be achieved by defining them as skips.

```
MCSKIP[
MCSKIP]
```

It is also usually convenient to cause all tab characters in the source text to be ignored. This can also be done by defining a suitable skip.

A mapping macro for a simple statement might be

```
MCDEF LAV N1 OPT, N1 OR NL ALL
AS< LOAD %A1.
    >
```

The delimiter structure defines LAV as the macro name, which is followed by an indefinitely long sequence of arguments separated by commas. The macro generates a LOAD instruction. If we wanted to be clever and eliminate the LOAD instruction if the second argument was R (for redundant) then we might have written the replacement text

$$<\text{MCGO LO IF } \%\text{A2.} = \text{R}$$
$$\text{LOAD } \%\text{A1.}$$
$$>$$

(MCGO LO means exit from the macro.) Alternatively it might be preferred
to generate a comment in the case when a LAV statement was ignored. A
suitable comment might be

ACCUMULATOR ALREADY CONTAINS ...

While on the subject of comments, it is often helpful to place the source
LOWL statement as a comment on the assembly language instructions that it
generates.

Some LOWL statements might not be replaced by in-line code but might
generate a call to a subroutine. Thus if it required six instructions to effect
the FMOVE statement then the mapping macro for FMOVE might be
written

$$\text{MCDEF FMOVE NL}$$
$$\text{AS} < \text{ CALL FMVSUB}$$
$$>$$

where FMVSUB was a subroutine consisting of the six required instructions.
(The NL in the delimiter structure of FMOVE stands for 'newline'. The text
in between, in this case null, counts as the argument.) It may be convenient to
combine such subroutines as FMVSUB with the MD-logic.

Lastly, we will show the mapping macro for the MESS statement, since
this has rather special properties. We will assume

MESS 'ABC'

is mapped into

$$\text{CALL} \quad \text{MESSUB}$$
$$\text{TEXT} \quad \text{``ABC\&''}$$

where the &, not being a character used in LOWL, acts as an end marker for
the message. The mapping macro might be written

$$\text{MCDEF MESS WITH TAB WITH' 'NL}$$
$$\text{SSAS} < \text{ CALL MESSUB}$$
$$\text{TEXT ``}\%\text{WB1.\&''}$$
$$>$$

Here the macro name is MESS followed by a tab and quote (even if tab has
been defined as a skip this would not affect a tab within a macro name), the
first delimiter is quote and the final delimiter is newline (—this allows for any

subsidiary arguments that might be added). The SSAS in place ᴗ
means that the macro is 'straight scan', i.e. no account is takeı.
macro calls when scanning for delimiters of this macro. The notation
means insert argument one exactly as written and include any spaceꜱ
occur at the beginning and end. It is assumed that the MESSUB subroutᵢ.
takes care of the conversion of dollar signs within messages to newlines.

Documentation

The implementor will need to provide a *User's Manual* of the software
he has implemented. In addition, he should provide some documentation
on the implementation process, as mentioned earlier.

Critical evaluations of the mapping process are also of value. Interesting
questions are

(a) How efficient is the final implementation?
(b) Where do the inefficiencies lie?
(c) How long did the implementation take?
(d) How much machine time does a mapping take?
(e) What features of LOWL proved difficult to map?
(f) Was the mapping tool adequate?
(g) Could the software have been better implemented some other way?

Chapter 3.5

The LOWL Kernel Test Program

LOWLTEST is a program to test the mapping macros for the kernel of LOWL. It was designed and written by R. C. Saunders, working on a project supported by a research grant from the Science Research Council.

The first action of LOWLTEST is to print an introductory message using the MESS statement. It then tests the following seven statements

(1) GO
(2) LAL
(3) CAL
(4) GONE
(5) GOEQ
(6) STV with X as second argument
(7) LAV

If any of these tests fail, LOWLTEST prints a suitable error message, for example

+ + + ERROR IN LAL OR CAL WITH NON-ZERO ARGUMENT

and abandons the run.

After this LOWLTEST tries to test the remaining LOWL statements independently of one another, relying on the use of the seven statements that have already been tested together with the MESS statement. If an error is found at this stage, a message is printed but the run continues. However some of the later tests may be omitted, since they may be dependent on an incorrect statement (e.g. UNSTK depends on BSTK). *The implementor must therefore continue to run LOWLTEST until it works completely.*

Mountain walkers, when traversing dangerous territory, should leave behind a message such as 'We are climbing to Windy Ridge and then crossing Suckfoot Bog to Creakbridge'. This helps the rescue party to find them. LOWLTEST adopts a similar policy, and its output, after the introductory message, should consist of a series of messages like

... TESTING GOADD ...

If the program is working correctly each of these should be followed by the acknowledgement OK or FOUND. These tests are followed, at the very end, by five lines of output that should read

ABCDEFGHIJKLMNOPQRSTUVWXYZ 0123456789
.,;:()*/ − + =   ”
SHOULD BE THE SAME AS
ABCDEFGHIJKLMNOPQRSTUVWXYZ 0123456789
.,;:()*/ − + =   TAB AND QUOTE

If there are any error messages, these will begin with the characters + + +.

Extensions, the MD-logic and I/O

By its very nature LOWLTEST requires no extensions to LOWL but it does require a small MD-logic. The input/output requirements are minimal, namely one output stream, which is the message stream used by MESS statements, and no input stream.

The MD-logic consists of two subroutines and some initialization code. The subroutines are as follows.

(1) MDERCH. Output the character in the C register on the message stream. The character set is exactly the LOWL character set.
(2) MDQUIT. As defined in the description of LOWL.

The initialization code is exactly the common initialization code given in the description of LOWL.

Chapter 3.6

Listing of LOWLTEST

This chapter contains a complete listing of LOWLTEST. This listing needs to be converted to a suitable form to be input to the computer on which the mapping is to be performed. When describing how this might be done, we will assume the listing is to be punched onto cards. Similar considerations apply to most other media.

Certainly the best approach to this data preparation problem is to find someone else who has done a mapping and get a copy of his card deck. Someone with a similar machine whose installation is local enough to avoid the use of long-distance mail services is ideal. Failing this, one has to smile bravely and do it oneself. (Actually one is not all that much worse off. There are often problems in reading other people's data into one's own computer, and the punching to be done is not excessive—most of the lines are short and some are even blank.) The most important point is that all material should be carefully checked and verified. One of the advantages of a DLIMP is that it is a relatively error-free means of software implementation, and this advantage can be totally nullified by shoddy data preparation.

The exact format of the punching is at the discretion of the implementor. Note that the line numbers on the listings are *not* part of the LOWL program, but merely an aid to readability and referencing. They should therefore either be totally omitted from the cards or placed in a field that is to be ignored (e.g. the sequence number field). The label field, therefore, should normally start in what is effectively column one. The standard LOWL separator between fields is the tab character. However this is seldom available on cards and it is therefore best to separate fields by spaces. The number of spaces that is typed can be chosen to fit in with the conventions of the macro processor to be used. Note that the label field consists of at most eight characters (a six-character label plus two brackets), the operation field consists of at most five characters and the operand field at most fifty characters. Thus, for example, the implementor might start the label field in column one of his card, the operation field in column ten and the operand field in column seventeen. The lines

$$212 \qquad \text{LAV} \qquad \text{SPT,X}$$
$$213 \quad [\text{XYZ}] \quad \text{MESS} \quad ' \text{ ABC } '$$

would then be punched as

⌴⌴⌴⌴⌴⌴⌴⌴⌴⌴⌴LAV⌴⌴⌴⌴⌴SPT,X
[XYZ]⌴⌴⌴⌴⌴MESS⌴⌴⌴'ABC'

where ⌴ represents a blank column.

The listing follows. (*Note.* Due to a peculiarity of the printer on which this listing, and that in Chapter 3.8, was produced, a single quote (') is printed on the slant and looks like a prime (').)

```
 1
 2            PRGST       'LOWLTEST'
 3            NB          'LOWL STATEMENTS TO TEST LOWL MACROS'
 4            DCL         AA
 5            DCL         BB
 6            DCL         PARNM
 7            NB          'THE FOLLOWING MUST BE STORED CONTIGUOUSLY'
 8            DCL         PVNUM
 9            DCL         PVARPT
10            NB          'END OF CONTIGUOUS BLOCK OF VARIABLES'
11            DCL         ENDPT
12            DCL         FFPT
13            DCL         LFPT
14            EQU         KK,AA
15            DCL         SRCPT
16            DCL         DSTPT
17            DCL         CC
18            DCL         DD
19            DCL·        EE
20            DCL         FF
21            DCL         GG
22            DCL         HH
23            DCL         II
24            DCL         JJ
25            DCL         LINKPT
26            DCL         SPT
27            DCL         IDLEN
28            DCL         IDPT
29            DCL         ERNOB
30            DCL         ERNOD
31            DCL         ERNOG
32            DCL         ERNOH
33            DCL         LOTEMP
34            IDENT       SEVTH,73
35 [TABFST]   CON         0
36 [TBCH]     STR         'X'
37 [TBNUM]    CON         -6
38 [LL34]     NCH         NLREP
39            STR         'ABCDEFGHIJKLMNOPQRSTUVWXYZ'
40            NCH         SPREP
41 [NUMS]     STR         '0123456789'
42            NCH         NLREP
43            STR         '.,;:()*/-+='
44            NCH         TABREP
45            NCH         QUTREP
46            NCH         NLREP
```

```
 47 [LL35]      CON        10
 48             STR        'GOSUB'
 49
 50 [BEGIN]     MESS       '$TEST OF LOWL'
 51             MESS       ' MAPPING$...DEC 1973$$...TESTING FORWARD GO..$'
 52             GO         LL1,3,X,X
 53             MESS       '+++FORWARD GO HAS NO EFFECT$'
 54 [LL99]      MESS       'OK$...TESTING LONG GO..$'
 55             GO         LL98,3,X,X
 56 [LL1]       MESS       'OK$...TESTING BACKWARD GO..$'
 57             GO         LL99,-4,X,X
 58             MESS       '+++BACKWARD GO HAS NO EFFECT$'
 59 [LL98]      GO         LL27,542,X,X
 60 [LL28]      MESS       'OK$...TESTING LAL,CAL,GONE,GOEQ,STV,LAV..$'
 61             LAL        0
 62             NB         'TEST LAL AND CAL ZERO'
 63             CAL        0
 64             GONE       ER1,539,X,X
 65             LAL        0
 66 [LL29]      CAL        0
 67             GOEQ       LL2,1,X,X
 68             MESS       '+++GOEQ NOT BRANCHING$'
 69 [LL2]       LAL        0
 70             STV        AA,X
 71             LAV        AA,X
 72             CAL        0
 73             GONE       ER2,532,X,X
 74             LAV        AA,X
 75             STV        AA,P
 76             CAL        0
 77             GONE       ER3,530,X,X
 78 [LL17]      LAV        AA,X
 79             CAL        0
 80             GONE       ER4,529,X,X
 81 [LL18]      LAL        8
 82             CAL        8
 83             GONE       ER5,528,X,X
 84             LAL        64
 85             AAL        0
 86             STV        BB,X
 87             LAV        BB,X
 88             CAL        64
 89             GONE       ER6,524,X,X
 90 [LL19]      LAL        0
 91             STV        ERNOB,X
 92             LAL        0
 93             STV        ERNOD,X
 94             LAL        0
 95             STV        ERNOG,X
 96             LAL        0
 97             STV        ERNOH,X
 98             LAL        64
 99             CAV        BB,X
100             GONE       ER7,515,X,X
101 [LL93]      MESS       'OK$...TESTING ARITHMETIC AND CONDITIONAL GOS..$'
102             LAL        0
103             AAV        BB
104             CAL        64
105             GONE       ER8,514,X,X
106 [LL92]      LAV        BB,X
107             SAL        64
108             CAL        0
109             GONE       ER9,512,X,X
110 [LL91]      LAL        64
111             SAV        BB
112             CAL        0
113             GONE       ER10,512,X,X
114 [LL20]      LAL        65
115             CAL        64
116             GOGR       LL3,1,X,X
117             MESS       '+++ERROR IN GOGR$'
```

```
118 [LL3]        LAL        65
119              GAL        64
120              GOGE       LL4,1,X,X
121              MESS       '+++GOGE ERROR   GR FAILS$'
122 [LL4]        LAL        64
123              CAL        64
124              GOGE       LL5,1,X,X
125              MESS       '+++GOGE ERROR   EQ FAILS$'
126 [LL5]        LAL        64
127              CAL        65
128              GOLE       LL6,1,X,X
129              MESS       '+++GOLE ERROR   LT FAILS$'
130 [LL6]        LAL        64
131              CAL        64
132              GOLE       LL7,1,X,X
133              MESS       '+++GOLE ERROR   EQ FAILS$'
134 [LL7]        LAL        64
135              CAL        65
136              GOLT       LL8,1,X,X
137              MESS       '+++GOLT ERROR$'
138 [LL8]        MESS       'OK...TESTING GOSUB AND EXIT 1..$'
139              GOSUB      SR1,384
140              MESS       'K$...TESTING EXITS 2,3 AND 4.,$'
141 [LL96]       GOSUB      SR2,387
142              GO         ER11,485,X,C
143              GO         LL39,2,X,C
144              GO         ER11,483,X,C
145              GO         ER11,482,X,X
146 [LL39]       MESS       '0'
147 [LL21]       LAL        0
148              STV        BB,X
149              GOSUB      SR2,379
150              GO         ER56,479,X,C
151              GO         ER56,478,X,C
152              GO         LL47,1,X,C
153              GO         ER56,476,X,X
154 [LL47]       MESS       'K'
155 [LL56]       LAL        8
156              STV        BB,X
157              GOSUB      SR2,371
158              GO         ER57,473,X,C
159              GO         ER57,472,X,C
160              GO         ER57,471,X,C
161              MESS       '$'
162 [LL57]       LAL        65
163              STV        BB,X
164              GOSUB      SR2,364
165              GO         LL9,3,X,C
166              GO         ER58,1,X,C
167              GO         ER58,0,X,C
168 [ER58]       MESS       '+++EXIT1 ERROR FROM SR2$'
169 [LL9]        LAL        65
170              GOSUB      SR3,374
171              LAL        0
172              GOSUB      SR4,392
173 [LL94]       LAL        15
174              STV        AA,X
175              LAL        102
176              ANDV       AA
177              CAL        6
178              GONE       ER12,455,X,X
179              LAV        AA,X
180              CAL        15
181              GONE       ER26,454,X,X
182 [LL22]       LAL        15
183              ANDL       102
184              CAL        6
185              GONE       ER13,452,X,X
186 [LL24]       CLEAR      AA
187              LAV        AA,X
188              CAL        0
```

```
189           GONE    ER15,450,X,X
190  [LL25]   BUMP    AA,65
191           BUMP    AA,8
192           LAV     AA,X
193           CAL     SEVTH
194           GONE    ER16,449,X,X
195  [LL46]   LAL     3
196           STV     CC,X
197           MESS    '...TESTING GOADD..$
198           GOADD   CC
199           GO      ER37,507,X,T
200           GO      ER37,506,X,T
201           GO      ER37,505,X,T
202           GO      LL10,1,X,T
203           GO      ER37,503,X,T
204  [LL10]   MESS    'OKS'
205           LAL     65
206           AAL     8
207           CAL     73
208           GONE    ER17,437,X,X
209  [LL90]   LAL     OF(2*LCH)
210           CAL     OF(LCH+LCH)
211           GONE    ER18,438,X,X
212           LAL     OF(LNM+LCH)
213           SAL     OF(LCH)
214           CAL     OF(LNM)
215           GONE    ER19,436,X,X
216           LAL     OF(3*LNM+LCH)
217           SAL     OF(2*LNM-LCH)
218           CAL     OF(2*LCH+LNM)
219           GONE    ER18,430,X,X
220           LAL     OF(LCH-LCH)
221           CAL     0
222           GONE    ER20,431,X,X
223  [LL88]   LAV     ERNOD,X
224           CAL     0
225           GONE    LL86,122,X,X
226           LAA     PVNUM,D
227           AAL     OF(LNM)
228           STV     AA,X
229           LAA     PVARPT,D
230           CAV     AA,A
231           GONE    ER22,424,X,X
232           LAL     27
233           STV     KK,X
234           LAA     KK,D
235           STV     BB,X
236           LAI     BB,X
237           CAL     27
238           GONE    ER23,421,X,X
239  [LL84]   LBV     BB
240           LAM     0
241           CAL     27
242           GONE    ER24,421,X,X
243  [LL83]   LAV     ERNOB,X
244           CAL     0
245           GONE    LL81,51,X,X
246           LAL     19
247           SAL     58
248           STV     AA,X
249           LAL     1
250           SAL     40
251           CAV     AA,X
252           GONE    ER59,492,X,X
253  [LL61]   LAV     ERNOG,X
254           CAL     0
255           GONE    LL81,41,X,X
256           LAV     FFPT,X
257           STV     PVARPT,X
258           LAV     LFPT,X
259           STV     ENDPT,X
```

```
260            LAL      69
261            STV      PVNUM,X
262            MESS     '...TESTING FSTK..$'
263            LAV      PVNUM,X
264            FSTK
265            LAV      FFPT,X
266            SAL      OF(LNM)
267            STV      CC,X
268            LAI      CC,X
269            CAV      PVNUM,X
270            GONE     ER25,397,X,X
271            MESS     'OK$...TESTING BSTK..$'
272 [LL82]     LAV      PVNUM,X
273            BSTK
274            LAI      LFPT,X
275            CAV      PVNUM,X
276            GONE     ER27,403,X,X
277            LAV      LFPT,X
278            AAL      OF(LNM)
279            STV      LFPT,X
280            LAV      LFPT,X
281            CAV      ENDPT,A
282            GONE     ER28,406,X,X
283            MESS     'OK$'
284            LAV      ERNOB,X
285            CAL      0
286            GONE     LL81,10,X,X
287            LAV      LFPT,X
288            SAL      OF(LNM)
289            STV      LFPT,X
290            UNSTK    CC
291            LAV      CC,X
292            CAV      PVNUM,X
293            GONE     ER29,397,X,X
294            LAV      LFPT,X
295            CAV      ENDPT,A
296            GONE     ER30,396,X,X
297 [LL81]     LAA      CC,D
298            STV      SRCPT,X
299            LAL      1
300            STV      CC,X
301            LAL      2
302            STV      DD,X
303            LAL      3
304            STV      EE,X
305            LAA      HH,D
306            STV      DSTPT,X
307            LAL      OF(3*LNM)
308            FMOVE
309            LAV      HH,X
310            CAL      1
311            GONE     ER31,383,X,X
312            LAV      II,X
313            CAL      2
314            GONE     ER31,380,X,X
315            LAV      JJ,X
316            CAL      3
317            GONE     ER31,377,X,X
318 [LL77]     LAA      HH,D
319            STV      SRCPT,X
320            LAA      FF,D
321            STV      DSTPT,X
322            LAL      OF(3*LNM)
323            FMOVE
324            LAV      FF,X
325            CAL      1
326            GONE     ER32,370,X,X
327            LAV      GG,X
328            CAL      2
329            GONE     ER32,367,X,X
330            LAV      HH,X
```

```
331              CAL     3
332              GONE    ER32,364,X,X
333 [LL76]       LAA     FF,D
334              STV     SRCPT,X
335              LAA     GG,D
336              STV     DSTPT,X
337              LAL     OF(3*LNM)
338              BMOVE
339              LAV     GG,X
340              CAL     1
341              GONE    ER33,357,X,X
342              LAV     HH,X
343              CAL     2
344              GONE    ER33,354,X,X
345              LAV     II,X
346              CAL     3
347              GONE    ER33,351,X,X
348 [LL86]       LAV     CC,X
349              MULTL   OF(LNM-LNM)
350              CAL     0
351              GONE    ER34,349,X,X
352 [LL44]       LAL     64
353              MULTL   1
354              CAL     64
355              GONE    ER35,347,X,X
356 [LL45]       LAL     28
357              MULTL   3
358              CAL     84
359              GONE    ER36,345,X,X
360 [LL85]       LAV     ERNOD,X
361              CAL     0
362              GONE    END,389,X,X
363              LAA     DD,D
364              GTV     JJ,X
365              LAV     ERNOH,X
366              CAL     0
367              GONE    LL80,6,X,X
368              LAL     3
369              STV     CC,X
370              LBV     JJ
371              LAM     OF(2*LNM)
372              CAV     FF,X
373              GONE    ER38,335,X,X
374 [LL80]       LAL     10
375              STI     JJ,X
376              LAV     DD,X
377              CAL     10
378              GONE    ER39,332,X,X
379 [LL75]       LAL     20
380              STI     JJ,P
381              CAL     20
382              GONE    ER40,330,X,X
383 [LL74]       LAV     ERNOH,X
384              CAL     0
385              GONE    LL54,19,X,X
386              LBV     JJ
387              SBL     OF(LNM)
388              LAM     0
389              CAL     3
390              GONE    ER42,324,X,X
391 [LL52]       LAL     OF(2*LNM)
392              STV     II,X
393              LBV     JJ
394              ABV     II
395              LAM     0
396              CAV     FF,X
397              GONE    ER43,319,X,X
398 [LL53]       LAL     OF(LNM)
399              STV     II,X
400              LBV     JJ
401              SBV     II
```

```
402              LAM      0
403              CAV      CC,X
404              GONE     ER44,314,X,X
405 [LL54]       LAV      DD,X
406              CAI      JJ,X
407              GONE     ER45,313,X,X
408 [LL101]      LAA      LL34,C
409              STV      CC,X
410              GOSUB    ADVNCE,182
411              LCI      SPT,X
412 [DUMA]       CCN      NLREP
413              GONE     ER47,309,X,X
414              LAL      0
415              STV      IDLEN,X
416              LAV      FFPT,X
417              STV      DD,X
418              LCI      SPT,X
419              CFSTK
420              LCI      DD,X
421              CCN      NLREP
422              GONE     ER51,308,X,X
423              LAV      DD,X
424              AAL      OF(LCH)
425              CAV      FFPT,A
426              GONE     ER52,306,X,X
427 [LL32]       LCN      NLREP
428              CCN      NLREP
429              GONE     ER53,309,X,X
430 [LL33]       GOSUB    ADVNCE,162
431              LCI      SPT,X
432 [DUMB]       CCL      'A'
433              GONE     ER48,291,X,X
434              MESS     '...SEARCHING FOR C.,S'
435 [LL13]       GOSUB    ADVNCE,157
436              LCI      SPT,X
437              CCL      'C'
438              GONE     LL13,-4,X,X
439              MESS     'FOUND$...SEARCHING FOR ZERO,.S'
440 [LL14]       GOSUB    ADVNCE,152
441              LCI      SPT,X
442              CCL      '0'
443              GONE     LL14,-4,X,X
444              MESS     'FOUND$...SEARCHING FOR PUNCT WITH GOPC..S'
445              LAV      SPT,X
446              STV      SRCPT,X
447              LAV      JJ,X
448              STV      DSTPT,X
449              LAL      OF(LCH)
450              FMOVE
451              LCI      SPT,X
452              CCI      JJ
453              GONE     ER49,273,X,X
454 [LL16]       GOSUB    ADVNCE,138
455              LCI      SPT,X
456              GOPC     LL15,1,X,X
457              GO       LL16,-4,X,X
458 [LL15]       MESS     'FOUND$...SEARCHING FOR NLREP..S'
459 [LL26]       GOSUB    ADVNCE,133
460              LCI      SPT,X
461              CCN      NLREP
462              GONE     LL26,-4,X,X
463              MESS     'FOUND$'
464              LAV      ERNOH,X
465              CAL      0
466              GONE     LL60,4,X,X
467              LBV      JJ
468              LCM      0
469              CCL      '0'
470              GONE     ER50,258,X,X
471 [LL60]       LAA      NUMS,C
472              STV      SPT,X
```

```
473            LCI      SPT,X
474            GOND     GONDER,11,X,X
475            CAL      0
476            GONE     GONDER,8,X,X
477            LBV      SPT
478            LCM      OF(9*LCH)
479            GOND     GONDER,6,X,X
480            CAL      9
481            GONE     GONDER,3,X,X
482            LBV      SPT
483            LCM      OF(10*LCH)
484            GOND     TSCON,1,X,X
485 [GONDER]   MESS     '***GOND OR STR ERRORS'
486            NB       'NOW TEST CON'
487 [TSCON]    LAV      ERNOG,X
488            CAL      0
489            GONE     TSAL,5,X,X
490            LAA      LL35,C
491            STV      CC,X
492            LAI      CC,X
493            CAL      10
494            GONE     ER54,247,X,X
495 [TSAL]     LAA      TRCH,C
496            AAL      OF(LCH)
497            ALIGN
498            STV      IDPT,X
499            LAI      IDPT,X
500            AAL      6
501            CAL      0
502            GONE     ER55,241,X,X
503            LAV      IDPT,X
504            ALIGN
505            CAV      IDPT,A
506            GONE     ER55,237,X,X
507 [LL37]     LAA      LL34,C
508            STV      IDPT,X
509            LAL      0
510            STV      JJ,X
511 [LL41]     LCI      IDPT,X
512            GOSUB    MDERCH,X
513            LAV      JJ,X
514            AAL      OF(LCH)
515            STV      JJ,X
516            LAV      IDPT,X
517            AAL      OF(LCH)
518            STV      IDPT,X
519            LAV      JJ,X
520            CAV      IDLEN,X
521            GONE     LL41,-11,X,X
522            MESS     'SSHOULD BE THE SAME ASSABCDEFGHIJKLMNOPQRSTUVWX'
523            MESS     'YZ 0123456789S.,;:()*/-*= TAB AND QUOTE SIGNS'
524            GOSUB    MDQUIT,X
525
526
527            SUBR     SR1,X,1
528            MESS     '0'
529            EXIT     1,SR1
530            MESS     '***POSSIBLY EXIT NOT TRANSFERRING CONTROLS'
531            GO       LL96,-388,X,X
532
533
534            SUBR     SR2,X,4
535            LAV      BB,X
536            CAL      64
537            GONE     SS1,1,X,X
538            EXIT     2,SR2
539 [SS1]      LAV      BB,X
540            CAL      0
541            GONE     SS2,1,X,X
542            EXIT     3,SR2
543 [SS2]      LAV      BB,X
```

```
544              CAL      8
545              GONE     SS3,1,X,X
546              EXIT     4,SR2
547 [SS3]        EXIT     1,SR2
548              MESS     '+++POSSIBLY EXIT NOT TRANSFERRING CONTROLS'
549              GO       LL21,-398,X,X
550
551
552              SUBR     SR3,PARNM,1
553              STV      AA,X
554              LAV      AA,X
555              CAL      65
556              GONE     ER100,5,X,X
557              LAV      PARNM,X
558              CAL      65
559              GONE     ER101,5,X,X
560              EXIT     1,SR3
561              GO       LL94,-382,X,X
562 [ER100]      MESS     '+++A CLOBBERED WHEN ENTERING SUBROUTINES'
563              EXIT     1,SR3
564              GO       LL94,-385,X,X
565 [ER101]      MESS     '+++A NOT STORED IN PARNM ON SR ENTRYS'
566              EXIT     1,SR3
567              GO       LL94,-388,X,X
568
569
570              SUBR     SRNEST,X,1
571              LAL      2
572              STV      IDLEN,X
573              EXIT     1,SRNEST
574
575
576              SUBR     SR4,PARNM,1
577              CAL      0
578              GONE     ER1,36,E,X
579              BUMP     PARNM,2
580              GOSUB    SRNEST,-9
581              LAV      PARNM,X
582              CAV      IDLEN,X
583              GOEQ     S4EX,1,X,X
584              MESS     '+++ERROR IN NESTED SUBROUTINE CALLS'
585 [S4EX]       EXIT     1,SR4
586
587
588              SUBR     BUMPFF,PARNM,1
589              CAL      0
590              GOEQ     ER1,26,E,X
591              LAV      FFPT,X
592              AAL      OF(LNM)
593              STV      FFPT,X
594              LAV      FFPT,X
595              CAV      LFPT,A
596              GOGE     ERLSO,167,E,X
597              EXIT     1,BUMPFF
598
599
600              SUBR     DECLF,PARNM,1
601              LAV      LFPT,X
602              SAL      OF(LNM)
603              STV      LFPT,X
604              LAV      FFPT,X
605              CAV      LFPT,A
606              GOGE     ERLSO,159,E,X
607              EXIT     1,DECLF
608
609
610              SUBR     ADVNCE,X,1
611              LAV      CC,X
612              STV      SPT,X
613              LAV      CC,X
614              AAL      OF(LCH)
```

```
615                 STV         CC,X
616                 LAV         IDLEN,X
617                 AAL         OF(LCH)
618                 STV         IDLEN,X
619                 EXIT        1,ADVNCE
620
621
622
623 [LL27]          GO          LL28,-543,X,X
624
625 [ER1]           MESS        '*+*ERROR IN LAL OR CAL WITH ZERO ARG OR GONES'
626                 GO          END,146,X,X
627 [ER2]           MESS        '*+*ERROR IN STV V,X OR LAVS'
628                 GO          END,144,X,X
629 [ER3]           MESS        '*+*ERROR IN STV V,P   A NOT PRESERVEDS'
630                 GO          LL17,-532,X,X
631 [ER4]           MESS        '*+*ERROR IN STV V,P   (NOT STORING)S'
632                 GO          LL18,-531,X,X
633 [ER5]           MESS        '*+*ERROR IN LAL OR CAL WITH NON=ZERO ARGS'
634                 GO          END,138,X,X
635 [ER6]           MESS        '*+*ERROR IN AAL WITH ZERO ARGS'
636                 GO          LL19,-526,X,X
637 [ER7]           MESS        '*+*CAV ERRORS'
638                 LAL         4
639                 STV         ERNOD,X
640                 GO          LL93,-519,X,X
641 [ER8]           MESS        '*+*AAV ERRORS'
642                 GO          LL92,-516,X,X
643 [ER9]           MESS        '*+*SAL ERRORS'
644                 LAL         2
645                 STV         ERNOB,X
646                 GO          LL91,-516,X,X
647 [ER10]          MESS        '*+*SAV ERRORS'
648                 GO          LL20,-514,X,X
649 [ER11]          MESS        '*+*EXIT2 ERRORS'
650                 GO          LL21,-483,X,X
651 [ER56]          MESS        '*+*EXIT3 ERRORS'
652                 GO          LL56,-477,X,X
653 [ER57]          MESS        '*+*EXIT4 ERRORS'
654                 GO          LL57,-472,X,X
655 [ER12]          MESS        '*+*ANDV ERRORS'
656                 GO          LL22,-454,X,X
657 [ER26]          MESS        '*+*VALUE OF V CLOBBERED IN ANDVS'
658                 GO          LL22,-456,X,X
659 [ER13]          MESS        '*+*ANDL ERRORS'
660                 GO          LL24,-454,X,X
661 [ER15]          MESS        '*+*CLEAR ERRORS'
662                 LAL         0
663                 STV         AA,X
664                 GO          LL25,-454,X,X
665 [ER16]          MESS        '*+*BUMP OR IDENT  ERRORS'
666                 GO          LL46,-451,X,X
667 [ER17]          MESS        '*+*AAL ERRORS'
668                 LAL         4
669                 STV         ERNOD,X
670                 GO          LL90,-441,X,X
671 [ER18]          MESS        '*+*OF ERROR * OR +S'
672                 GO          END,100,X,X
673 [ER19]          MESS        '*+*OF ERROR ADDITIONS'
674                 GO          END,98,X,X
675 [ER20]          MESS        '*+*OF ERROR SUBTRACTIONS'
676                 GO          END,96,X,X
677 [ER22]          MESS        '*+*LAA L,D ERROR OR VALUE OF LNM INCORRECTS'
678                 LAL         4
679                 STV         ERNOD,X
680                 GO          LL86,-312,X,X
681 [ER23]          MESS        '*+*LAI ERRORS'
682                 LAL         7
683                 STV         ERNOG,X
684                 GO          LL84,-425,X,X
685 [ER24]          MESS        '*+*LBV OR LAM 0 ERRORS'
```

```
686                LAL        8
687                STV        ERNOH,X
688                GO         LL83,-425,X,X
689  [ER25]        MESS       '+++FSTK ERROR
690                LAV        PVARPT,X
691                AAL        OF(LNM)
692                CAV        FFPT,A
693                GONE       LL79,2,X,X
694                MESS       'BUT FFPT BUMPED CORRECTLY$'
695                GO         LL82,-403,X,X
696  [LL79]        MESS       'FFPT INCORRECT$'
697                LAV        PVARPT,X
698                AAL        OF(LNM)
699                STV        FFPT,X
700                GO         LL82,-408,X,X
701  [ER27]        MESS       '+++BSTK ERROR
702                LAV        LFPT,X
703                AAL        OF(LNM)
704                CAV        ENDPT,A
705                GONE       LL78,2,X,X
706                MESS       'BUT LFPT CORRECT$'
707                GO         LL81,-390,X,X
708  [LL78]        MESS       'LFPT INCORRECT$'
709                GO         LL81,-392,X,X
710  [ER28]        MESS       '+++LFPT NOT DEBUMPED CORRECTLY IN BSTK$'
711                GO         LL81,-394,X,X
712  [ER29]        MESS       '+++UNSTK ERROR$'
713                GO         LL81,-396,X,X
714  [ER39]        MESS       '+++LFPT NOT BUMPED CORRECTLY IN UNSTK$'
715                GO         LL81,-398,X,X
716  [ER31]        MESS       '+++FMOVE ERROR(NON-OVERLAPPING CASE)$'
717                GO         LL77,-379,X,X
718  [ER32]        MESS       '+++FMOVE ERROR(OVERLAPPING CASE)$'
719                GO         LL76,-365,X,X
720  [ER33]        MESS       '+++BMOVE ERROR$'
721                GO         LL86,-353,X,X
722  [ER34]        MESS       '+++MULTL ERROR WITH ZERO ARG$'
723                GO         LL44,-351,X,X
724  [ER35]        MESS       '+++MULTL ERROR WITH ONE AS ARG$'
725                GO         LL45,-349,X,X
726  [ER36]        MESS       '+++MULTL ERROR WITH 3 AS ARG$'
727                GO         LL85,-347,X,X
728  [ER37]        MESS       '+++GOADD ERROR$'
729                GO         LL10,-505,X,X
730  [ER38]        MESS       '+++LAM ERROR$'
731                GO         LL80,-337,X,X
732  [ER39]        MESS       '+++STI ERROR$'
733                GO         LL75,-334,X,X
734  [ER40]        MESS       '+++A NOT PRESERVED IN STI V,P$'
735                GO         LL74,-332,X,X
736  [ER42]        MESS       '+++SBL ERROR$'
737                GO         LL52,-326,X,X
738  [ER43]        MESS       '+++ABV ERROR$'
739                GO         LL53,-321,X,X
740  [ER44]        MESS       '+++SBV ERROR$'
741                GO         LL54,-316,X,X
742  [ER45]        MESS       '+++CAI ERROR$'
743                GO         LL101,-315,X,X
744  [ER47]        MESS       '+++NCH,LCI OR CCN NLREP ERROR$'
745                GO         END,27,X,X
746  [ER48]        MESS       '+++CCL A ERROR$'
747                GO         END,25,X,X
748  [ER49]        MESS       '+++CCI ERROR$'
749                GO         LL16,-275,X,X
750  [ER50]        MESS       '+++LCM ERROR$'
751                GO         LL60,-260,X,X
752  [ER51]        MESS       '+++CFSTK ERROR$'
753                GO         LL32,-306,X,X
754  [ER52]        MESS       '+++FFPT NOT BUMPED CORRECTLY IN CFSTK, POSSIBLY'
755                MESS       ' LCH VALUE IS WRONG$'
756                LAV        CC,X
```

```
757              AAL        OF(LCH)
758              STV        FFPT,X
759              GO         LL32,-312,X,X
760 [ER53]       MESS       '+++LCN NLREP ERROR$'
761              GO         LL33,-311,X,X
762 [ER54]       MESS       '+++CON ERROR$'
763              GO         TSAL,-249,X,X
764 [ER55]       MESS       '+++ALIGNMENT ERROR$'
765              GO         LL37,-239,X,X
766 [ER59]       MESS       '+++ERROR IN MOVING OR COMPARING'
767              MESS       ' NEGATIVE INTEGERS$'
768              GO         LL61,-495,X,X
769              LCI        SPT,X
770              CCL        '<'
771              GONE       LL29,-685,X,X
772 [ERLSO]      MESS       '+++STACK OVERFLOW$'
773 [END]        MESS       '...CORRECT ABOVE ERROR(S) AND RUN AGAIN$'
774              GOSUB      MDQUIT,X
775              PRGEN
776
777
```

Chapter 3.7

MD-logic and LOWL Extensions
for ALGEBRA

This chapter describes the MD-logic of ALGEBRA and the LOWL extensions it needs. Although not described here, all the other pieces of software encoded in LOWL have their own MD-logic and LOWL extensions, just as ALGEBRA has.

I/O requirements

ALGEBRA logically requires three output streams and one input stream. The output streams are the message and results streams, as described in Chapter 3.3, and the *questions stream*, which is used to output all the questions that ALGEBRA asks of its user (e.g. " VALUES = "). In a simple conversational implementation all four I/O streams may correspond to the same device, an on-line console. However, provision may be made for the results stream, which is used for output produced by the TABLE and TRY statements, to go to a line-printer or perhaps to backing storage.

In a non-conversational environment the questions stream requires special treatment as it is not possible to communicate directly with the user. One possible approach is to suppress all questions. This is trivial to implement. A second approach is to require the input lines to contain both the question and the answer. Thus an input line, a card say, might read

VALUES = TRUE FALSE

The question part can be used as an error check to prevent the input getting out of phase with what ALGEBRA expects. This second approach requires significant extra work for the implementor, which in detail is as follows. Questions should be sent to an intermediate buffer, and, when an input line is read, the following action would be taken:

(a) If the questions buffer is empty go to step (e).

(b) Check the questions buffer character-by-character against the input line, ignoring spaces. If there is a mis-match before the end of the questions buffer is reached, output an error message and stop.
(c) Clear the questions buffer.
(d) Update pointers, etc., so that the question part is not treated as part of the input line.
(e) Proceed with the input in the normal way.

Breaks

If ALGEBRA is to run in a conversational environment, it is desirable to cater for 'breaks', i.e. cases where the user stops ALGEBRA by pressing some special key. The user may, for example, wish to break ALGEBRA when it is outputting a very large table so that he can make some change. The MI-logic has been designed so that it can accept such breaks at any time without losing any information (i.e. the names of values and the definitions of operators).

If an implementor decides to cater for breaks it is suggested he writes MD-logic code to perform the following action at each break:

```
MESS      '$***BREAK$'
LAV       INFFPT,X
CAL       0
GONE      NEXTLN, ...   (label in MI-logic)
GOSUB     MDQUIT,X
```

This means abandon the run if no values have yet been defined, otherwise go to the code in the MI-logic which resumes operation by reading the next line of input.

Extensions to LOWL

ALGEBRA requires two extra statements in addition to the kernel of LOWL. These are the RMESS and QMESS statements, which are identical in form to the MESS statement except that the string is output, respectively, on the results and questions streams. Examples are

```
QMESS    'VALUES='
RMESS    'IS A CONTINGENCY$'
```

ALGEBRA is actually one of the smallest pieces of software coded in LOWL. As a result of this it makes relatively small demands on the kernel of LOWL, and a few statements of the kernel (e.g. the CON statement) are not used at all. The extra effort of implementing these statements in order to satisfy LOWLTEST is a penalty that the implementor of ALGEBRA pays for the generality of LOWL.

The form of the MD-logic

Immediately on being entered, ALGEBRA should zeroize the variable INFFPT. This is done to tell the routine that caters for breaks, if it exists, that no values have yet been defined. Breaks can be accepted at any time after INFFPT has been cleared. The common initialization code, as given in the LOWL manual, should then be performed. The stack area need not be large—300 words should be adequate unless use with complicated multi-valued logics is envisaged. However, at least eighty words should be allocated.

In addition to this, the MD-logic of ALGEBRA requires the MDQUIT subroutine, as described in Chapter 3.3, and the subroutines described below.

The MDERCH, MDRCH, MDQCH subroutines

The MDERCH, MDRCH, MDQCH subroutines output the character in C on the message, results and questions stream, respectively. Each has a single exit.

The MDLINE subroutine

MDLINE is a subroutine with two exits. It reads lines of input. If input is exhausted it uses exit 1. Otherwise it reads a line of input into a buffer, sets IBFPT to point at the first character of the buffer and uses exit 2. (IBFPT should be reset on each call of MDLINE, since the MI-logic changes it.) The text in the buffer should be terminated with a newline character (as represented by NLREP). Thus, for example, a null input line would cause the buffer to contain simply a single newline character.

MDLINE is used both for answers to questions and for ordinary input. In the case of questions it is desirable for the answer to be on the same line as the question. Hence when a question is output (using QMESS and/or MDQCH) it is not terminated with a newline.

If the implementor wishes to produce a gold-plated version of ALGEBRA, he should cater for switches of input stream. Users may wish to input some definitions from a non-conversational device, for example from backing storage or from a paper-tape reader, and then to use these at an on-line console. This has implications on the coding of MDLINE and perhaps also of the initialization code.

Documentation

When ALGEBRA is working, a Users' Manual needs to be written for it. This manual should contain a specification of ALGEBRA itself—this can, if desired be an almost identical copy of the material in Chapter 3.2—together with a description of features peculiar to the implementation. These should include:

(a) how a run of ALGEBRA is started and stopped,
(b) what I/O options are available and how they can be set,
(c) the treatment of breaks.

How ALGEBRA works

Ideally an implementor should not need to make the effort of finding out how ALGEBRA works. Occasionally, however, the curing of an intractable bug may require such knowledge, so this section is provided for implementors who have such a misfortune.

The most important data structure is the *LID* (Length and *ID*entifier), which represents a symbol. A LID consists of a numerical field giving the length of the symbol, followed by the symbol itself. For example the LOWL statements to define the LID for the symbol PIG would be

```
CON   OF(3*LCH)
STR   'PIG'
```

Actually all ALGEBRA symbols are created dynamically at run time, so none is defined in LOWL. In some situations a list of LIDs is stored end to end immediately following one another. The length of one LID can be used to calculate the position of the next. A length field of zero is used to terminate a list.

In particular such a list is used to store the value names defined by the user at the start of an ALGEBRA session. Thus if he supplied the symbols TRUE and F in reply to the 'VALUES =' question, these would be stored internally as the equivalent of the LOWL statements

```
CON   OF(4*LCH)
STR   'TRUE'
CON   OF(LCH)
STR   'F'
CON   0
```

Throughout the logic, values are represented not by the names supplied by the user but by their index in the internal list. The first name has the index zero, the second index one, and so on. Thus we will use the terminology Value (0), Value (1), etc. to stand for the value names supplied by the user. Similarly, the names of variables used in an expression are stored internally as a LID list, and we will speak of them as Variable (0), Variable (1), etc.

During execution, ALGEBRA creates a dictionary on the forwards stack, which consists of LIDs and other information relating to values, operators and variables. When it is supplied an expression as the argument to a TABLE or TRY statement it first compiles the expression into a Reverse Polish form. This is built up on the backwards stack. Figure 3.7A shows the detailed form of the stacks and the pointers which reference them.

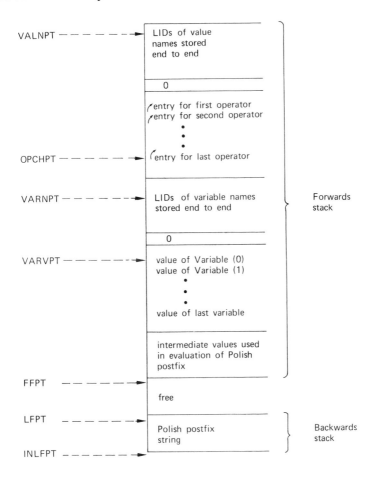

Fig. 3.7A. Use of stacks by ALGEBRA

At the end of each statement the backwards stack is completely cleared and the forwards stack is cleared down to where VARNPT points. The formats of the operator entries and of the Reverse Polish string are described in detail in subsequent sections. The area pointed at by VARVPT is used during expression evaluation. At that stage it is necessary to loop through all possible values of each of the variables. Each value is, as usual, represented by the index of the corresponding symbol in the list of names. The ith number beyond VARVPT indicates the value of Variable (i).

In addition to the stacks shown, ALGEBRA uses a separate stack, called TEMPSTACK, during the creation of the Polish string. The storage for this stack is taken off the main stack during initialization.

Operator entries

The operator entries are chained together in a linked list (as distinct from the end-to-end list used for value and variable names) in the way shown in Figure 3.7A. The chain works backwards so that if an operator is redefined the new definition comes before the old on the chain. Each operator entry consists of the following sequence of items:

(a) pointer to next operator entry on the chain,
(b) LID of operator,
(c) 0 if binary, 1 if unary,
(d) precedence,
(e) table of values.

If there are N values, then the table of values contains N entries in the case of a unary operator and $N \times N$ entries for a binary operator. In the unary case the ith position in the table (counting the first position as 0) gives the index of the value that results from applying the operator to Value (i). For example if there are two values and the operator NEG is such that

$$\text{NEG Value (0)} = \text{Value (1)}$$
$$\text{NEG Value (1)} = \text{Value (0)}$$

then the table for NEG will consist of the two entries 1, 0.

In the binary case the $(i \times N + j)$th position in the table gives the index of the value that results from applying the operator with Value (i) on the left and Value (j) on the right. For example if there are two values and the operator AND is defined such that

$$\text{Value (0) AND Value (0)} = \text{Value (0)}$$
$$\text{Value (0) AND Value (1)} = \text{Value (0)}$$
$$\text{Value (1) AND Value (0)} = \text{Value (0)}$$
$$\text{Value (1) AND Value (1)} = \text{Value (1)}$$

then the table for AND will consist of the four values 0, 0, 0, 1.

The Reverse Polish string

Each item in the Polish string consists of a pair of numbers. The first (i.e. the one with the *higher* stack address, since the Polish string lies on the backwards stack) indicates the type of the item. Type zero means a variable, type one means a value and type two means an operator. The value three is used as an end marker for the Polish string. In the case of a variable or value the type field is followed by the index of the item in the list of corresponding names. In the case of an operator the type field is followed by a stack pointer to field (c) of the operator entry as given in the previous section.

For example the Polish string for the expression

Value (1) AND Variable (0)

would be

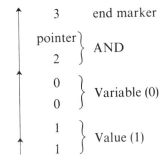

Variable names

The following is a list of those variables in the logic of ALGEBRA that have fixed meanings. The remaining variables serve miscellaneous temporary roles. An asterisk against a name means that it appears in Figure 3.7A.

Name	Meaning
IDPT	points at first character of current symbol
IDLEN	length of current symbol
ENDSPT	points at end of current symbol
FFPT*	points at first free of forwards stack
INFFPT	used to reset FFPT
VALNPT*	points at LID of Value (0)
VARNPT*	points at LID of Variable (0); 0 if none exists
OPCHPT*	head of chain of operator entries
VARVPT*	points at vector of variable values
LFPT*	current top of backwards stack
INLFPT*	points beyond end of backwards stack
TSFFPT	points at first free of TEMPSTACK
TSTKPT	points at start of TEMPSTACK
TSMXPT	points beyond end of TEMPSTACK
IBFPT	input buffer pointer

ISTABL	1 if TABLE statement, 0 if TRY
ISUNRY	1 if unary operator, 0 if binary
VALCT	number of values
VARCT	number of variables

Chapter 3.8

Listing of ALGEBRA

A listing of ALGEBRA in LOWL follows. It is in the same format as the listing of LOWLTEST in Chapter 3.6.

```
 1
 2         PRGST      'ALGEBRA'
 3         NB         'ALGEBRA PROGRAM   APR 9 1973'
 4
 5
 6         NB         'VARIABLES DESCRIBING THE CURRENT SYMBOL'
 7         NB         'SET BY GETSYM ROUTINE'
 8
 9         DCL        IDPT
10         DCL        IDLEN
11         DCL        ENDSPT
12
13         NB         'MISCELLANEOUS TEMPORARIES'
14
15         DCL        PARNM
16         DCL        TEMPT
17         DCL        DICTPT
18         DCL        VALUE
19         DCL        NUOPPT
20         DCL        TEMP
21         DCL        TEM1PT
22         DCL        TEM2PT
23         DCL        TYPE
24         DCL        COUNT
25
26         NB         'POINTERS TO FSTACK, BSTACK AND TEMPSTACK'
27
28         DCL        FFPT
29         DCL        INFFPT
30         DCL        VALNPT
31         DCL        VARNPT
32         DCL        OPCHPT
33         DCL        VARVPT
34         DCL        LFPT
35         DCL        INLFPT
36         DCL        TSFFPT
37         DCL        TSTKPT
38         DCL        TSMXPT
39
40         NB         'MISCELLANEOUS'
41
42         DCL        IBFPT
43         DCL        ISTABL
44         DCL        ISUNRY
45         DCL        VALCT
46         DCL        VARCT
```

```
 47              DCL       SRCPT
 48              DCL       DSTPT
 49              DCL       LOTEMP
 50
 51
 52
 53
 54
 55
 56
 57              NB        'FIRST ASK FOR VALUES TO BE DEFINED'
 58
 59 [BEGIN]      LAL       0
 60              STV       VARNPT,P
 61              STV       OPCHPT,P
 62              STV       INFFPT,X
 63              LAV       FFPT,X
 64              STV       TSTKPT,P
 65              AAL       OF(30*LNM)
 66              STV       ISMXPT,P
 67              STV       VALNPT,P
 68              STV       FFPT,P
 69              CAV       LFPT,A
 70              GOGE      ERLSO,617,X,X
 71 [ASKVAL]     LAV       VALNPT,X
 72              STV       FFPT,X
 73              LAL       0
 74              ISTK
 75              CLEAR     VALCT
 76              QMESS     'VALUES='
 77              GOSUB     MDLINE,X
 78              GO        GIVEUP,606,X,C
 79 [VALOOP]     GOSUB     TSTSYM,556
 80              GO        ENVAL,15,X,C
 81              GO        ERLCLA,604,X,C
 82              GO        OK1,1,X,C
 83              GO        ERLCLA,602,X,X
 84 [OK1]        GOSUB     TESTCH,530
 85              GO        OK2,2,X,C
 86              GO        OK2,1,X,C
 87              GO        ERLILL,602,X,X
 88 [OK2]        LAV       FFPT,X
 89              SAL       OF(LNM)
 90              GTV       FFPT,X
 91              GOSUB     STKSYM,506
 92              LAL       0
 93              FSTK
 94              RUMP      VALCT,1
 95              GU        VALOOP,-17,X,X
 96
 97              NB        'END OF LIST OF VALUES'
 98
 99 [ENVAL]      LAV       VALCT,X
100              CAL       0
101              GOEU      ERLINC,595,X,X
102              LAV       FFPT,X
103              STV       INFFPT,X
104              LAV       LFPT,X
105              GTV       INLFPT,X
106
107
108
109              NB        'MAIN SCANNING ROUTINE'
110              NB        'READS A LINE AND THEN GOES TO ...'
111              NB        '...ROUTINE TO ANALYSE STATEMENT'
112
113 [NEXTLN]     GOSUB     MDLINE,X
114              GO        GIVEUP,580,X,C
115              GOSUB     GETSYM,421
116              GU        NEXTLN,-4,X,C
117              CLEAR     VARNPT
```

```
118              LAV        INFFPT,X
119              STV        FFPT,X
120              LAV        INLFPT,X
121              STV        LFPT,X
122              CLEAR      ISTABL
123              LCI        IDPT,X
124              CCL        'O'
125              GUNE       GL1,4,X,X
126              LBV        IDPT
127              LCM        OF(LCH)
128              CCL        'P'
129              GUEQ       OP,13,X,X
130  [GL1]       LCI        IDPT,X
131              CCL        'T'
132              GUNE       ERLSTA,569,X,X
133              BUMP       IDPT,OF(LCH)
134              LCI        IDPT,X
135              CCL        'R'
136              GUEQ       TABTRY,116,X,X
137              LAL        1
138              STV        ISTABL,X
139              LCI        IDPT,X
140              CCL        'A'
141              GUEQ       TABTRY,111,X,X
142              GU         ERLSTA,559,X,X
143
144
145
146              NB         'PROCESSING OF OPERATOR STATEMENT'
147
148  [OP]        GOSUB      TSTSYM,502
149              GO         ERLINC,559,X,C
150              GO         ERLCLA,550,X,C
151              GO         OPOK,3,X,C
152              LAV        TYPE,X
153              LAL        2
154              GUGE       ERLCLA,546,X,X
155  [OPOK]      GOSUB      CHKEND,342
156              GU         ERLILL,548,X,C
157              LAV        FFPT,X
158              STV        NUOPPT,X
159              LAV        OPCHPT,X
160              FSTK
161              GOSUB      STKSYM,451
162  [FNUNB]     CLEAR      ISUNRY
163              QMESS      'UNARY OR BINARY='
164              GOSUB      MDLINE,X
165              GU         GIVEUP,534,X,C
166              GOSUB      GETSYM,375
167              GU         EHUNB,18,X,C
168              GOSUB      CHKEND,329
169              GU         EHUNB,16,X,C
170              LCI        IDPT,X
171              CCL        'R'
172              GUNE       GL2,4,X,X
173              LBV        IDPT
174              LCM        OF(LCH)
175              CCL        'I'
176              GUEQ       STKUNB,11,X,X
177  [GL2]       LAL        1
178              STV        ISUNRY,X
179              LCI        IDPT,X
180              CCL        'U'
181              GUNE       EHUNB,4,X,X
182              LBV        IDPT
183              LCM        OF(LCH)
184              CCL        'N'
185              GUEQ       STKUNB,2,X,X
186  [EHUNB]     MESS       'EHS'
187              GO         FNUNB,-26,X,X
188
```

```
189              NB          'STACK UNARY OR BINARY MARKER AND FIND PRECEDENCE'
190
191 [STKUNB]     LAV         ISUNRY,X
192              FSTK
193 [FNPREC]     QMESS       'PRECEDENCE='
194              GOSUB       MDLINE,X
195              GO          GIVEUP,507,X,C
196              GOSUB       GETSYM,348
197              GO          EHPREC,7,X,C
198              GOSUB       LOGNUM,538
199              GO          EHPREC,5,X,C
200              GOSUB       CHKEND,300
201              GO          EHPREC,3,X,C
202              LAV         VALUE,X
203              FSTK
204              GO          GTVALS,2,X,X
205 [EHPREC]     MESS        'EHS'
206              GO          FNPREC,-14,X,X
207
208              NB          'NOW GO THROUGH ALL POSSIBLE VALUE COMBINATIONS'
209
210 [GTVALS]     LAV         VALNPT,X
211              STV         TEM2PT,P
212              STV         TEM1PT,X
213 [REASK]      LAV         ISUNRY,X
214              CAL         0
215              GONE        UNOPT,3,X,X
216              LAV         TEM1PT,X
217              GOSUB       LOQLID,575
218              QMESS       ' '
219 [UNOPT]      LAV         NUOPPT,X
220              AAL         OF(LNM)
221              GOSUB       LOQLID,571
222              QMESS       ' '
223              LAV         TEM2PT,X
224              GOSUB       LOQLID,568
225              QMESS       ' '
226              GOSUB       MDLINE,X
227              GO          GIVEUP,478,X,C
228              GOSUB       TSTSYM,428
229              GO          EHVAL,2,X,C
230              GO          OKVAL,3,X,C
231              GO          EHVAL,0,X,C
232 [EHVAL]      MESS        'EHS'
233              GO          REASK,-21,X,X
234
235 [OKVAL]      GOSUB       CHKEND,269
236              GO          EHVAL,-4,X,C
237              LAV         VALUE,X
238              FSTK
239              LAI         TEM2PT,X
240              AAV         TEM2PT
241              AAL         OF(LNM)
242              ALIGN
243              STV         TEM2PT,X
244              LAI         TEM2PT,X
245              GAL         0
246              GONE        REASK,-33,X,X
247              LAV         ISUNRY,X
248              CAL         0
249              GONE        ENDVLS,10,X,X
250              LAV         VALNPT,X
251              STV         TEM2PT,X
252              LAI         TEM1PT,X
253              AAV         TEM1PT
254              AAL         OF(LNM)
255              ALIGN
256              STV         TEM1PT,X
257              LAI         TEM1PT,X
258              CAL         0
259              GONE        REASK,-46,X,X
```

```
260
261             NB          'SUCCESSFUL DEFINITION. NOW ADD OPERATOR TO CHAIN'
262
263 [ENDVLS]    LAV         FFPT,X
264             STV         INFFPT,X
265             LAV         NUOPPT,X
266             STV         OPCHPT,X
267             GU          NEXTLN,-140,X,X
268
269
270
271             NB          'PROCESSING OF TABLE AND TRY STATEMENTS'
272             NB          'FIRST CONVERT EXPRESSION TO POLISH POSTFIX'
273             NB          'ALL VARIABLE NAMES ARE STACKED END TO END'
274             NB          'POLISH STRING IS BUILT UP ON BSTACK'
275
276 [TABTRY]    LAV         ISTKPT,X
277             STV         TSFFPT,X
278             LAV         FFPT,X
279             STV         VARUPT,X
280             LAL         0
281             ISTK
282             CLEAR       VARCT
283
284
285             NB          'STATE 1 -- EXPECTING OPERAND'
286
287 [OPRAND]    GOSUB       TSTSYM,385
288             GU          ERLINC,442,X,C
289             GU          VAL,21,X,C
290             GU          NEW,6,X,C
291             GUADD       TYPE
292             GU          ERLNB,446,X,T
293             GO          STKOP,23,X,T
294             GU          LPAR,21,X,T
295             GU          ERLPAR,439,X,T
296             GU          VAR,9,X,T
297
298             NB          'NEW VARIABLE'
299
300 [NEW]       LAV         VARCT,X
301             STV         VALUE,X
302             BUMP        VARCT,1
303             LAV         FFPT,X
304             SAL         OF(LNM)
305             STV         FFPT,X
306             GOSUB       STKSYM,331
307             LAL         0
308             ISTK
309
310             NB          'EXISTING VARIABLE -- ADD TO POLISH STRING'
311
312 [VAR]       LAL         0
313             BSTK
314             LAV         VALUE,X
315             BSTK
316             GU          OPRATE,13,X,X
317
318             NB          'VALUE -- ADD TO POLISH STRING'
319
320 [VAL]       LAL         1
321             BSTK
322             LAV         VALUE,X
323             BSTK
324             GU          OPRATE,8,X,X
325
326             NB          'LEFT PARENTHESIS -- ADD MARKER TO TEMPSTACK'
327
328 [LPAR]      CLEAR       DICTPT
329
330             NB          'UNARY OPERATOR -- ADD TO TEMPSTACK'
```

```
331
332 [STKOP]    LAV        DICTPT,X
333            STI        TSFFPT,X
334            BUMP       TSFFPT,OF(LNM)
335            LAV        TSFFPT,X
336            CAV        TSMXPT,A
337            GOGE       ERLCMP,414,X,X
338            GO         OPRAND,-37,X,X
339
340
341            NB         'STATE 2 -- EXPECTING OPERATOR'
342
343 [OPRATE]   GOSUB      TSTSYM,348
344            GO         ENDST,27,X,C
345            GO         ERLVLO,418,X,C
346            GO         ERLVRO,415,X,C
347            GOADD      TYPE
348            GO         BINOP,8,X,T
349            GO         ERLWU,410,X,T
350            GO         ERLPAR,403,X,T
351            GO         RPAR,1,X,T
352            GO         ERLVRO,409,X,T
353
354            NB         'RIGHT PAREN -- MOVE OPERATORS ...'
355            NB         '...FROM TEMPSTACK TO POLISH STRING'
356
357 [RPAR]     GOSUB      GETTS,254
358            GO         ERLPAR,399,X,C
359            GO         OPRATE,-13,X,C
360            GO         RPAR,-4,X,X
361
362            NB         'BINARY OPERATOR -- COMPARE PRECEDENCE WITH ...'
363            NB         '...TOP OF TEMPSTACK UNTIL GREATER'
364
365 [BINOP]    GOSUB      GETTS,250
366            GO         STKOP,-23,X,C
367            GO         BIN1,10,X,C
368            LAI        TSFFPT,X
369            STV        TEM1PT,X
370            LBV        TEM1PT
371            LAM        OF(LNM)
372            AIV        LOTEMP,X
373            LBV        DICTPT
374            LAM        OF(LNM)
375            CAV        LOTEMP,X
376            GOLE       BINOP,-12,X,X
377
378            NB         'UNDO PREVIOUS GETTS'
379            NB         'ADD NEW OPERATOR TO TEMPSTACK'
380
381            BUMP       LFPT,OF(LNM+LNM)
382 [BIN1]     BUMP       TSFFPT,OF(LNM)
383            GO         STKOP,-36,X,X
384
385            NB         'END OF STATEMENT -- CLEAR TEMPSTACK'
386
387 [ENDST]    GOSUB      GETTS,235
388            GO         FIN,2,X,C
389            GO         ERLPAR,379,X,C
390            GO         ENDST,-4,X,X
391
392            NB         'ADD END MARKER TO POLISH STRING'
393
394 [FIN]      LAL        3
395            PSTK
396
397            NB         'NOW EVALUATE POLISH STRING'
398            NB         'CYCLE THROUGH ALL POSSIBLE VALUES OF VARIABLES'
399            NB         'USE TOP OF FSTACK TO STORE CURRENT SET OF VALUES'
400            NB         'FIRST SET ALL TO ZERO'
401
```

```
402              LAV      FFPT,X
403              STV      VARVPT,X
404              CLEAR    COUNT
405 [STLOOP]     LAV      COUNT,X
406              CAV      VARCT,X
407              GOEQ     STL1,4,X,X
408              LAL      0
409              FSTK
410              BUMP     COUNT,1
411              CO       STLOOP,-7,X,X
412
413              NB       'INITIALIZE VALUE TO -1 ( MEANING UNDEFINED)'
414
415 [STL1]       LAL      0
416              SAL      1
417              STV      VALUE,X
418              LAV      ISTABL,X
419              CAL      0
420              GOEQ     EVAL,38,X,X
421              LAV      VARCT,X
422              CAL      0
423              GOEQ     ERLNOV,355,X,X
424
425              NB       'PRINT OUT TABLE HEADING'
426              RMESS    '$'
427              LAV      VARNPT,X
428              STV      TEM1PT,X
429 [HDLOOP]     LAI      TEM1PT,X
430              CAL      0
431              GOEQ     ENDHD,10,X,X
432              LAV      TEM1PT,X
433              GOSUB    LORLID,403
434              LAV      TEM1PT,X
435              GOSUB    PRTAB,218
436              LAI      TEM1PT,X
437              AAV      TEM1PT
438              AAL      OF(LNM)
439              ALIGN
440              STV      TEM1PT,X
441              GO       HDLOOP,-13,X,X
442
443 [ENDHD]      RMESS    ': VALUES'
444              CLEAR    COUNT
445 [UNDLP]      RMESS    '------'
446              BUMP     COUNT,1
447              LAV      COUNT,X
448              CAV      VARCT,X
449              GONE     UNDLP,-5,X,X
450              RMESS    '!------$'
451
452              NB       'NOW PRINT OUT LINE OF TABLE'
453
454 [PTLINE]     LAV      VARVPT,X
455              STV      TEM1PT,X
456 [PLLOOP]     LAV      TEM1PT,X
457              CAV      FFPT,A
458              GOEQ     EVAL,6,X,X
459              LAI      TEM1PT,X
460              GOSUB    PRVAL,208
461              LAV      DICTPT,X
462              GOSUB    PRTAB,195
463              BUMP     TEM1PT,OF(LNM)
464              GO       PLLOOP,-9,X,X
465
466              NB       'EVALUATE POLISH STRING FOR CURRENT SET OF VALUES'
467
468 [EVAL]       LAV      INLFPT,X
469              SAL      OF(LNM)
470              STV      TEM1PT,X
471 [EVLOOP]     LAI      TEM1PT,X
472              STV      TEMP,X
```

```
473                    LAV          TEM1PT,X
474                    SAL          OF(LNM)
475                    STV          TEM1PT,X
476                    GUADD        TEMP
477                    GU           PLVAR,3,X,T
478                    GU           PLVAL,9,X,T
479                    GU           PLOP,16,X,T
480                    GO           PLEND,45,X,T
481
482                    NB           'CASE OF VARIABLE'
483
484   [PLVAR]          LAI          TEM1PT,X
485                    MULTL        OF(LNM)
486                    AAV          VARVPT
487                    STV          TEM2PT,X
488                    LAI          TEM2PT,X
489                    STV          TEMP,X
490                    GU           PLV1,2,X,X
491
492                    NB           'CASE OF VALUE'
493
494   [PLVAL]          LAI          TEM1PT,X
495                    STV          TEMP,X
496   [PLV1]           LAV          TEM1PT,X
497                    SAL          OF(LNM)
498                    STV          TEM1PT,X
499   [PLV2]           LAV          TEMP,X
500                    FSTK
501                    GU           EVLOOP,-25,X,X
502
503                    NB           'CASE OF OPERATOR -- APPLY TO ITEMS AT STACK TOP'
504
505   [PLOP]           LAI          TEM1PT,X
506                    STV          TEM2PT,X
507                    LAV          TEM1PT,X
508                    SAL          OF(LNM)
509                    STV          TEM1PT,X
510                    GOSUB        GETEMP,135
511                    LAV          TEMP,X
512                    MULTL        OF(LNM)
513                    STV          TEMP,P
514                    AAV          TEM2PT
515                    AAL          OF(LNM+LNM)
516                    STV          DICTPT,X
517                    LAI          TEM2PT,X
518                    CAL          0
519                    GONE         PLUNOP,12,X,X
520
521                    NB           'BINARY OPERATOR -- GET LEFT OPERAND'
522
523                    GOSUB        GETEMP,125
524                    CLEAR        COUNT
525                    LAV          TEMP,X
526                    MULTL        OF(LNM)
527                    STV          TEMP,X
528   [MULLP]          LAV          DICTPT,X
529                    AAV          TEMP
530                    STV          DICTPT,X
531                    BUMP         COUNT,1
532                    LAV          COUNT,X
533                    CAV          VALCT,X
534                    GONE         MULLP,-7,X,X
535   [PLUNOP]         LAI          DICTPT,X
536                    STV          TEMP,X
537                    GO           PLV2,-33,X,X
538
539                    NB           'END OF EVALUATION'
540
541   [PLEND]          GOSUB        GETEMP,110
542                    LAV          ISTABL,X
543                    CAL          0
```

```
544              GONE       TABVAL,11,X,X
545              LAV        VALUE,X
546              GAL        0
547              GOGE       VALSET,3,X,X
548
549              NB         'FIRST SETTING OF EXPRESSION VALUE'
550
551              LAV        TEMP,X
552              STV        VALUE,X
553              GO         NEXVAL,9,X,X
554
555              NB         'COMPARE CURRENT VALUE WITH PREVIOUS ONE'
556
557 [VALSET]     LAV        TEMP,X
558              GAV        VALUE,X
559              GOEQ       NEXVAL,6,X,X
560              RMESS      'IS A CONTINGENCY$$'
561              GO         NEXTLN,-346,X,X
562
563              NB         'CASE OF TABLE -- PRINT VALUE'
564
565 [TABVAL]     RMESS        :
566              LAV        TEMP,X
567              GOSUB      PRVAL,128
568              RMESS      '$'
569
570              NB         'PROCEED TO NEXT SET OF VALUES'
571
572 [NEXVAL]     LAV        FFPT,X
573              STV        TEM1PT,X
574 [NXLOOP]     LAV        TEM1PT,X
575              CAV        VARVPT,A
576              GOEQ       COMPLT,16,X,X
577              LAV        TEM1PT,R
578              SAL        OF(LNM)
579              STV        TEM1PT,X
580              LAI        TEM1PT,X
581              AAL        1
582              STI        TEM1PT,X
583              LAI        TEM1PT,X
584              CAV        VALCT,X
585              GONE       NX1,3,X,X
586              LAL        0
587              STI        TEM1PT,X
588              GO         NXLOOP,-15,X,X
589 [NX1]        LAV        ISTABL,X
590              CAL        0
591              GOEQ       EVAL,-97,X,X
592              GO         PTLINE,-109,X,X
593
594              NB         'CASE WHERE EVALUATION IS COMPLETE'
595
596 [COMPLT]     LAV        ISTABL,X
597              CAL        0
598              GONE       COMTAB,4,X,X
599              RMESS      '■ '
600              LAV        VALUE,X
601              COSUB      PRVAL,100
602              RMESS      '$'
603 [COMTAB]     RMESS      '$'
604              GO         NEXTLN,-380,X,X
605
606
607
608
609
610
611
612
613              SUBR       CHKEND,X,2
614
```

```
615                 NB          'HAS 2 EXITS AND NO PARAMETER'
616                 NB          'CHECKS IF IBFPT IS AT THE END OF INPUT BUFFER'
617                 NB          'IF NOT USES EXIT 1'
618                 NB          'IF SO USES EXIT 2'
619
620 [CREDO]         GOSUB       TESTCH,130
621                 GO          CHKOK,2,X,C
622                 GO          CREDO,-3,X,C
623                 EXIT        1,CHKEND
624 [CHKOK]         EXIT        2,CHKEND
625
626
627
628
629                 SUBR        CMPARE,PARNM,2
630
631                 NB          'HAS 2 EXITS AND A POINTER PARAMETER'
632                 NB          'COMPARES CURRENT SYMBOL WITH LID ...'
633                 NB          '...POINTED AT BY PARAMETER'
634                 NB          'IF A MATCH USES EXIT 1, OHERWISE USES EXIT 2'
635
636                 LAV         IDLEN,X
637                 GAI         PARNM,X
638                 GUEQ        GL4,1,X,X
639                 EXIT        2,CMPARE
640 [GL4]           LAV         IDPT,X
641                 STV         TEMPT,X
642                 BUMP        PARNM,OF(LNM)
643 [CMLOOP]        LAV         TEMPT,X
644                 CAV         ENDSPT,A
645                 GUNE        GL5,1,X,X
646                 EXIT        1,CMPARE
647 [GL5]           LCI         TEMPT,X
648                 CCI         PARNM
649                 GOEQ        GL6,1,X,X
650                 EXIT        2,CMPARE
651 [GL6]           BUMP        TEMPT,OF(LCH)
652                 BUMP        PARNM,OF(LCH)
653                 GO          CMLOOP,-11,X,X
654
655
656
657
658                 SUBR        CMPLST,PARNM,2
659
660                 NB          'HAS 2 EXITS AND A POINTER PARAMETER'
661                 NB          'PARAMATER POINTS AT LIST OF LIDS - END TO END'
662                 NB          'LIST IS TERMINATED BY ZERO LENGTH'
663                 NB          'CURRENT SYMBOL IS COMPARED WITH THE LIST'
664                 NB          'USES EXIT 2 IF NO MATCH'
665                 NB          'ELSE USES EXIT 1 AND SETS VALUE=0 IF MATCH ...'
666                 NB          '...IS FIRST LID, =1 IF SECOND, ETC.'
667
668                 CLEAR       VALUE
669                 LAV         PARNM,X
670                 STV         DICTPT,X
671 [CTLOOP]        LAI         DICTPT,X
672                 CAL         0
673                 GUNE        GL7,1,X,X
674                 EXIT        2,CMPLST
675 [GL7]           LAV         DICTPT,X
676                 GOSUB       CMPARE,-29
677                 GO          GOTIT,7,X,C
678                 BUMP        VALUE,1
679                 LAI         DICTPT,X
680                 AAV         DICTPT
681                 AAL         OF(LNM)
682                 ALIGN
683                 STV         DICTPT,X
684                 GO          CTLOOP,-14,X,X
685
```

```
686 [GOTIT]    EXIT        1,CMPLST
687
688
689
690
691            SUBR        GETSYM,X,2
692
693            NB          'HAS 2 EXITS AND NO PARAMETERS'
694            NB          'GETS A SYMBOL FROM THE INPUT BUFFER'
695            NB          'IGNORES ANY SEPARATORS AT THE START'
696            NB          'USES EXIT 1 IF TERMINATOR IS FOUND'
697            NB          'ELSE USES EXIT 2 AND SETS VARIABLES AS FOLLOWS'
698            NB          'SETS IDPT TO POINT AT FIRST CHARACTER OF SYMBOL'
699            NB          'SETS ENDSPT TO POINT BEYOND LAST CHAR OF SYMBOL'
700            NB          'SETS IDLEN AS LENGTH OF SYMBOL'
701
702 [REDO]     LAV         IBFPT,X
703            STV         IDPT,X
704            LCI         IDPT,X
705            GOPC        ISPUNC,4,X,X
706 [GTLOOP]   BUMP        IBFPT,OF(LCH)
707            LCI         IBFPT,X
708            GOPC        ENDSYM,4,X,X
709            GO          GTLOOP,-4,X,X
710
711 [ISPUNC]   GOSUB       TESTCH,78
712            GO          GTEXIT,6,X,C
713            GO          REDO,-11,X,C
714 [ENDSYM]   LAV         IBFPT,X
715            STV         ENDSPT,P
716            SAV         IDPT
717            STV         IDLEN,X
718            EXIT        2,GETSYM
719
720 [GTEXIT]   EXIT        1,GETSYM
721
722
723
724
725            SUBR        GETEMP,X,1
726
727            NB          'HAS 1 EXIT AND NO PARAMETER'
728            NB          'UNSTACKS NUMBER FROM FSTACK AND PUTS IT IN TEMP'
729
730            LAV         FFPT,X
731            SAL         OF(LNM)
732            STV         FFPT,X
733            LAI         FFPT,X
734            STV         TEMP,X
735            EXIT        1,GETEMP
736
737
738
739
740            SUBR        GETTS,X,3
741
742            NB          'HAS 3 EXITS AND NO PARAMETER'
743            NB          'UNSTACKS POINTER FROM TOP OF TEMPORARY STACK'
744            NB          'IF STACK EMPTY USES EXIT1'
745            NB          'IF POINTER IS NULL (MEANING LEFT PAREN) USES ...'
746            NB          'EXIT 2. ELSE ADDS POINTER TO ...'
747            NB          '...POLISH STRING AND USES EXIT 3'
748
749            LAV         TSFFPT,X
750            CAV         TSTKPT,A
751            GUNE        GL8,1,X,X
752            EXIT        1,GETTS
753 [GL8]      LAV         TSFFPT,X
754            SAL         OF(LNM)
755            STV         TSFFPT,X
756            LAI         TSFFPT,X
```

```
757                CAL      0
758                GONE     GL9,1,X,X
759                EXIT     2,GETTS
760 [GL9]          LAL      2
761                BSTK
762                LAI      TSFFPT,X
763                BSTK
764                EXIT     3,GETTS
765
766
767
768
769                SUBR     PRTAB,PARNM,1
770
771                NB       'HAS 1 EXIT AND POINTER PARAMETER'
772                NB       'PARAM POINTS AT LID THAT HAS JUST BEEN PRINTED'
773                NB       'PRINTS ENOUGH SPACES TO GIVE AN 8-COLUMN TAB'
774
775                LAI      PARNM,X
776                STV      TEMP,X
777                RMESS    '  '
778 [PRTLP]        LAV      TEMP,X
779                CAL      OF(6*LCH)
780                GOLT     GL10,1,X,X
781                EXIT     1,PRTAB
782 [GL10]         BUMP     TEMP,OF(LCH)
783                RMESS    '  '
784                GO       PRTLP,-7,X,X
785
786
787
788
789                SUBR     PRVAL,PARNM,1
790
791                NB       'HAS 1 EXIT AND NUMERICAL PARAMETER'
792                NB       'PRINTS NAME OF N-TH VALUE ...'
793                NB       '...WHERE N+1 IS VALUE OF PARAMETER'
794
795                LAV      VALNPT,X
796                STV      DICTPT,X
797 [PRVLP]        LAV      PARNM,X
798                CAL      0
799                GOEQ     NMFND,9,X,X
800                LAV      PARNM,R
801                SAL      1
802                STV      PARNM,X
803                LAI      DICTPT,X
804                AAV      DICTPT
805                AAL      OF(LNM)
806                ALIGN
807                STV      DICTPT,X
808                GO       PRVLP,-12,X,X
809
810 [NMFND]        LAV      DICTPT,X
811                GOSUB    LORLID,155
812                EXIT     1,PRVAL
813
814
815
816
817                SUBR     STKSYM,X,1
818
819                NB       'HAS 1 EXIT AND NO PARAMETERS'
820                NB       'STACKS CURRENT SYMBOL ON FORWARDS STACK'
821
822                LAV      IDLEN,X
823                ESTK
824                LAV      FFPT,X
825                STV      TEM2PT,P
826                AAV      IDLEN
827                ALIGN
```

```
828              STV       FFPT,P
829              CAV       LFPT,A
830              GOGE      ERLSO,80,E,X
831              LAV       IDPT,X
832              GTV       SRCPT,X
833              LAV       TEM2PT,X
834              STV       DSTPT,X
835              LAV       IDLEN,X
836              FMOVE
837              EXIT      1,STKSYM
838
839
840
841
842              SUBR      TESTCH,X,3
843
844              NB        'HAS 3 EXITS AND NO PARAMETERS'
845              NB        'GETS AND CLASSIFIES NEXT INPUT CHARACTER'
846              NB        'IF A TERMINATOR USES EXIT 1'
847              NB        'IF A SEPARATOR ADVANCES IBFPT AND USES EXIT 2'
848              NB        'OTHERWISE ADVANCES IBFPT AND USES EXIT 3'
849
850
851              LCI       IBFPT,X
852              CCL       ';'
853              GUEQ      TS1,14,X,X
854              LCI       IBFPT,R
855              CCN       NLREP
856              GUEQ      TS1,11,X,X
857              LCI       IBFPT,R
858              CCN       SPREP
859              GOEQ      TS2,9,X,X
860              LCI       IBFPT,R
861              CCL       ','
862              GUEQ      TS2,6,X,X
863              LCI       IBFPT,R
864              CCN       TABREP
865              GUEQ      TS2,3,X,X
866              BUMP      IBFPT,OF(LCH)
867              EXIT      3,TESTCH
868
869    [TS1]     EXIT      1,TESTCH
870
871    [TS2]     BUMP      IBFPT,OF(LCH)
872              EXIT      2,TESTCH
873
874
875
876
877              SUBR      TSTSYM,X,4
878
879              NB        'HAS 4 EXITS AND NO PARAMETER'
880              NB        'GETS AND CLASSIFIES NEXT INPUT SYMBOL'
881              NB        'USES EXIT 1 IF TERMINATOR IS FOUND'
882              NB        'USES EXIT 2 IF SYMBOL IS A VALUE'
883              NB        'USES EXIT 3 IF SYMBOL IS UNDEFINED'
884              NB        'OHERWISE USES EXIT 4 AND SETS TYPE AS FOLLOWS'
885              NB        'TYPE=0 MEANS SYMBOL IS A BINARY OPERATOR'
886              NB        'TYPE=1 MEANS SYMBOL IS A UNARY OPERATOR'
887              NB        'TYPE=2 MEANS SYMBOL IS A LEFT PARENTHESIS'
888              NB        'TYPE=3 MEANS SYMBOL IS A RIGHT PARENTHESIS'
889              NB        'TYPE=4 MEANS SYMBOL IS UNDEFINED'
890              NB        'IF SYMBOL IS A VARIABLE OR VALUE THEN VALUE ...'
891              NB        '...IS SET AS FOR CMPLST. IF SYMBOL IS AN ...'
892              NB        '...OPERATOR THEN DICTPT IS SET TO POINT ...'
893              NB        '...AT THE INFORMATION AFTER ITS LID'
894
895              GOSUB     GETSYM,-111
896              GO        NOSYM,43,X,C
897              LAL       2
898              STV       TYPE,X
```

```
899              LCI        IDPT,X
900              CCL        '('
901              GOEQ       USE4,37,X,X
902              LAL        3
903              STV        TYPE,X
904              LCI        IDPT,X
905              CCL        ')'
906              GOEQ       USE4,32,X,X
907              LAV        VALNPT,X
908              GOSUB      CMPLST,-143
909              GU         ISVAL,31,X,C
910              LAL        4
911              STV        TYPE,X
912              LAV        VARNPT,X
913              CAL        U
914              GOEQ       GL11,3,X,X
915              LAV        VARNPT,R
916              GOSUB      CMPLST,-151
917              GO         USE4,21,X,C
918  [GL11]      LAV        UPCHPT,X
919              STV        DICTPT,X
920  [OPLOOP]    LAV        DICTPT,X
921              CAL        U
922              GONE       GL12,1,X,X
923              EXIT       3,TSTSYM
924  [GL12]      LAV        DICTPT,X
925              AAL        OF(LNM)
926              GOSUB      CMPARE,-18J
927              GO         ISOP,3,X,C
928              LAI        DICTPT,X
929              STV        DICTPT,X
930              GO         OPLUOP,-11,X,X
931
932              NB         'CASE OF OPERATOR'
933
934  [ISOP]      BUMP       DICTPT,OF(LNM)
935              LAI        DICTPT,X
936              AAV        DICTPT
937              AAL        UF(LNM)
938              ALIGN
939              STV        DICTPT,X
940              LAI        DICTPT,X
941              STV        TYPE,X
942  [USE4]      EXIT       4,TSTSYM
943
944  [NOSYM]     EXIT       1,TSTSYM
945  [ISVAL]     EXIT       2,TSTSYM
946
947
948
949
950
951
952
953
954  [ERLSYS]    MESS       'SOFTWARE ERROR$'
955  [GIVEUP]    GOSUB      MDQUIT,X
956
957  [ERLCLA]    MESS       'ERROR -- CLASHING USE OF SYMBOL$'
958              GO         ERLCOM,27,X,X
959
960  [ERLS0]     MESS       '$ERROR -- INSUFFICIENT WORKSPACE$'
961              GU         GIVEUP,-5,X,X
962
963  [ERLILL]    MESS       'ERROR -- ILLEGAL SYMBOL$'
964              GO         ERLCOM,23,X,X
965
966  [ERLSTA]    MESS       'ERROR -- UNRECOGNIZED STATEMENT$'
967              GO         ERLCOM,21,X,X
968
969  [ERLINC]    MESS       'ERROR -- INCOMPLETE LINES'
```

```
970                 GO          ERLCOM,19,X,X
971
972  [ERLNOV]       MESS        'ERROR -- NO VARIABLESS'
973                 GO          ERLCOM,17,X,X
974
975  [ERLPAR]       MESS        'ERROR IN USE OF PARENTHESESS'
976                 GO          ERLCOM,15,X,X
977
978  [ERLCMP]       MESS        'ERROR -- EXPRESSION TOO COMPLICATEDS'
979                 GO          ERLCOM,13,X,X
980
981  [ERLNB]        MESS        'ERROR IN USE OF BINARY OPERATOR '
982                 GO          ERLNAM,5,X,X
983
984  [ERLWU]        MESS        'ERROR IN USE OF UNARY OPERATOR '
985                 GO          ERLNAM,3,X,X
986  [ERLVRO]       MESS        'ERROR IN USE OF VARIABLE '
987                 GO          ERLNAM,1,X,X
988
989  [EPLVLO]       MESS        'ERROR IN USE OF VALUE '
990
991                 NB          'PRINT NAME OF OFFENDING SYMBOL'
992
993  [ERLNAM]       LAV         FFPT,X
994                 STV         TEM1PT,X
995                 GOSUB       STKSYM,-114
996                 LAV         TEM1PT,X
997                 GOSUB       LOELID,24
998                 MESS        'S'
999
1000                NB          'COMMON ACTION AFTER ERROR'
1001
1002 [ERLCOM]       LAV         INFFPT,X
1003                CAL         0
1004                GOEQ        ASKVAL,-647,X,X
1005                GO          NEXTLN,-616,X,X
1006
1007
1008                NB          'SPECIAL ADDITIONAL CODE FOR LOWL ALGEBRA'
1009
1010
1011                SUBR        LOGNUM,X,2
1012
1013                NB          'PERFORMS CHARACTER TO NUMERICAL CONVERSION'
1014                CLEAR       VALUE
1015                LAV         IDPT,X
1016                AAL         OF(3*LCH)
1017                CAV         ENDSPT,A
1018                GOLT        NUMEX,12,X,X
1019 [NUMLP]        LCI         IDPT,X
1020                GOND        NUMEX,10,X,X
1021                STV         TEMP,X
1022                LAV         VALUE,X
1023                MULTL       10
1024                AAV         TEMP
1025                STV         VALUE,X
1026                BUMP        IDPT,OF(LCH)
1027                LAV         IDPT,X
1028                CAV         ENDSPT,A
1029                GONE        NUMLP,-11,X,X
1030                EXIT        2,LOGNUM
1031
1032 [NUMEX]        EXIT        1,LOGNUM
1033
1034
1035                SUBR        LOELID,PARNM,1
1036                NB          'OUTPUTS A LID ON THE ERROR STREAM'
1037
1038                LAI         PARNM,X
1039                AAV         PARNM
1040                AAL         OF(LNM)
```

```
1041                STV        LOTEMP,X
1042                BUMP       PARNM,OF(LNM)
1043 [LOELP]        LAV        PARNM,X
1044                CAV        LOTEMP,A
1045                GOEQ       LOEEX,4,X,X
1046                LCI        PARNM,X
1047                GOSUB      MDERCH,X
1048                BUMP       PARNM,OF(LCH)
1049                GO         LOELP,-7,X,X
1050
1051 [LOEEX]        EXIT       1,LOELID
1052
1053
1054                SUBR       LORLID,PARNM,1
1055                NB         'OUTPUTS A LID ON RESULTS STREAM'
1056
1057                LAI        PARNM,X
1058                STV        LOTEMP,P
1059                GAL        OF(6*LCH)
1060                GOLE       NOTRUN,2,X,X
1061                LAL        OF(6*LCH)
1062                STV        LOTEMP,X
1063 [NOTRUN]       LAV        LOTEMP,X
1064                AAV        PARNM
1065                AAL        OF(LNM)
1066                STV        LOTEMP,X
1067                BUMP       PARNM,OF(LNM)
1068 [LORLP]        LAV        PARNM,X
1069                CAV        LOTEMP,A
1070                GOEQ       LOREX,4,X,X
1071                LCI        PARNM,X
1072                GOSUB      MDRCH,X
1073                BUMP       PARNM,OF(LCH)
1074                GO         LORLP,-7,X,X
1075
1076 [LOREX]        EXIT       1,LORLID
1077
1078
1079                SUBR       LOQLID,PARNM,1
1080                NB         'OUTPUTS A LID ON QUESTION STREAM'
1081
1082                LAI        PARNM,X
1083                AAV        PARNM
1084                AAL        OF(LNM)
1085                STV        LOTEMP,X
1086                BUMP       PARNM,OF(LNM)
1087 [LOQLP]        LAV        PARNM,X
1088                CAV        LOTEMP,A
1089                GOEQ       LOQEX,4,X,X
1090                LCI        PARNM,X
1091                GOSUB      MDQCH,X
1092                BUMP       PARNM,OF(LCH)
1093                GO         LOQLP,-7,X,X
1094
1095 [LOQEX]        EXIT       1,LOQLID
1096
1097                PRGEN
1098
1099
1100
```

Chapter 3.9

Testing an Implementation of ALGEBRA

This chapter contains some test data which can be used to validate an implementation of ALGEBRA. This data needs to be supplemented by tests of the machine-dependent features of the implementation. Unfortunately the nature of ALGEBRA does not allow the data to be self-checking in any way, so the implementor needs to go through the output from the test line by line to check that the output is what it should be. (Alternatively a program might be written to perform this comparison, the inputs being what the implementation should produce as output and what it actually does produce. It is very doubtful, however, whether the effort needed to produce this program and punch up the data for it would be worthwhile, unless part of a larger project.)

The test data

The test data consists of three separate tests, convering one-valued, two-valued and three-valued logics. It is reasonable to suppose that if these work then all multi-valued logics will work.

In the descriptions that follow, the inputs and outputs of each test are interspersed, exactly as they would appear on an on-line typewriter listing. In order to indicate the nature of each line to the reader, input lines have been prefixed by three dots and output lines produced on the message stream by three asterisks. Output lines produced on the results stream have no prefix. Where an input is the answer to the question, the question is prefixed to the input line (after the dots). For example the initial input line might be specified

$$\dots \text{VALUES} = \text{T} \quad \text{F}$$

The first test deals with a one-valued logic and is simply a path-finding test to make sure the main features of ALGEBRA are working. The test is as follows.

```
   ...VALUES=SINGLE
   ...OP +
   ...UNARY OR BINARY=BINARY
   ...PRECEDENCE=15
   ...SINGLE + SINGLE=SINGLE
   ...TRY A+B
   =SINGLE
   ...TABLE AA+BB
```

AA	BB	:VALUE
------	------	:-----
SINGLE	SINGLE	:SINGLE

```
   ...OP NOT
   ...UNARY OR BINARY=UNARY
   ...PRECEDENCE=1
   ...NOT SINGLE=SINGLE
   ...TABLE + ; ERROR LINE
***ERROR IN USE OF BINARY OPERATOR +
   ...TRY NOT A+B
   = SINGLE
   ...;END OF TEST
```

The second test, which is a comprehensive one, covers a two-valued logic. The test proceeds as follows. Firstly a set of operators is defined, a large number of errors being made, and corrected, during this process. There follows a series of statements, all of which contain errors. The TRY statement is then tested, firstly with a series of expressions all of which should be true, then with a series of FALSE expressions and finally with some contingencies. This is followed by a series of tables, which need to be carefully checked by the tester. The test concludes by redefining an existing operator, and checking the new definition. In detail, the test is as follows.

```
   ...VALUES=(
***ERROR -- CLASHING USE OF SYMBOL
   ...VALUES=X+
***ERROR -- ILLEGAL SYMBOL
   ...VALUES=
***ERROR -- INCOMPLETE LINE
   ...VALUES=TRUE FALSE
   ...
   ...;*********FIRST DEFINE SOME OPERATORS*********
   ...OP    +; EXCLUSIVE OR
   ...UNARY OR BINARY=
```

```
***EH
...UNARY OR BINARY=UN X
***EH
...UNARY OR BINARY=UXARY
***EH
...UNARY OR BINARY=BINARY
...PRECEDENCE=
***EH
...PRECEDENCE=5X
***EH
...PRECEDENCE=-1
***EH
...PRECEDENCE=1 X
***EH
...PRECEDENCE=1001
***EH
...PRECEDENCE=1
...TRUE + TRUE=
***EH
...TRUE + TRUE=TRUE X
***EH
...TRUE + TRUE=+
***EH
...TRUE + TRUE=FALSE
...TRUE + FALSE=TRUE
...FALSE + TRUE=TRUE
...FALSE + FALSE=FALSE
...;
...OPERATOR-
...UNARY OR BINARY=UNARY
...PRECEDENCE=999
...-TRUE=FALS
***EH
...-TRUE=FALSE
...-FALSE=
***EH
...-FALSE=+
***EH
...-FALSE=TRUE
...OPERATOR NOT; LOW PRECEDENCE NEGATION
...UNARY OR BINARY=UNARY
...PRECEDENCE=0
...NOT TRUE=FALSE
```

```
...NOT FALSE=TRUE
...OPER X
...UNARY OR BINARY=BIN
...PRECEDENCE=2
...TRUE X TRUE=TRUE
...TRUE X FALSE=FALSE
...FALSE X TRUE=FALSE
...FALSE X FALSE=FALSE
...OPERATOR >; IMPLIES OPERATOR
...UNARY OR BINARY=BIN
...PRECEDENCE=3
...TRUE > TRUE=TRUE
...TRUE > FALSE=FALSE
...FALSE > TRUE=TRUE
...FALSE > FALSE=TRUE
...
...;*********THE FOLLOWING STATEMENTS ALL CONTAIN
    ERRORS*********
...BBB
***ERROR -- UNRECOGNIZED STATEMENT
...XYZ+Q
***ERROR -- UNRECOGNIZED STATEMENT
...OP TRUE
***ERROR -- CLASHING USE OF SYMBOL
...OP
***ERROR -- INCOMPLETE LINE
...OP(
***ERROR -- CLASHING USE OF SYMBOL
...TABLE
***ERROR -- INCOMPLETE LINE
...TABLE A+
***ERROR -- INCOMPLETE LINE
...TABLE TRUE+FALSE
***ERROR -- NO VARIABLES
...TABLE AX B
***ERROR IN USE OF VARIABLE B
...TABLE AX FALSE
***ERROR IN USE OF VALUE FALSE
...TABLE A(B+A)
***ERROR IN USE OF PARENTHESES
...TABLE A+B)
***ERROR IN USE OF PARENTHESES
...TABLE)
```

```
***ERROR IN USE OF PARENTHESES
...TABLE A NOR
***ERROR IN USE OF VARIABLE NOR
...TABLE A NOT B
***ERROR IN USE OF UNARY OPERATOR NOT
...TABLE +B
***ERROR IN USE OF BINARY OPERATOR +
...TABLE F+(+B)
***ERROR IN USE OF BINARY OPERATOR +
...TABLE (A
***ERROR IN USE OF PARENTHESES
...TABLE ((NOT A) > (B)
***ERROR IN USE OF PARENTHESES
...TRY
***ERROR -- INCOMPLETE LINE
...TRY----------------------------------------X
***ERROR -- EXPRESSION TOO COMPLICATED
...
....:*********THE FOLLOWING SHOULD ALL BE
    TRUE*********
...TRY TRUE
= TRUE

...TR NOT FALSE
= TRUE

...TRYFORMEPLEASE NOT-TRUE
= TRUE

...TRY TRUE X TRUE
= TRUE

...TRY,,TRUE, ,X,NOT,,,FALSE,,:
= TRUE

...TRY NOT - - FALSE X TRUE
= TRUE

...TRY FALSE>(TRUE+TRUE)
= TRUE

...TRY (TRUE+FALSE)>TRUE
= TRUE

...TRY A+ -A+XX+ -XX+C+(-(C) )
= TRUE
```

```
...TRY TRUE+A X  −A
= TRUE

...TRY NOT FALSE X FALSE
= TRUE

...TRY((((TRUE)))X TRUE)
= TRUE

...

...;*********THE FOLLOWING SHOULD ALL BE
     FALSE*********
...TRY FALSE>TRUE+TRUE; > IS DONE FIRST
= FALSE

...TRY TRUE+FALSE>TRUE
= FALSE

...TRY A X−A
= FALSE

... TRY A X−A
= FALSE

...,,,TRY A + A
= FALSE

...TRY −A X A
= FALSE

...

...;*********THE FOLLOWING SHOULD ALL BE
     CONTINGENCIES*********
...TRY PIG
IS A CONTINGENCY

...TRY NOT A X A
IS A CONTINGENCY

...TRY A+B+C+D+E+F+G
IS A CONTINGENCY

...

...;*********TEST THE TABLE STATEMENT*********
...TA XYZ
```

XYZ	:VALUE
TRUE	:TRUE
FALSE	:FALSE

...TABLE A + − B

A	B	:VALUE
TRUE	TRUE	:TRUE
TRUE	FALSE	:FALSE
FALSE	TRUE	:FALSE
FALSE	FALSE	:TRUE

...TABLE Z>(LONGNAME+C)X(−TRUE X C)>D+Z)

Z	LONGNA	C	D	:VALUE
TRUE	TRUE	TRUE	TRUE	:FALSE
TRUE	TRUE	TRUE	FALSE	:FALSE
TRUE	TRUE	FALSE	TRUE	:TRUE
TRUE	TRUE	FALSE	FALSE	:TRUE
TRUE	FALSE	TRUE	TRUE	:TRUE
TRUE	FALSE	TRUE	FALSE	:TRUE
TRUE	FALSE	FALSE	TRUE	:FALSE
TRUE	FALSE	FALSE	FALSE	:FALSE
FALSE	TRUE	TRUE	TRUE	:TRUE
FALSE	TRUE	TRUE	FALSE	:TRUE
FALSE	TRUE	FALSE	TRUE	:TRUE
FALSE	TRUE	FALSE	FALSE	:TRUE
FALSE	FALSE	TRUE	TRUE	:TRUE
FALSE	FALSE	TRUE	FALSE	:TRUE
FALSE	FALSE	FALSE	TRUE	:TRUE
FALSE	FALSE	FALSE	FALSE	:TRUE

```
...
....:*********REDEFINE AN OPERATOR*********
...OP >
...UNARY OR BINARY=BI
...PRECEDENCE=10
...TRUE > TRUE=FALSE
...TRUE > FALSE=TRUE
...FALSE > TRUE=FALSE
...FALSE > FALSE=FALSE
...TRY A>A;  THIS SHOULD NOW BE FALSE
= FALSE
...:END OF TEST
```

The third and last test covers a three-valued logic. The test is short and contains little that is not covered by the previous test, and thus should cause few problems. It is as follows.

```
...VALUES=0,1,2
...OPERATOR-
...UNARY OR BINARY=BINARY
...PRECEDENCE=2
...0 - 0=0
...0 - 1=2
...0 - 2=1
...1 - 0=1
...1 - 1=0
...1 - 2=2
...2 - 0=2
...2 - 1=1
...2 - 2=0
...
...;*********THE FOLLOWING SHOULD ALL BE 0*********
...TRY 0
=0

...TRY FISH-FISH
=0

...TRY 2-1-1
=0

...TRY 2-(1-1)-2
=0

...;*********NOW PRINT A TABLE*********
...TABLE (A-B)-(C-A)
```

A	B	C	:VALUE
0	0	0	:0
0	0	1	:2
0	0	2	:1
0	1	0	:2
0	1	1	:1
0	1	2	:0
0	2	0	:1
0	2	1	:0
0	2	2	:2
1	0	0	:2
1	0	1	:1
1	0	2	:0

1	1	0	:1
1	1	1	:0
1	1	2	:2
1	2	0	:0
1	2	1	:2
1	2	2	:1
2	0	0	:1
2	0	1	:0
2	0	2	:2
2	1	0	:0
2	1	1	:2
2	1	2	:1
2	2	0	:2
2	2	1	:1
2	2	2	:0

. . . ;END OF TEST

Testing of implementation-dependent features

The given test data needs to be supplemented by tests of implementation-dependent features. Areas to be tested may include:

(a) Operating system interface. Entry, exit, sudden termination (e.g. in the middle of an operator definition), a null run, a run with little or no storage for the stack area.

(b) Breaks. Breaks during input, output and in reply to a question. Breaks before values have been defined. Recovery from breaks.

(c) Input/output. I/O options, incorrectly specified I/O devices, overflow conditions (lines too long, etc.), switching of input stream (if available).

Chapter 3.10

Writing Software in LOWL

It has often happened that implementors, at the end of one project, wish to carry the process one stage further and implement their own software in LOWL. I would be the last to discourage this, but it is necessary to make two caveats. Firstly, the implementor must be absolutely sure that LOWL, with suitable extensions, is a good descriptive language for his software. If it is not, he is tailoring his software to a language rather than vice-versa and the whole point of the exercise is lost. If LOWL is basically unsuitable then the implementor should design his own descriptive language.

The second caveat is that portability is expensive for the first implementation. There are two situations to be considered: firstly the implementor may be designing a new piece of software and he may decide to make it portable; secondly he may wish to recode an existing piece of software in a portable way. If we consider the first situation it might take nearly twice as long to produce the first implementation using LOWL as it would by coding the software in a machine-dependent way. The pay-off only comes when further implementations are made. The extra overheads for the first implementation include

(a) the design of the necessary LOWL extensions,
(b) the separation of the MI-logic from the MD-logic,
(c) documentation of the portability method,
(d) debugging.

In the second situation, the recoding of an existing piece of software, the relative overheads are even higher, because the original step of implementing the software in a machine-dependent way was wasted work. Even so, portability is usually worth the effort.

Coding in LOWL

One of the prime aims of LOWL is that it should be easy to implement. Sometimes this adds to the effort of writing programs in LOWL. The most obvious instances of this are supplementary arguments, which force the original program writer to supply extra information which may well be redundant for the implementation he has in mind. The only case, however, where supplementary arguments present a real problem, as distinct from a minor overhead, to the software writer are the arguments on branching statements that specify how far away the designated labels are. It is totally impractical for these to be supplied by hand, and it is therefore necessary to write a program which fills them in automatically. This can be done in many ways. One way that has been used in practice is to write a set of ML/I macros, which work in two passes. The first pass counts LOWL statements, ignoring comments and blank lines, recording the position of each label. The second pass again counts LOWL statements, and fills in the relative distances on all references to the labels.

This adaptation of LOWL to make things easier for the program writer can be carried much further. LOWL, like any other language, can be improved by a macro pre-pass. In fact several of the pieces of software that are available in LOWL, including ALGEBRA, were originally encoded in a much higher-level language (the language L mentioned in Part 2) and mapped by macros into LOWL. (This is the reason for the occasional pieces of crude code that the implementor may have noticed in the LOWL encoding of ALGEBRA.)

As regards the rules for writing programs in LOWL, these are all stated in the definition of LOWL. Special points to be noted are the layout, with the labels TABFST and BEGIN at the start of the table items and executable code, respectively, and the requirement for a section of code labelled ERLSO to take a suitable action on stack overflow (e.g. print a message and call MDQUIT).

Debugging

Testing the correctness of software encoded in LOWL is a non-trivial job. The first task is to make sure the software works on one machine, but this is not, of course, a full test. Some of the supplementary arguments not used by that machine might be wrong. Moreover the program may work on a machine 'by coincidence'. For example a bug where LNM was used in place of LCH would not show up on a machine where LNM and LCH had the same value, and, more sinister, a bug where LCH was assumed to be one would only show up on those rare machines where LCH was not one. Hence an extensive testing procedure is needed. This does not, however, require the availability of many different computers as the various properties under test can be simulated on a single computer. Thus on one run LCH might be one and on another run two. Such tests are not trivial to organize as they may require changes or extra parameterization in the MD-logic as well as adjustments to the mapping macros.

A further series of trials would need to test supplementary arguments. One such trial might deliberately clobber the values of all registers after the evaluation of each LOWL statement that did not require preservation of registers. Thus every store statement would clobber registers unless it had P as its supplementary argument.

It is tasks like this that make the work of implementing software in an easily portable form so much greater than the work to produce a single machine-dependent implementation.

References

Arden, B. W., B. A. Galler and R. M. Graham (1969). 'The MAD definition facility', *Comm. ACM*, **12**, 8, 432–439.

Barron, D. W. and I. R. Jackson (1972). 'The evolution of job control languages', *Software—Practice and Experience*, **2**, 143–164.

Brown, P. J. (1967). 'The ML/I macro processor', *Comm. ACM*, **10**, 10, 618–623.

Brown, P. J. (1969). 'Using a macro processor to aid software implementation', *Computer Journal*, **12**, 4, 327–331.

Brown, P. J. (1970). *ML/I User's Manual*, 4th Edition, University of Kent at Canterbury.

Brown, P. J. (1971a). 'Design of the ML/I macro processor', *Symposium on Software Engineering held at Culham Laboratory*, HMSO, London, 48–54.

Brown, P. J. (1971b). 'A survey of macro processors', *Annual Review in Automatic Programming*, Vol. 6, Pergamon Press, Oxford, 37–88.

Brown, P. J. (1972a). 'SCAN—a simple conversational programming language for text analysis', *Computers and the Humanities*, **6**, 4, 223–227.

Brown, P. J. (1972b). 'Levels of language for portable software', *Comm. ACM*, **13**, 12, 1059–1062.

Brown, P. J. (1972c). 'Extending high-level languages by macros—a practical case evaluation', *Proceedings of Software 72 Conference*, Transcripta Books, London, 95–99.

Brown, P. J. and J. D. Lowe (1971). 'A computer program for symbolic logic', *Bulletin IMA*, **7**, 11, 320–322.

Brown, W. S. (1969). 'Software portability', *Software Engineering Techniques*, report on a Conference sponsored by the NATO Science Committee, Brussels, 80–84.

Cheetham, T. E. (1966). 'The introduction of definitional facilities into higher level programming languages', *AFIPS Conference Proceedings*, **29**, 623–637.

Ferguson, D. E. (1966). 'The evolution of the meta-assembly program', *Comm. ACM*, **9**, 3, 190–193.

Fletcher, J. G. (1965). 'A program to solve the pentomino problem by the recursive use of macros', *Comm. ACM*, **8**, 10, 621–623.

Freeman, D. N. (1966). 'Macro language design for System/360', *IBM Systems Journal*, **5**, 2, 63–77.

Galler, B. A. and A. J. Perlis (1970). *A view of programming languages*, Addison-Wesley, Reading, Mass.

Grant, C. A. (1971). 'Syntax translation with context macros, or macros without arguments', *SIGPLAN Notices*, **6**, 12, 48–50.

Griswold, R. E. (1972). *The macro implementation of SNOBOL4*, Freeman, San Francisco.

IBM (1968). *Student Text: An Introduction to the Compile-time Facilities of PL/I*, Form C20–1689–0, IBM Corporation, White Plains, New York.

Irons, E. T. (1970). 'Experience with an extensible language', *Comm. ACM*, **13**, 1, 31–40.

Kent, W. (1969). 'Assembler-language macroprogramming: a tutorial oriented toward the IBM 360', *Computing Surveys*, **1**, 4, 183–196.

Lindstrom, G. (1973). 'Control extensions in a recursive language', *BIT*, **13**, 50–70.

Macleod, J. A. (1971). 'MP/I—a FORTRAN macroprocessor', *Computer Journal*, **14**, 3, 229–231.

Mandil, S. H. (1972). 'A general-purpose "problem-to-program" translator', *Computer Bulletin*, **16**, 10, 492–496.

Masterson, K. S. (1960). 'Compilation for two computers using NELIAC', *Comm. ACM*, **3**, 11, 607–611.

Maurer, W. D. (1969). 'The compiled macro assembler', *AFIPS Conference Proceedings*, **34**, 89–93.

McIlroy, M. D. (1960). 'Macro instruction extensions of compiler languages', *Comm. ACM*, **3**, 4, 214–220.

McKinnon Wood, T. R. (1968). 'A multi-access implementation of an interpretive text processing language', *Information Processing 68*, Vol. 1, North-Holland, Amsterdam, 373–377.

Mock, O. *et al.* (1958). 'The problem of programming communications with changing machines: a proposed solution', *Comm. ACM*, **1**, 8, 12–18.

Molnar, G. (1971). 'SEL—a self-extensible programming language', *Computer Journal*, **14**, 3, 238–242.

Mooers, C. N. and L. P. Deutsch (1965). 'TRAC, a text handling language', *Proceedings 20th ACM National Conference*, 229–246.

Mooers, C. N. (1966). 'TRAC, procedure describing language for the reactive typewriter', *Comm. ACM*, **9**, 3, 215–219.

Mooers, C. N. (1968). 'How some fundamental problems are treated in the design of the TRAC language', in D. Bobrow (Ed.), *Symbol Manipulation Lanuages and Techniques*, North-Holland, Amsterdam, 178–190.

Newey, M. C., P. C. Poole and W. M. Waite (1972). 'Abstract machine modelling to produce portable software—a review and evaluation', *Software—Practice and Experience*, **2**, 107–136.

Nicholls, J. (1969). 'PL/I compile time extensibility', *SIGPLAN Notices*, **4**, 8, 40–44.

Poole, P. C. (1971). 'Hierarchical abstract machines', *Symposium on Software Engineering held at Culham Laboratory*, HMSO, London, 1–9.

Richards, M. (1969). 'BCPL: a tool for compiler writing and system programming', *AFIPS Conference Proceedings*, **34**, 557–566.

Richards, M. (1971). 'The portability of the BCPL compiler', *Software—Practice and Experience*, **1**, 135–146.

Scowen, R. S. (1971). 'Babel, an application of extensible compilers', *SIGPLAN Notices*, **6**, 12, 1–7.

Solntseff, N. (1972). 'Classification of extensible programming languages', *Information Processing Letters*, **1**, 3, 91–96.

Standish, T. A. (1971). 'PPL—an extensible language that failed', *SIGPLAN Notices*, **6**, 12, 144–145.

Steel, T. B. (1961). 'Uncol: the myth and the fact', *Annual Review in Automatic Programming*, Vol. 2, Pergamon Press, Oxford, 325–344.

Strachey, C. (1965). 'A general purpose macrogenerator', *Computer Journal*, **8**, 3, 225–241.

Waite, W. M. (1967). 'A language-independent macro processor', *Comm. ACM*, **10**, 7, 433–440.

Waite, W. M. (1970a). 'Building a mobile programming system', *Computer Journal*, **13**, 1, 28–31.

Waite, W. M. (1970b). 'The mobile programming system: STAGE2', *Comm. ACM*, **13**, 7, 415–421.

Warshall, S. (1972). 'Language independence?', *Incompatibility*, Infotech State of the Art Report 9, Maidenhead, England, 233–244.

Wilkes, M. V. (1964). 'An experiment with a self-compiling compiler for a simple list processing language', *Annual Review in Automatic Programming*, Vol. 4, Pergamon Press, Oxford, 1–48.

Wilkes, M. V. (1968). 'The outer and inner syntax of a programming language', *Computer Journal*, **11**, 3, 260–263.

Williams, R. (1968). 'A concise notation for the TRAC scanning algorithm', *SIGPLAN Notices*, **3**, 7, 31–32.

Wirth, N. (1968). 'PL360, a programming language for the 360 computers', *Journal ACM*, **15**, 1, 37–74.

Wirth, N. (1970). 'Program development by stepwise refinement', *Comm. ACM*, **14**, 4, 221–227.

Wulf, W. S., D. B. Russell and A. N. Habermann (1971). 'BLISS: a language for systems programming', *Comm. ACM*, **14**, 12, 780–790.

Index